INDIA 2020

VIKING
Penguin India

INDIA 2020

A Vision for the New Millennium

A.P.J. Abdul Kalam

with

Y.S. Rajan

VIKING

VIKING

Penguin Books India (P) Ltd., 11 Community Centre, Panchsheel Park, New Delhi 110 017, India
Penguin Books Ltd., 27 Wrights Lane, London W8 5TZ, UK
Penguin Books USA Inc., 375 Hudson Street, New York, NY 10014, USA
Penguin Books Australia Ltd., Ringwood, Victoria, Australia
Penguin Books Canada Ltd., 10 Alcorn Avenue, Suite 300, Toronto, Ontario M4V 3B2, Canada
Penguin Books (NZ) Ltd., 182-190 Wairau Road, Auckland 10, New Zealand

First published in Viking by Penguin Books India (P) Ltd. 1998

10

Typeset in *Nebraska* by SÚRYA, New Delhi
Printed at Rekha Printers Pvt. Ltd., New Delhi

After one of the talks delivered by Dr Kalam, a ten-year-old girl came up to him for his autograph. 'What is your ambition?' he asked her. 'I want to live in a developed India,' she replied without hesitation. This book is dedicated to her and the millions of Indians who share her aspiration.

If those who think to achieve,
Have a firm and focussed mind,
They will realize what they thought of,
And even as they have thought of.

—Thirukkural

Contents

Contents

Contents

Acknowledgements

In writing this book, our ideas have been shaped by several hundred Indians—some very well known. Each interaction enriched our experience and added a new dimension to understanding India's developmental needs and actions required. It is difficult to list every name. First and foremost, we are thankful to the Chairpersons and Co-chairpersons of the various Technology Vision 2020 Task Forces and Panels as well as the Coordinators and the key TIFAC persons who helped in the whole Vision 2020 exercise. Their names are listed in an Appendix to this book. In addition, the members of the Governing Council of TIFAC continue to be a source of encouragement. There are many members of the Technology Vision 2020 Task Forces, Panels, recently constituted Action Team members and the staff of TIFAC. We thank them for their dedicated work. Results of their work have been the source of a number of useful inputs in writing this book. We thank Prof V.S. Ramamurthy, Secretary, Department of Science and Technology, for the encouragement and the permission given to use the material from TIFAC reports.

While embarking on this journey of writing a book, we realized the magnitude of various detailed activities starting with the manuscript. The book would not have taken this shape without the sincere, untiring and dedicated effort put forth by H. Sheridon, beyond his long office hours. His laptop computer was always busy for the past several months. We also thank Krishan Chopra of Penguin Books for his excellent project management in shaping the book to its final form.

Y.S. Rajan would like to thank his wife Gomati, who has been a great source of strength through her affection and tender care and through the candid expression of her insights into real-life situations.

A.P.J. Abdul Kalam would like to place on record his thanks to the thousands of Indians who write to him on several occasions and inspire him to undertake several technological tasks for India.

Preface

Both of us were born when India was still struggling for her independence. One was in the final year of school when Jawaharlal Nehru made his famous speech about India waking up to make her tryst with destiny; the other was a child speaking a first few words. Our families were not known for riches or power. Destiny in the form of the progressive measures taken by independent India to harness science and technology in order to develop a modern nation brought us together.

It was the vision of the great Vikram Sarabhai, supported by Nehru and Homi Bhabha, which gave us the opportunity to work on the space programme. The programme was aimed at carrying developmental messages into homes all over the country, especially in the 6 lakh villages, by leap-frogging many traditional routes. The programme also aimed at surveying the natural resources of the country so that they could be harnessed to benefit our people. Many in India must have considered these objectives an unattainable dream in the early '60s when the space programme was born. We, however, along with many of our colleagues, saw these aims as a vision real and attainable. What followed was a shared mission. Every person in ISRO believed that they were born to realize all that space technology can bring to the country and its people.

For us, then, there was no going back. There were days and nights of work. Many failures and a few hard-won successes. The systems which were designed, developed, fabricated and tested were directed towards a common goal—a strong India, a developed and proud India with the benefits available all over the country. It is gratifying to note the vision, in relation to space technology, has come true now especially in terms of reaching out to the people; providing communication through networks in remote areas; disaster warning systems; quick resource surveys to target ground water, save our forest cover and so on. And, of course, in areas of certain strategic strengths, vital to India in a world which respects only strength.

We are also proud and happy that the dreams of many Indians in the agricultural, scientific, artistic, cultural and social fields have also come true. However, the vision of a prosperous India without poverty, an India strong in trade and commerce, an India strong in many fields of science and technology, an India with innovative industry and with health and education for all, has remained just partially realized. In some areas, in fact, pessimism has taken deep roots.

We have completed the fiftieth year of our independence, with a large majority born after independence. Every year about twenty million Indians are being added to the nation. What vision can they have? Should we, like some, question the very concept of development and leave our people to the same condition of stagnation which existed for centuries? Or think only of the upper strata of society and leave the rest to their fate, employing such nice sounding phrases as 'market driven strategies' and 'competitiveness'? Or leave the initiative to various globalizing forces? Where should we see India (and its people) going in the next two decades? In the next five decades? And more?

The authors were fortunate to have been associated with a large number of persons who were interested in posing these questions and finding some answers. These came substantially through a novel organization, the Technology Information, Forecasting and Assessment Council (TIFAC), which launched a major exercise called Technology Vision for India up to 2020.

About 500 experts with unique experience in industry, academia, laboratories and government administration were deeply involved in the exercise. Experts and socially aware persons also participated. About 5000 people contributed indirectly through responses to questionnaires and other inputs.

Subsequently, while the teams deliberated on various issues and the draft reports, and later when the report was released by the Prime Minister on 2 August 1996, we had numerous opportunities to interact with many others about a vision for India. We had the benefit of various inputs ranging from encouraging suggestions for specific actions to pessimistic comments about the inability of systems to act on anything focussed and long term. We travelled widely to interact with different sections of people in variegated parts of the country. We also reflected on the imperatives for India in a changing world.

We are aware of our systems of governance and social and political compulsions. We are fortunate to have gained experience in implementing projects involving people of various strata as beneficiaries, as well as projects entailing strong commercial pressures and those that are high profile, such as a satellite or a launch vehicle or missile project. The execution of these schemes provided varied experiences, which worked as base line knowledge for the shaping of this book.

Having taken these factors into account and after studying several vision reports of India and other countries, we still believe firmly that India can reach a developed country status by 2020. The Indian people can rise well above the present poverty and contribute more productively to their country because of their own improved health, education and self-esteem. India can have considerable technological strengths, so crucial for its strategic strengths and for economic and trade-related strengths.

In this book we have attempted to share some of these thoughts. We have also disclosed elements of a few action plans, which can be missions for many young people in the country. We hope that these will help to stimulate young Indians and ignite their minds in the same way that we were ignited by the space programme three decades ago. Our vision ahead for the country and the missions we see before us make us feel young even now.

A developed India, by 2020 or even earlier is not a dream. It need not even be a mere aspiration in the minds of many

Indians. It is a mission we can all take up—and accomplish.

Ignited young minds, we feel, are a powerful resource. This resource is mightier than any resource on the earth, in the sky and under the sea. We must all work together to transform our 'developing India' into a 'developed India', and the revolution required for this effort must start in our minds. This book, *India 2020*, will hopefully be the source for igniting many minds.

10 July 1998

Chapter 1

Can India Become a Developed Country?

All the brothers of the poor despise him, how much more do his friends go far from him! He pursues them with words, but they are gone.

—Old Testament Proverb 19:7

What makes a country developed? The obvious indicators are the wealth of the nation, the prosperity of its people and its standing in the international forum. There are many indicators regarding the wealth of a nation: the Gross National Product (GNP), the Gross Domestic Product (GDP), the Balance of Payments, foreign exchange reserves, rate of economic growth, per capita income, etc. In addition, the volume of trade, the share in international trade (both imports and exports) and rate of growth in both of these also provides an idea about the strength of the economy and its ability to sustain the wealth created and to create more. Economic indicators are important, but they provide only a part of the picture. The numbers, impressive though they may appear, can veil considerable human misery, especially that of the common people. In this context, I and Rajan have often discussed something I observed during my stint at the Defence Research & Development Laboratory (DRDL), Hyderabad. I came across three persons there who became in my mind points of reference that called me back unceasingly to certain issues. Venkat had two sons and a daughter. All were graduates and employed. Living in the same area was Kuppu who had three sons. He succeeded in educating only one. He lived in a rented dwelling. Karuppan had two daughters and one son. He was semi-employed, could not educate any of them because of poverty and had no regular dwelling place. Was it not possible for him to merely give a normal life to his offspring and not an unrealistic or extraordinary one? A reasonable lifespan, an occupation that would provide them basic comforts and good health care? This is our dream of a developed India.

Per capita income can indicate the wealth in the hands of people. Per capita income does not indicate that they all have the same amount of money. It is the average of the rich and poor. The same per capita figure also does not indicate the amount of well-being within a country or even within a state or region. For purposes of global comparisons, a new parameter, such as purchasing power parity, is nowadays being used. Complex models are also being discussed, debated and used as indices of human development. All of them only present certain facets of living conditions. These statistics do not indicate the long-term sustainability of the quality of life achieved by people.

People and development

Many parameters are utilized to indicate how well people are fed; their overall nutritional status; the availability of good nutrition during various phases of their growth and lives; the average life expectancy; the infant mortality rate; the availability of sanitation; the availability of drinking water and its quality; the quantum of living space; broad categories of human habitat; the incidence of various diseases, dysfunctions, disorders or disabilities; the access to medical facilities; literacy; the availability of schools and educational facilities; various levels of skills to cope with fast-changing economic and social demands; and so on.

One can include many other indicators of the quality of life. Still there is a nagging worry when we apply the talisman prescribed by Gandhiji. Gandhiji's strikingly simple criterion was that every action proposed or contemplated, should in its implementation wipe the tears of a poor and downtrodden person. He emphasized that only when we have wiped the tears from the faces of all, have we truly arrived as a nation.

Even when one applies the much less stringent Nehruvian vision for the elimination of ignorance, illiteracy, poverty, disease and inequalities in opportunities, the task of realizing such a vision through the missions that would follow appears difficult. They did not appear difficult at the time of our independence. Most Indians were ignited by the vision of our tryst with destiny. Are we as nation still inspired with that vision after fifty years? We are not unaware of the growing pessimism and even cynicism when one discusses the question of India reaching the status of a developed nation. We believe, moreover, that while aggregated indicators are important, *it does not make sense to achieve a 'developed' status without a major and continuing upliftment of all Indians who exist today and of the many more millions who would be added in the years to come.* They should all have a secure and enjoyable 'present' and also be in a position to look forward to a better 'future'. Such a developed India is what we are looking for.

I was in my teens when India became independent. The headmaster of my school used to take us to hear the news on the only available radio. We used to hear of the events in Delhi, and many speeches and commentaries. I used to distribute the morning newspaper *Dinamani* to households in Rameswaram, to help my brother with his work. While going on my daily morning round I also read the news items. One report which particularly struck me appeared in the heady days following independence. It was a time of celebration and the country's leaders were gathered in Delhi, addressing themselves to the momentous tasks that faced the government. At this moment, however, far from being at the centre of power, the father of the nation, Mahatma Gandhi, was away in Noakhali caring for the riot victims and trying to heal the wounds inflicted by communal rioting. How many persons would have such courage of conviction as did Gandhiji at a time when the nation was at his command? It is that kind of deep and unshakeable commitment to the well-being of all Indians that underlies the vision of a developed India.

Strategic strengths

The achievement of independence was of utmost importance to us. The implications of subservience to another power remain as abhorent today in this era of economic rather than military domination. Globalization, which means integration with the world economy, brings the influence of external forces into our society. Some experts may point out that these are economic or trade or market forces and they have beneficial influence in terms of developing our 'core competencies' in areas in which we have 'comparative advantage'. We also share the view that competition, both internally and with other global players would be useful to make the country efficient and strong. But we would also like to point out that developed countries have set up several non-tariff barriers which strike at the roots of 'ideal' competition based on 'market' forces. These are mostly aimed at denying opportunities to other countries to reach a developed status. Even when one country prepares to cope with a set of barriers introduced by these developed countries, either through their own laws or through multilateral treaties, a new set of complex barriers crops up. Even a simple analysis of many of these international or global transactions indicates a much deeper fact: the continuous process of domination over others by a few nations. India has to be prepared to face such selectively targeted actions by more powerful players even when it tries to march ahead to realize its vision of reaching a developed status.

Issues of national security are no longer simple considerations of defence but are closely intertwined with many aspects of trade, commerce, investment as well as creation and use of a knowledge base. What appears to be emerging is a new kind of warfare. If a country does *not* learn to master these new realities of life, all our aspirations to ensure the prosperity of our people may come to nought. This does not mean the advocacy of isolation or going back to the concepts of a nuts-and-bolts form of self-reliance. We need to address newer and more sophisticated concepts of protecting our strategic interests.

I recently spoke on our vision of national security. I said, '. . . a nation is made great by its people, and people in turn become important citizens of that great nation. By importing non-strategic systems for defence (strategic systems will not be available), a nation will not be able to defend both its economic freedom and security as this will only perpetuate the dependence on other nations. A country's strength to protect its security and evolve an independent foreign policy is dependent on the degree to which the nation is able to underpin this with self-reliance in defence and defence systems. India's core competence in certain technological areas and scientific technological manpower has to be harnessed. Through our sustained efforts for growth of core competence and self-reliance in critical technologies, we can transform our nation. We have to recognize that technology is the tool that brings faster economic growth and needed inputs for national security. The successful experience of certain technological leaders reveals that we have to demand from our institutions the impossible, and the possible will emerge.'*

A developed India should be able to take care of its strategic interests through its internal strengths and its ability to adjust itself to the new realities. For this it will need the strength of its healthy, educated and prosperous people, the strength of its economy, as well as the strength to protect its strategic interests of the day and in the long term.

---

*(Extracted from the USI National Security Lecture 1996, delivered by A.P.J. Abdul Kalam to the members of USI on 12 December, 1996; *Journal of the United Service Institution of India*, Vol CXXVI, No 526, October-December 1996).

Technologies as a core strength of the nation

In this book we focus on the technological imperatives for India to develop her internal strengths, keeping in mind three dynamic dimensions:

— the people
— the overall economy
— the strategic interests.

These technological imperatives also take into account a 'fourth' dimension, time, an offshoot of modern-day dynamism in business, trade, and technology that leads to continually shifting targets. We believe that technological strengths are especially crucial in dealing with this fourth dimension underlying continuous change (of the aspirations of people, of the economy in the global context, and of the strategic interests).

The progress of technology lies at the heart of human history, as illustrated in table 1.1. Technological strengths are the key to creating more productive employment in an increasingly competitive market place and to continually upgrade human skills. Without a pervasive use of technologies, we cannot achieve overall development of our people in the years to come. Technology is important as well in combating the dangers posed by existing and newer forms of diseases.

The direct linkages of technology to the nation's strategic strengths are becoming more and more clear, especially since the last decade. India's own strength in a number of core areas still puts it in a position of reasonable strength in geo-political terms. Any nation aspiring to become a developed one needs to have strengths in various strategic technologies and also the ability to continually upgrade them through its own creative strengths.

For people-oriented actions as well, whether for the creation of large-scale productive employment or for ensuring nutritional and health security for people, or for better living conditions, technology is the only vital input. From the early discoveries of X-ray as a diagnostic tool or penicillin as an antibiotic or

TABLE 1.1

Growth of technologies and human impact

Approximate Time (Years preceding 1998)	Innovation/ Breakthrough	Consequence/Reason
100000	Making and using gear for hunting	Extending human capabilities
40000	Making and using weapons	
3500	Boats and sailboats	
800	The clock, compass and other measurement instruments	Reducing and/or making manual work easier
360	Mechanical calculators	
190	Railroads/using coal and oil for energy	Facilitating and/or making mental work easier
160	Electricity	
140	Image and sound reproduction	
		Improving comfort and/or speed of transportation
100	Telecommunications/ X-rays	
95	Aircraft	Increased speed and/or availability of telecommunications
80	Automobiles and roads	
70	Mass-produced chemical products	

Approximate Time (Years preceding 1998)	Innovation/ Breakthrough	Consequence/Reason
55	Nuclear weapons/ energy	
50	Computers	Improving the quality of arts and entertainment
45	Mass-produced home appliances	Improving material quality of life
40	Extensive use of fertilizers/ oral contraceptives	
35	Lasers	
30	The moon landing/ tissues and organ transplants	
20	The CT(CAT or Body) Scan	
10	Genetically engineered plants/Internet	Increased knowledge base and applications

Adapted from: 'Forecasting, Planning & Strategy for the 21st Century' *by Spyros G. Makrindakis (Free Press, a division of Macmillan, Inc., New York)*

vaccination for preventive health care, we have come a long way. There are many specialized and affordable diagnostic tools, new medicines with negligible side-effects; and there are many possibilities on the horizon with the emergence of molecular biology. The absence of greater technological impetus could lead to lower productivity and wastage of precious natural resources. Activities with low productivity or low value addition, in the final analysis, hurt the poorest the most.

Just as in any other human activity, there would also be some side-effects accompanying the application of some technologies. These need to be removed: partly through a better knowledge of all our people and partly through technological solutions. There is a tendency nowadays to highlight the problems of technology which borders on defeatism. Environmental pollution does tend to increase with unbridled technological growth. China is a telling example. Yet, technology can also provide a cost-effective solution to pollution when the same factories are linked to a cleaner technology. The technological imperatives to lift our people to a new life, and to a life they are entitled to, is an important theme which is elaborated in all chapters of this book.

The linkages between technologies and economic strengths have been well researched for over two decades. The economic imperatives for acquiring technological strengths do not warrant repetition here. However, this connection has *not* become a part of the thinking of many in positions of leadership, whether in government, industry or elsewhere. An India aspiring to become a major economic player in terms of trade and increase in GDP cannot do it on the strength of turnkey projects designed and built abroad or only through large-scale imports of plant machinery, equipment and knowhow. Even while being alive to the short-term realities, medium- and long-term strategies to develop core technological strengths within our industry are vital for envisioning a developed India. Our studies indicate that the vision for the nation is only possible through identifying such core strengths and building on them.

Thus, looking at all four dimensions, i.e. (1) people, (2) economy, (3) strategic strengths and (4) ability to sustain and improve on these over very long periods of time in the future—it would appear that mastering of technologies is the key task to which the country and its people have to give importance. This can be considered to be the very essence of development. An India aspiring to a developed status must have a technology vision. The dynamics of this vision are discussed and developed in further chapters.

A vision for the economy

A Technology Vision for a nation may be constituted by

integrating data on the overall economy with social dimensions of development. The background of the TIFAC study were several studies done within India, some detailed and some already focussed on in the plan documents. The authors also had the benefit of discussions with a number of persons to understand the realities, constraints and aspirations behind various projections of growth rates. In addition, underlying the overall economic indicators are several assumptions about implementation which involve investment, enabling administrative, fiscal or legal measures, ability to mobilize human resources and so on. It is not possible to envision all the details of implementation. A vision, in fact, should *not* be a feasibility report, just as it cannot be a mere slogan or play of words. But it would be worthwhile to examine projections for a few economic indicators of a developed India against this background. The authors are grateful to T.K. Bhaumik and his team for providing them with a number of analyses and derived information.

In 1994 the world GDP was about $25224 billion. Assuming a growth rate of 2.5 per cent for 1995–2000, 3 per cent for 2000–2010 and 3.5 per cent for 2010–2020, we can project world GDP to be $55453 billion. The faster growth rates projected for the beginning of the twenty-first century are based on the appearance of newly emerging fast-growing economies (including that of India). The recent problems affecting the South-east Asian economies would change these figures; however, the overall pointers vis-à-vis India's development would still be valid.

Worldwide, considering countries with GDP of $100 billion and above to be countries in the Big League, India was already in this league during the 1980s along with China, Mexico and others. The collective GDP of these nineteen countries in 1980 was about $8168 billion and India's share was only 1.74 per cent. In the decade of the 1990s, there are new entrants and a few exits, bringing the Big League Countries (BLC) to twenty-four. In 1990, the collective GDP of the BLCs was about $17625 billion, but India's share was 1.44 per cent only, a fall compared to better achievers in the world. In 1994, the BLCs were twenty-eight in number including Thailand, South Africa and Turkey with collective GDP of $22348 billion. India's share fell to 1.31 per cent.

TABLE 1.2

World GDP

Years	US$ Billion
1995	25854.08
1998	27842.02
2000	29251.52
2002	31032.94
2005	33910.53
2007	35975.68
2010	39311.60
2015	46689.85
2020	55452.90

Note : Assuming growth rate of 2.5 per cent for 1995-2000, 3 per cent for 2000–2010 and 3.5 per cent for 2010–2020. Courtesy: T.K. Bhaumik, Senior Adviser, Confederation of Indian Industry

TABLE 1.3

Big league of the world economy

Countries	Collective GDP (US$ million)	Share of India (%)
1980 (Total 19)		
India, China, Brazil, Mexico, Argentina, Saudi Arabia, Spain, Italy, U.K., Australia, Japan, Canada, U.S., Netherlands, France, Belgium, Sweden, Germany, Switzerland	8168190	1.74

Countries	Collective GDP (US$ million)	Share of India (%)
1990 (Total 24)		
New Entrants *Exits* Indonesia, Argentina, Iran, Saudi Arabia Denmark, Austria, Korea, Norway, Finland	17624570	1.44
1994 (Total 28)		
New Entrants *Exits* Thailand, Iran South Africa, Saudi Arabia, Argentina, Turkey	22347726	1.31
2000 (Total 33)		
New Entrants Poland, Malaysia, Portugal, Israel, Finland	25943552.7	1.68
2010 (Total 38)		
New Entrants Philippines, Colombia, Pakistan, Iran, Chile	34831636.5	2.62
2020 (Total 42)		
New Entrants Peru, Hungary, Venezuela, Greece	52488568.2	4.07

Note: Countries with GDP of $100 bn and above are considered countries in the Big League. Courtesy T.K. Bhaumik, Senior Adviser, CII

Considering the present trends of economic growth, it is projected that by 2000 there will be 33 BLCs and India's share can rise to 1.68 per cent; and by 2020 there would be 42 BLCs with India's share projected at 4.07 per cent (see table 1.3). Figure 1.1 indicates how this march could proceed.

Even this preliminary exercise would indicate the challenges before us. The assumed growth rates are not impossible to achieve, nor are they easy. To achieve the fourth position may mean more challenging growth rates of 10 per cent–13 per cent in the later years, as indicated in figure 1.1. The recent problems facing the South-east Asian economies can be seen as a newer challenge or even as a greater opportunity.

We believe that we as a nation should aim to reach at least the fourth position by the year 2020. True, there are many factors we have to take into account. For instance, other countries may perform better than is anticipated. Also, as we grow, competition in international transactions (be it in trade or finance or technology or any other) may take different forms than those which exist today. Unfair grouping against Indian interests cannot be totally ruled out despite several multilateral or bilateral arrangements. But then, growing up and being counted are not easy tasks. It is therefore imperative that to keep up our growth we manage our exports and imports and ensure our endogenous competitive strengths within the agricultural, industrial and service sectors. All these have to be achieved without compromising on our primary goal: the benefits of well-being percolating down to all our people and as speedily as possible. Let us have a look at how the distribution of wealth may appear. Table 1.4 provides a possible scenario.

Naturally, we need to look at population growth. World population is estimated to be 7 billion by the year 2000 and projected to be 9.4 billion by the year 2020. In India the current population growth rate of 1.8 per cent can be envisioned as coming down to 1.5 per cent by 2020. Investment in primary education and basic health care facilities is vital if the rate is to be brought down, as it must be if we are to achieve the vision of a developed India. With certain assumptions it is possible to

FIGURE 1.1

India in the Big League
1996–2020

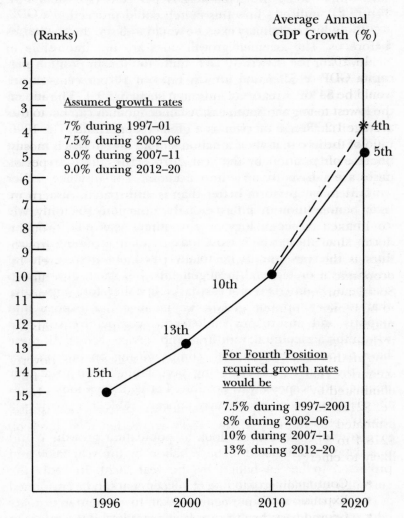

(Ranks)

Average Annual
GDP Growth (%)

Assumed growth rates

7% during 1997–01
7.5% during 2002–06
8.0% during 2007–11
9.0% during 2012–20

* 4th
5th

10th

13th

15th

For Fourth Position
required growth rates
would be

7.5% during 1997–2001
8% during 2002–06
10% during 2007–11
13% during 2012–20

1996   2000   2010   2020

Courtesy: T.K. Bhaumik
Senior Adviser CII

envision a population of about 1.2 billion by 2010 and therefore a per capita GDP of $762 at constant prices (being $3146 with purchasing power parity—PPP); and a population of about 1.4 billion by 2020 and per capita $1540 at current prices ($6355 with PPP). Similarly, distribution of GDP and per capita GDP according to the income class can be envisaged to be as in table 1.4.

In 2020, the lowest 10 per cent would then have a per capita GDP of $569 and for the top ten percentile group it would be $4369, with overall average being $1569. The ratio of the lowest to the highest would be about 1:7.7; the lowest to the average 1:2.75; and the average to the highest 1:2.78. The 1996 ratio of the lowest to the top was about the same. This is mostly because of linearity implied in the projections. These types of ratios are also similar in other countries.

It is to be noted that the income distribution pattern in India between 1960 and 1994 has *not* changed significantly. We would like to recommend that these ratios are further brought down. How this can be done without affecting overall growth rates is the question. Equity cannot be achieved merely by economic measures or fiscal policies or technologies alone. Social awareness and action is also called for. However, it needs to be remembered that to provide any meaningful equity, it is necessary that the economy be strong and the right mix of technologies is deployed.

Another crucial human element relates to the poverty scenario. There are good chances that poverty can be fully eliminated by 2007/8 using the present poverty line as a base, i.e. $212.8 at 1996 prices. Personal disposable income is also estimated to increase considerably from the 1996 level of $278.4 to $1717.1. Other features of the economy which are likely to emerge are:

- Continually expanding domestic market
- Expansion of the wage economy
- Growing tendency towards self-employment
- Expanding informal economy despite growth of formal sector

TABLE 1.4

INDIA VISION 2020

Distribution of GDP and per capita GDP (according to income class)

Income Class	GDP ($ Billion)				Per Capita GDP ($)			
	1996	2000	2010	2020	1996	2000	2010	2020
Lowest 10 %	12.47	16.1	33.7	79.1	130.1	158.8	281.9	569.2
Next 10 %	16.02	20.9	43.8	102.6	169.2	206.0	365.7	738.5
IInd Quintile	40.30	52.8	110.3	258.7	212.8	259.7	461.0	930.8
IIIrd Quintile	52.60	68.9	144.0	337.9	278.8	339.0	601.8	1215.4
IVth Quintile	70.30	92.1	192.4	451.2	371.1	452.8	803.7	1623.1
Vth Quintile	141.90	185.9	388.4	911.0	749.1	914.2	1622.7	3277.1
Top 10 %	94.60	124.0	258.9	607.3	998.9	1218.9	2163.6	4369.4
Overall	333.0	436.4	911.72	2140.5	351.7	429.2	761.8	1538.5

Note: (i) Based on income distribution pattern observed in 1994. (ii) It is observed that growth and inequality have very little correlation (iii) All the countries are seen to have a more or less similar income distribution pattern (data on China is not available but it is understood that inequality is growing with high income growth). Courtesy: T.K. Bhaumik, Senior Adviser, CII

- Simultaneous growth of both production and service sector
- Modernized agriculture—qualitative transition in the rural economy
- Emergence of non-cropping economic activities on a large scale
- Substantial increase in small and medium entrepreneurship with technocrats/professionals leading entrepreneurship
- An era of financial revolution
- Technological upsurge in manufacturing, finance, R&D integration
- India leading the world in certain sectors, e.g. mineral-based industries (steel, aluminium, special alloys, cement), automobiles, electronics, industries based on human knowledge and skills (software, media, financial services), food processing, drugs & pharmaceuticals, etc.

Some social indicators

The literacy rate can be expected to improve from 52 per cent in 1991 to roughly 80 per cent in 2020. The life expectancy at birth is expected to improve substantially. There is likely to be a large population of young people with aspirations of a better lifestyle. There would be a large reservoir of literate and skilled persons. There is also a greater likelihood of more women taking part in direct economic activities including entrepreneurship.

Even while there will be greater urbanization, there would also be greater rural-urban integration economically and socially. Integration with the world economy is also likely to bring a number of different consumption styles and value systems. With increasing prosperity there would also be greater attention to protection of environment. It will be possible to ensure better nutritional and health standards for all our people.

Economic growth, urbanization and exposure to foreign value systems can also bring in various conflicts and alienation.

These are aspects which need to be attended to on the social and cultural planes. Perhaps India may have to devise suitable organizational and educational systems and the media to address social and cultural aspects of life. No doubt our ancient wisdom and traditional knowledge would prove invaluable in this effort. Newer information technologies can help in capturing this knowledge and experience of our common people in various parts of the country and make it available to others to learn from.

As we endeavour towards a developed India through economic reforms and other measures, it is worthwhile to recall what the distinguished economist Amartya Sen has said of this:

> The central issue is to expand the social opportunities open to people. In so far as these opportunities are compromised by counter-productive regulations and bureaucratic controls, the removal of these hindrances must be seen to be extremely important. But the creation of social opportunities on a broad basis requires much more than the 'freeing' of markets. It calls, in particular, for expansion of educational facilities and health care for all (irrespective of incomes and means), and public provisions for nutritional support and social security. It also demands a general political, economic, and social programme for reducing the inequalities that blot out social opportunities from the lives of so many hundreds of millions of Indian citizens.

The vision, as would be unfolded in the subsequent chapters, is based on an assessment of the Indian people and India's resources. India's core strengths are derived from our resources—national and human. The technological vision is aimed at increasing social and economic opportunities for our people and to build on the strengths derived from them. A symbolic representation of the vision may be depicted as in fig. 1.2. The figure indicates not only GDP, per capita, trade and strategic strengths but also reflects achievements in nutrition, in health, in education, in skill, and in providing various social and cultural opportunities for all Indians.

FIGURE 1.2

Towards A Technologically Strong India

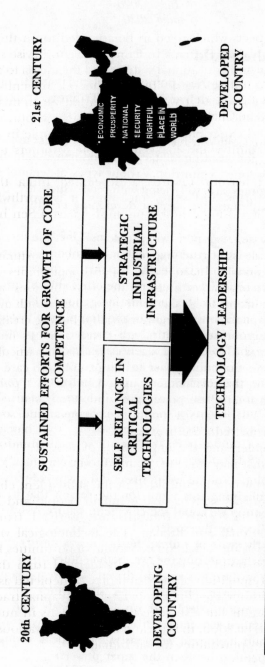

20th CENTURY

DEVELOPING COUNTRY

21st CENTURY

- ECONOMIC PROSPERITY
- NATIONAL SECURITY
- RIGHTFUL PLACE IN WORLD

DEVELOPED COUNTRY

SUSTAINED EFFORTS FOR GROWTH OF CORE COMPETENCE

SELF RELIANCE IN CRITICAL TECHNOLOGIES

STRATEGIC INDUSTRIAL INFRASTRUCTURE

TECHNOLOGY LEADERSHIP

TECHNOLOGY VISION 2020

India and the world

I have been discussing these points and related issues frequently. I quote from a talk delivered at the Tribune Trust on 22 February 1998 at Chandigarh.

> Though the Cold War has ended, selective tactics are still continuing for ensuring military and economic dominance of the developed countries. Various types of technology denial regimes are still being enforced which are now being mainly targeted against developing countries like India.
>
> Today we encounter twin problems. One side there is a large scale strengthening of our neighbours through supply of arms and clandestine support to their nuclear and missile programmes and on the other side all efforts are being made to weaken our indigenous technology growth through control regimes and dumping of low-tech systems, accompanied with high commercial pitch in critical areas. Growth of indigenous technology and self-reliance are the only answer to the problem.
>
> Thus in the environment around India, the number of missiles and nuclear powers are continuously increasing and destructive weapons continue to pile up around us, in spite of arms reduction treaties.
>
> To understand the implications of various types of warfares that may affect us, we need to take a quick look at the evolution of war weaponry and the types of warfare. I am highlighting this point for the reason that in less than a century we could see change in nature of warfare and its effect on the society.
>
> In early years of human history it was mostly direct human warfare. During the twentieth century up to about 1990, the warfare was weapon driven. The weapons used were guns, tanks, aircraft, ships, submarines and the nuclear weapons deployed on land/sea/air and also reconnaissance spacecraft. Proliferation of conventional, nuclear and biological weapons was at a peak owing to the competition between the super powers.

The next phase, in a new form, has just started from 1990 onwards. The world has graduated into economic warfare. The means used is control of market forces through high technology. The participating nations, apart from the USA, are Japan, the UK, France, Germany, certain South-east Asian countries and a few others. The driving force is the generation of wealth with certain type of economical doctrine.

The urgent issue that we need to address collectively as a nation is, how do we handle the tactics of economic and military dominance in this new form coming from the back door. Today technology is the main driver of economic development at the national level. Therefore, we have to develop indigenous technologies to enhance our competitive edge and to generate national wealth in all segments of economy. Therefore, the need of the hour is *arm India with technology.*

Vision for the nation

Nations are built by the imagination and untiring enthusiastic efforts of generations. One generation transfers the fruits of its toil to another which then takes forward the mission. As the coming generation also has its dreams and aspirations for the nation's future, it therefore adds something from its side to the national vision; which the next generation strives hard to achieve. This process goes on and the nation climbs steps of glory and gains higher strengths.

The first vision: Freedom for India

Any organization, society or even a nation without a vision is like a ship cruising on the high seas without any aim or direction. It is clarity of national vision which constantly drives the people towards the goal.

Our last generation, the glorious generation of freedom fighters, led by Mahatma Gandhi, and many others set for the nation a vision of free India. This was the first vision, set by the people for the nation. It, therefore, went deep into the minds and the hearts of the masses and soon became the great inspiring and driving force for the people to collectively plunge into the struggle for freedom movement. The unified dedicated efforts of the people from every walk of life won freedom for the country.

The second vision: Developed India

The next generation (to which I also belong) has put India strongly on the path of economic, agricultural and technological development. But India has stood too long in the line of developing nations. *Let us, collectively, set the second national vision of Developed India.* I am confident that it is very much possible and can materialize in 15–20 years' time.

Developed status

What does the developed nation status mean in terms of the common man? It means the major transformation of our national economy to make it one of the largest economies in the world; where the countrymen live well above the poverty line, their education and health is of high standard; national security reasonably assured, and the core competence in certain major areas gets enhanced significantly so that the production of quality goods, including exports, is rising and thereby bringing all-round prosperity for the countrymen. What is the common link needed to realize these sub-goals? It is the technological strength of the nation, which is the key to reach this developed status.

Build around our strength

The next question that comes to the mind is, how can it be made possible? We have to build and strengthen our national infrastructure in an all-round manner, in a big way. Therefore, we should build around our existing strengths including the vast pool of talented scientists and technologists; and our abundant natural resources. The manpower resource should be optimally utilized to harness health care, services sectors and engineering goods sectors. We should concentrate on development of key areas, namely agriculture production, food processing, materials and also on the emerging niche areas like computer software, biotechnologies and so on. The common link required to bring this transformation is the human resources. Therefore, adequate attention needs to be paid to development of special human resource cadre in the country to meet these objectives.

Beyond 2020

The attainment of a developed status by 2020 does not mean that we can then rest on our laurels. It is an endless pursuit of well-being for all our people. Our vision of a developed nation integrates this element of time within it as well. Only people with many embodied skills and knowledge and with ignited minds can be ready for such a long-term vision. We believe that it is possible to develop our people to reach such a state, provided we can follow a steady path and make available to the people the benefits of change all through their lives. They should see their lives and those of others improving in actual terms, and not merely in statistical tables.

Actions

This means the vision should become a part of the nation, transcending governments—the present and the future. To make this happen, several actions are required. An important element of these efforts is to develop various endogenous technological strengths. After all, technologies are primarily manifestations of human experience and knowledge and thus are capable of further creative development, under enabling environments.

We have often asked ourselves and others why India in its several thousand years of history has rarely tried to expand its territories or to assume a dominating role. Many of the experts and others with whom we had a dialogue referred to some special features of the Indian psyche which could partly explain this: greater tolerance, less discipline, the lack of a sense of retaliation, more flexibility in accepting outsiders, great adherence to hierarchy, and emphasis on personal safety over adventure. Some felt that a combination of many of these features have affected our ability to pursue a vision tenaciously. We will give glimpses of these views in later chapters.

We believe that as a nation and as a people we need to shed our cynicism and initiate concrete action to realize the second vision for the nation. The first vision, seeded around 1857, was for India to become politically independent; the second one is to become a fully developed nation. Our successful action will lead to further action, bringing the vision much closer to reality. Perhaps in a decade from now we may even be judged as having been cautious and conservative! We will be happy if the action taken proves that they could have been still bolder in advocating a faster march towards a developed India!

We had written this chapter before the nuclear tests on 11 May 1998. The details of the numbers projected in the tables and figures may change but our belief in what we say there remains unchanged. In any case, they are meant to be indicative of directions for change. We have seen the reactions to the tests within the country in the Indian and foreign media. We have also had the benefit of private conversations with many Indians. In all these, I observed one striking feature: a number of persons in the fifty-plus bracket and especially those who are in powerful positions in government, industry, business and academia, seem to lack the will to face problems. They would like to be supported by other countries in every action we have to take in the country. This is not a good sign after fifty years of an independent India which has all along emphasized 'self-reliance'.

We are not advocating xenophobia nor isolation. But all of us have to be clear that nobody is going to hold our hands to lead us into the 'developed country club'. Nuclear tests are the culmination of efforts to apply nuclear technology for national security. When we carried out the tests in May 1998, India witnessed issuing of sanctions by a few developed countries. In the process, the same countries have purposely collapsed their own doctrine of global marketing, global finance systems and global village. Hence India has to evolve its own original economic policy, as well as development, business and marketing strategies.

It is not just that the Indian nuclear tests are resented. If tomorrow Indian software export achieves a sizable share in the global market, becoming third or fourth or fifth in size, we should expect different types of reactions. Today, we are a small percentage of the total trade in software or information technology. Similarly, if India becomes a large enough exporter of wheat or rice or agro-food products to take it into an exclusive club of four or five top foodgrain-exporting nations, various new issues would be raised couched in scientific and technical terms ranging from phyto-sanitary specifications to our contribution to global warming. Multilateral regimes to these effects exist in terms of General Agreement on Trade and Tariffs (GATT) and other environment related multilateral treaties. India cannot afford not to sign these treaties, though we could have done our homework a little better during the negotiations. We have to face what we have with us. We need to play the multilateral game, attract foreign investments, have joint ventures and be an active international player. Still, we have to remember that those who aim high, have to learn to walk alone too, when required.

There are economic and social problems in South-east Asia and Japan. Each country is trying to tackle them in its own way. There is a variety in the approaches. Some may overcome the difficulties and some may not. We believe India can still emerge a major developed country and all its people can contribute to and share in the prosperity. Our hope lies in the fact that even in the older generation, there are a number of persons who are ready to face the challenges. Most of the people are proud to see an India that is bold. In addition, the younger generation is ready to take action in such a complex environment. Many of them have to contend with difficult hierarchial structures in the Indian systems, whether in the private or public sector, in government or in academia. They are ready to rough it out. That is where our hopes lies for the realization of the Second Vision.

Chapter 2

What Other Countries Envision for Themselves

> *Believe nothing, merely because you have been told it, or because it is traditional or because you yourselves have imagined it. Do not believe what your teacher tells you merely out of respect for your teacher. But whatever after due consideration and analysis you find to be conducive to the good, the benefit, the welfare of all beings, that doctrine, believe and cling to and take it as your guide.*
>
> —The Buddha

As a country, we have not yet become bold enough to set a course of our own. When Gandhiji adopted ahimsa and satyagraha as methods of obtaining freedom, it was a great innovation. But today we want only to imitate what others have done, be it in economic policy, industry, trade, science, technology, media or even literature. India has never been averse to welcoming ideas and peoples from outside. It has assimilated many ideas, cultures and technologies after shaping them to suit its genius and its environment. Indians too have gone abroad and disseminated our culture. We have contributed to technology as well: the stirrup and the rocket, the numbers theory in mathematics, herbal medicine and metallurgy, to name some. Today we see a new situation, in which our high calibre scientists and technologists enrich the economies of the USA and European and other countries.

Somewhere down the line in our long history, we appear to have lost faith in ourselves. That mindset seems to persist. For a time we shut our doors to other ideas and mainly fought among ourselves. Then came a period when we blindly adopted whatever was foreign. We seem to have a blind admiration of anything done outside our borders and very little belief in our own abilities. It is a sad state to be in, after fifty years of independence. However, there are brighter spots too.

This mythical foreign superiority is vouched for, sometimes, by people who ought to know better. They simply cannot believe that we too can aspire for, and achieve, excellence in technology. I have in my possession a glossy, superbly produced German calendar with maps of Europe and Africa based on remote sensing. When people are told that the satellite that took the picture was the Indian Remote Sensing Satellite, they find it hard to believe. They have to be shown the credit line under the pictures.

When it is something relating to the past, things are even worse. I recall a dinner meeting with many participants and Indian guests where the discussion drifted to the early history of rocketry. The Chinese invented gunpowder a thousand years ago, and used powder-propelled fire arrows in battle during the thirteenth century. During the course of the discussion, I spoke of the effort I made to see Tippu's rockets in the Rotunda Museum at Woolwich near London which were used in the two battles of Seringapattam. I pointed out it was the first use of military-powered rockets anywhere in the world, and that the British studied these rockets and improved upon them for use in their battles in Europe. A senior Indian immediately concluded that the French had imparted their technology to Tippu. I had to politely tell him that this was not the case and that I would later show him a book authenticating what I said. The book, by the famous British scientist Sir Bernard Lovell, was entitled *The Origins and International Economics of Space Exploration.* William Congrave, studying Tippu's rockets, demonstrated the prototype of improved versions of rockets in September 1805 to Prime Minister William Pitt and

Secretary of War Lord Castlereagh. Impressed, they used these rockets in a British attack against Napoleon in the occupied parts near Boulogne harbour during October 1806. Subsequently, the rockets were used by the British in the attacks on Copenhagen during August-September 1807, and in April 1800 against the French fleet anchored near Rochefort.

The Indian guest looked at the book carefully, glanced through the parts I had pointed to, flipped a few pages and gave the book back, saying, 'Interesting.' Did it make him proud of India and Indian creativity? I do not know, but it is true that in India we have forgotten our creative heroes. The British have a meticulous record of all that William Congrave did to improve Tippu's rockets. We don't even know who Tippu's engineers were, nor how the rockets were manufactured on a large scale. A crucial task before us is to overcome this defeatist mentality that has crept into our intelligentsia and the powers-that-be, the fatalistic belief that Indians cannot do anything new in India.

It is good to read, hear and see what others have done. However, the conclusions regarding what is good for our country are to be shaped by our own people. With this in mind, we should look at how other countries have generated vision documents of their own.

The USA and Europe

The United States of America is a big economy that has grown over two centuries into a major industrial, commercial and military power. In addition to abundant natural resources and the hard work of an adventurous people, the two world wars also helped the USA to develop many technological strengths. There were many entrepreneurs who worked hard to realize their vision: Richard Branson, Andrew Carnegie, George Eastman, Thomas Edison, Henry Ford, King Gillette, Lee Iacocca, William Lear, Helena Rubenstein and recently Bill Gates, to name a few.

It is interesting to note the background of some of these great achievers. Richard Branson, who established an empire of music-related products, was from a family of lawyers and high school dropouts. Andrew Carnegie, a name synonymous with the American steel and iron empire, was a son of poor linen weavers and had no formal education. Henry Ford, who was a farmer's son with a modest background, not only established the largest company of his times but also revolutionized manufacturing techniques. One common feature of all these people is their commitment to a vision and tenacious hard work to achieve it. But it was not only the hard work of an ethnically diverse population and great natural resources that led to the nation becoming the world number one. It was also due to a national characteristic: to recognize the best and to get the best out of the best.

There were and are thousands of small-scale entrepreneurs and venture capitalists who daringly invested in their future missions. There were hundreds of researchers fuelled by a lifetime dedicated to extending the frontiers of science and technology. In addition, many companies or business organizations like Merck, Bell Labs, 3M, Hewlett-Packard, Martin Marietta, Du Pont, Citicorp, Wal-Mart, IBM and Compaq had a vision of long-term developments and invested huge funds in research aimed at technological excellence and core strengths. Such commitment to a long-term vision by American companies continued despite the fact that there were a number of failures. Thus in the American system, such vision in terms of technological leadership had been internalized at various levels of society, including the consumers. Therefore, the role of the government could be centred around major areas like defence, space and atomic energy.

John F. Kennedy's vision of an American on the moon, the USA's competitive challenge to the Soviet Union's first entry into space, is common knowledge. Gathering government and public support behind that one vision made possible its realization and also provided several spin-off benefits. Recent US presidents also emphasize that strengths in technology are the engines of growth and a crucial element in providing jobs for Americans. President Clinton has called for energy security:

to be independent of the need to import energy sources by the early part of the next century. So research and development in various new areas of energy as well as for energy conservation are being stepped up. Most American strategic military capabilities are also focussed on eliminating or drastically decreasing dependence on foreign governments for defensive purposes; therefore sophisticated and better technologies are being developed and deployed. What was demonstrated during the 1991 Gulf war is one facet of such capabilities.

Though in some areas its lead is being eroded by others, the USA continues to set the agenda in many fields of technology. Based on these strengths it also attempts to dominate the world: in politics, culture, trade and in almost every other sector.

In contrast, the UK (which once prided itself that the sun never set on the British empire) never declared any long-term vision. The UK has recently however started a Technology Foresight Programme supported by the government. Germany has also adopted some elements of the Japanese twenty-five-year Technology Vision Exercise in projecting the nation's future possibilities. In France the government has always played a proactive role in developing core technology strengths in many areas: military, aerospace, electronics, biotechnology and agro-food sectors. This role continues, and France is determined to be a major world player through the use of better technology. Much smaller countries like Finland with a population of just five million also emphasize their technological strengths. Finland is a leader in the production of ecofriendly paper, and in telecommunications.

All these visions draw on individual research, reports from private agencies as well as national governments. The European Union also places a strong emphasis on technological capability. Towards that end it has set up a number of technology forecasting institutions which produce regular reports. A common feature of the conclusions drawn in all these publications is the emphasis on the acquisition of internal capabilities in areas like advanced materials, electronics and information technologies, biotechnology, advanced manufacturing techniques which include design, robotics, and CAD/CAM (computer-aided design and computer-aided manufacture). As one author puts it, these areas of technology are commonly agreed upon from Tokyo to Brussels to New York. However, there are several variations in detail as well as in their emphasis on other technologies. Each country has to find its own balance of various requirements.

India has also similarly found its own balance through collective and creative thinking by over five thousand people. We will see that story in the subsequent chapters. In this chapter, we will analyse the approach of other countries which can offer us some lessons: Malaysia, China, Japan, Korea and Israel.

Malaysia

During the past decade Malaysia has made a mark in the world. Its people are much better off economically. It has successfully built upon the wealth of a mere plantation economy to be now considered one of the important industrialized economies of the modern world. This is because of the shared vision of its people—a vision articulated by the Malaysian prime minister, Mahathir Mohamed. On his visit to India in 1996, at one of the functions organized by the Confederation of Indian Industries, he saw glimpses of India's Technology Vision 2020 through a multi-media presentation. He also saw a special exhibition of India's Super Computer Anurag, and the CAD/ CAM software of the Aeronautics Development Agency (ADA). He asked questions about the cost-effectiveness of composite material products and titanium products. He later shared his country's Technology Mission 2020 with the Indian audience, remarking, 'Our 2020 also means perfect vision,' reminding us that he was originally a physician.

Malaysia has framed a strategic master plan to become a fully developed nation by the year 2020. This calls for concerted development in all areas—economic, social, political, spiritual, psychological and cultural. The balanced development of the nation encompassing 'its natural environment requires a strong capability in science and technology', as Mahathir Mohamed puts it. The Malaysian focus is not only on the major manufacturing sectors with heavy industries, such as steel and core manufacturing and petroleum and chemical sectors — it also concentrates on advanced micro-electronics, consumer goods, computers and telecommunications. The Malaysian vision envisages a role for foreign direct investment. It also wants to achieve complete design capability and to manufacture products using indigenous expertise. This emphasis is important: the ability to design on your own and manufacture products to your design is a crucial indicator of 'developed' capability.

In the goods and services sector, the aim is to enhance value addition in the production and delivery of goods. The areas targeted by Malaysia are: advanced materials (which is why the Malaysian prime minister asked questions about advanced composites and titanium products), advanced manufacturing technologies, microelectronics, information technologies and energy technologies. In its plans for science and technology, the Malaysian government envisages a doubling of the percentage of GDP devoted to research. The vision articulates the strategies through which Malaysia aspires to be in the forefront of certain areas of technology, not merely as a leading exporter of technology-intensive products, but also a generator of a few major technologies in microelectronics and in several other areas. The vision also provides a glimpse of the roles of various regions of Malaysia and some of its bigger dreams of becoming a multi-media supercorridor.

In addition, the vision addresses relevant environmental aspects. It points out that despite rapid progress, Malaysia's forest resources have not been sacrificed and 60 per cent of the land is still forest. The vision envisages a strong commitment to 'green' policies and it states that environmental problems cannot be dealt with unilaterally or even bilaterally; they must be approached holistically and multilaterally. The many facets of infrastructural development are also a part of Malaysia's vision. This nation is taking constant measures to drum up the enthusiasm of various interested parties in realizing this vision. Its present emphasis is on action.

China

It is difficult to compare countries because various factors such as size, culture, history, geography, natural endowments, geopolitics and internal polity come into play. There are some goals which can be achieved by smaller countries; but sometimes smaller countries find it difficult to embark upon certain big technological plans even if they have the funds because the size of the domestic market is too small. If we consider the bigger countries, the closest comparison to India is China, though there are many crucial differences.

The Chinese vision is to prepare the country for entry into the ranks of mid-level developed nations by the middle of the twenty-first century. Acceleration of the nation's economic growth and social development by relying on advances in science and technology is pivotal in this.

Documents describing the Chinese vision state that science and technology constitute premier productive forces and represent a great revolutionary power that can propel economic and social development. It is interesting to note that the main lessons the Chinese have drawn from their past performance is their failure to promote science and technology as strategic tools for empowerment. They also point to the absence of mechanisms and motivations in their economic activity to promote dependence on science and technology. Similarly, they hold that their scientific and technological efforts were not oriented towards economic growth. As a consequence, they conclude, a large number of scientific and technological achievements were not converted into productive forces as they were too far removed from China's immediate economic and social needs. The Chinese vision is therefore aimed at exploiting state-of-the-art science and technology to enhance the nation's overall power and strength, to improve the people's living standards, to focus on resolving problems encountered in large-scale industrial and agricultural production, and to effectively control and alleviate pressures brought on by population, resources, and the environment. By the year 2000, China aims at bringing the main industrial sectors up to the technological levels achieved by the developed countries in the 1970s or '80s, and by 2020 to the level they would have attained by the early twenty-first century. The aim is to bridge the overall gap with the advanced world. There is a special emphasis on research and development of high technologies that would find defence applications. Some of these technologies are critical for improving the features of key conventional weapons. Some technologies are meant for enhancing future military capabilities. Other efforts are aimed at maintaining the momentum to develop capabilities for cutting-edge defence technologies. They call for unremitting efforts in this regard with the aim of maintaining effective self-defence and nuclear deterrent capabilities, and to enable parity in defence, science and technology with the advanced world.

The underlying principle is that economic growth must be driven by science and technology and scientific and technological principles must be geared to economic growth, so as to foster the harmonious development of both.

Some glimpses of the Chinese vision documents are in order here, as they relate to various sectors of the Chinese economy. These are:

- Open all avenues for new sources of food and develop new protein resources and mixed animal feeds. Develop diversified food production and plant resources for the purpose of improving the diet of urban and rural residents.
- Take full advantage of hybrid and genetic engineering techniques to screen and breed new high-yield, fine quality, adversity-free animal and plant varieties.
- Strengthen research and development of various elements to drastically increase the quality and yield of agricultural products.
- Equip agricultural and township enterprises with

modern industrial technologies, develop technologies for storage, transport, processing, packaging, and comprehensive utilization of agricultural products.

- Guide the diversion of surplus rural labour to the development of a rural commodity economy.
- Accelerate research and development of core technologies for heavy-duty rail transport and rapid passenger transit lines over 200 km/hour.
- Strengthen the technological and industrial capabilities for electronic equipment and machine tools.
- Increase rate of innovation in the field of mechatronics.
- Increase science and technology inputs to the consumer goods industry. Improve the technical levels of village and township housing construction, design and management.
- Upgrade the technical level of social and public facilities and service industry.
- Micro-electronics and computer technologies: accelerate the development of micron and sub-micron silicon integrated circuits design, manufacturing, and testing centres and opto-electronic integration technologies; super high-performance parallel computers and commercial software engineering; new generation computers; artificial intelligence; robotics technology.
- Use of biotechnology as a powerful means of addressing food, health, resources, environmental, and other major problems.
- Advanced materials technology to make breakthroughs and to bring about fundamental changes.
- Aerospace technology: manned space flight and maintaining an international position in the field.
- Develop a network of gas pipelines to meet growing energy demand.
- Source energy supplies overseas.

As is seen in the later chapters of this book, there are a number of common elements in the Chinese long-term plans and the vision that has emerged for India, though these have been arrived at independently of each other.

Japan

In many ways, Japan can be considered the country that has pioneered the systematization of a long-term technological vision of the country as whole, and translated its vision into reality through trading agencies, industry, laboratories, universities, financial institutions and government agencies. The Japanese Science & Technology Agency has perfected various surveying techniques to assess what the Japanese experts forecast as future events and possibilities for a period of twenty-five years. Starting with the years from 1970 to '95, there is to be a revision every five years. The latest document available is 'The Fifth Technology Forecast Survey: Future Technology in Japan Toward the Year 2020' by the National Institute of Science and Technology Policy/Science and Technology Agency (Japan) and the Institute for Future Technology. It divides technological areas into the following broad headings (see table 2.1, below):

TABLE 2.1

Materials and processing	Information and electronics	Life science	Outer space
Particles	Marine science and earth science	Mineral and water resources	Energy
Environment	Agriculture, forestry, and fisheries	Production	Urbanization and construction
Communications	Transportation	Health and medical care	Lifestyles and culture

The technological possibilities, mostly given as a defined end-result or applications, are listed with figures indicating the probable year of occurrence, as per the analyses of expert opinions. The flatness or sharpness of the graphs indicates whether the expert opinions vary significantly or are nearly unanimous. These forecasts, methodologies for which have been perfected over more than two decades, are very strongly oriented in terms of Japan's domestic consumption or external trade. These national level forecasts are internalized in many businesses, industries and institutions to underpin their plans of action. It is remarkable that the nation is geared at various levels to be ready for meeting the challenges of the future as envisioned by experts.

If we look at the case of Japan, there are many indices through which Japanese growth can be judged and depicted. These are the GNP, GDP or per capita export growth. This growth has been achieved in a short period, a testimony to the Japanese vision. An important element which has been both the cause as well as the effect of Japan's grand vision, is the ability to deal with technologies. Japan made development of internal capability for technologies an essential component in every part of its vision.

In the sixties, the Japanese were not technological leaders. In fact, Japanese products during that period were known more for their poor quality. The country had to import technologies in a major way. But the Japanese made it a point, mostly through voluntary action by their industries and government agencies, to invest about four times more towards their own technology development for every unit of money they spent in importing technology. This was meant to develop internal technological core competencies in their industries and institutions. Over a period of about two decades they have reached the status of a net exporter of technology and become one of the world's great economic powers, though their own natural resources are practically negligible in most sectors.

As shown in figure 2.1, in 1975, Japan's bill for import of technologies was close to 20 billion yen, and receipts of money through export of technology was around 5 billion yen. Japan had a deficit of about 15 billion yen in technology trade in 1975. Imports increased as the economy was growing. But its export of technology began to increase much faster, especially from 1986–87 onwards—so much so that in 1995 Japanese export of technologies amounted to 56.21 billion yen, and

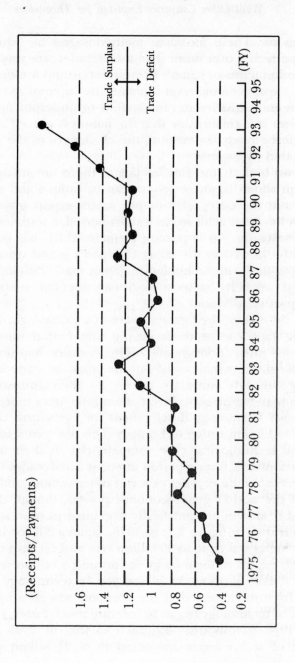

FIGURE 2.1

Technology balance of Japan (Ratio of receipts and payments)

Trade Surplus

Trade Deficit

(Receipts/Payments)

(FY)

1975 76 77 78 79 80 81 82 83 84 85 86 87 88 89 90 91 92 93 94 95

1.6 1.4 1.2 1 0.8 0.6 0.4 0.2

Source: General Coordination Agency, Japan

imports stood at 39.17 billion yen. As indicated in figure 2.2, after a few ups and down, Japan has had a continuous trade surplus in technology since 1993. In fact, it did achieve a trade surplus a few years earlier, but it fell subsequently. Then exports and imports became equal. Now, they have achieved a very clear margin of exports over imports.

Their strategy for export-import is not just one to one. When they import from a country, they do not necessarily have to export back to the same country in the same mode, because a vision should also have a certain realism. Their long-term goal was to become a net exporter of technology. Realizing that they were not ahead in many areas in the 1960s and '70s, Japan's strategy was to export to countries less developed than it and to import from countries which were more developed, to continue to use them, improve upon them and export products to the advanced countries as well. In terms of technologies, the Japanese were able to export to countries which were relatively less developed. In this process they managed to become overall exporters of technologies. But now, that is not enough for Japan: this nation always keeps aiming higher.

Recently the naval chief, who visited Japan and South Korea, explained to me that the Japanese have as part of their vision the aim to equal and surpass the United States in all aspects, whether it is in the generation and export of technologies or in the quality of life. Similarly, the Koreans confided to him that they would like to equal and surpass the Japanese!

How did Japan achieve this status? Not overnight, but over about two decades, with large teams in industries, laboratories, government, financial institutions, users, and consumers holding steadfast to their vision of a developed Japan and working hard to ensure that the vision was realized.

This vision was shared by politicians, administrators, diplomats, businessmen, scientists, engineers, technicians, bankers and people from several other occupations. Whenever a Japanese agency or industry imported a technology, they did not rest in peace. They worked hard to understand it and to

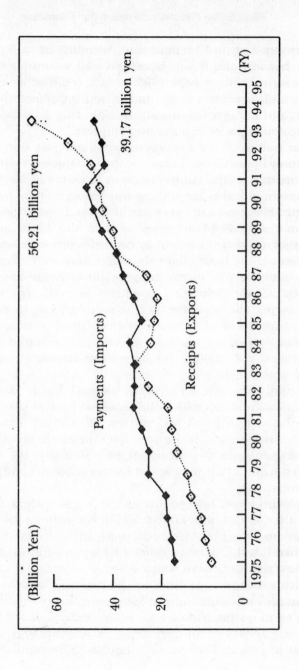

FIGURE 2.2

Technology trade of Japan (Payments and Receipts)

56.21 billion yen

39.17 billion yen

Payments (Imports)

Receipts (Exports)

(Billion Yen)

60

40

20

0

1975 76 77 78 79 80 81 82 83 84 85 86 87 88 89 90 91 92 93 94 95 (FY)

Source: General Coordination Agency, Japan

improve upon it. In the process they spent almost four times as much as the value of imported technology in generating their own technologies, because they knew that a developed Japan could become a reality only when it was technologically competent and when it could develop its own designs. The results are before us: a country devastated by war and two nuclear bombs, and subjected to humiliating conditions after the Second World War, is now accepted as one of the world's seven most powerful countries. Japan has very limited natural resources and was restricted in its attempts to acquire military strength. It has won through a technological race, inspired by a vision.

Other countries in the world have begun to emulate the Japanese example by developing core competencies in technologies to use as competitive tools in business. Even a powerful nation like the USA is often obsessed with containing Japan in trade and business.

For example, US businesses, which are ferociously independent and resent joint actions with the government, came together in 1991 under the Council of Competitiveness. In its report, *Gaining New Ground: Technology Priorities for America's Future*, the council noted that 'this project was characterized by uncommon cooperation and involvement on the part of public and private sectors'. The council conducted an in-depth analysis of nine major technology-intensive industries: aerospace, chemicals and allied products, computers and software, construction, drugs and pharmaceuticals, electronic components and equipment, machine tools, motor vehicles and telecommunications. Together, these sectors account for more than $11 trillion in sales and directly employ twelve million people. They have attempted to look 'beyond the parochial interest of each sector in the national interest'.

The 'remarkable consensus' for the 'first time between America's corporates, academic and the labour leaders' underscores a crucial point in the technology debate: the US needs to move beyond simply making lists. Instead, America needs a pragmatic plan for joint public and private sector action. The report compares Japan and Europe with the US and derives a plan for competition. It clearly acknowledges the lead of Japan in a number of areas in commercially viable technologies. Such is the power of Japan's commitment to concerted action as regards its technology vision for more than three decades.

A 1997 document by Keidarnan (Japan Federation of Economic Organizations) describes 'an attractive Japan', 'a country that gives the young hope for the future and is perceived by people around the world as a good place to live, do business and study'. The report also states that 'we must understand that Japan's future depends on the progress of science and technology'. We have a lot to learn from Japan's dedicated and sustained efforts in achieving technological excellence and leadership.

South Korea

About three decades ago, South Korea was not even considered a force to contend with. Korea received some attention during the Korean War in the 1950s and was generally forgotten soon after. The country had suffered extensive damage while it was occupied by Japan during the Second World War. It was considered by many nations, including India, to be a country so poor that there was no hope for it. It also suffered a partition. Despite this, South Korea created a vision by which it became a major global player in a few years in some major economic sectors that used modern technologies. These were steel production, shipbuilding, automobiles and electronics. There were many western economists who thought that this was a wrong strategy, because the country did not have a natural core competence in any of these areas. But South Korea was a nation with a will. It did achieve success in all these areas. South Koreans have gone on to become formidable multinationals in these areas as well as in several others. In electronics, South Koreans still use the 'reverse entry' technique in various areas. That is, they use themselves as a manufacturing base initially, and then use a few selected technologies of their own to create the subsequent models. And they have invested

FIGURE 2.3

Milk yield for major countries per head of cattle per year

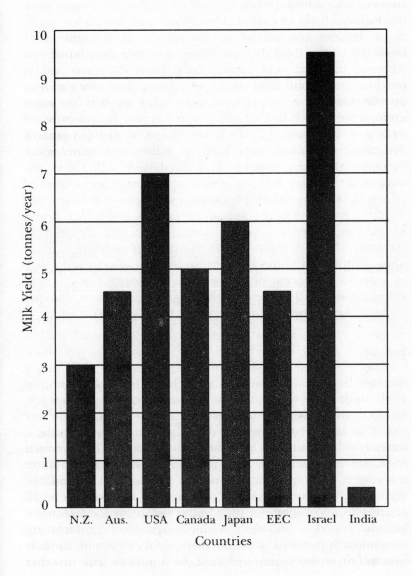

in R&D, enabling them to make major contributions in some areas, such as electronics. Their quality of life has improved tremendously over two decades, and per capita income has risen to about US$ 10000.

Koreans from an earlier generation recall that about two or three decades ago discussions around the dining table were confined to the food they ate in the morning or at lunch; or what was planned to be cooked later. Food was scarce, and a meal or some good food served as a strong incentive for most people. Just to be able to have three solid meals a day was a great achievement in that era. South Koreans have now gone well past that stage. Food is no longer a major point of discussion with them: now it is the globe—how many more successes they can achieve. A detailed study will show how massive technological input as well as concerted and sustained efforts in building core technological strengths in industry and business have been the prime propelling forces for South Korea's achievement. Considerable funds are devoted to research and development expenditure in industries. They have design capabilities in many areas. The authors are aware of some of the recent problems in South Korea. But the core strengths of South Korean technologies are so high that the country should be able to overcome these problems soon.

Israel

Another interesting country is Israel. It was born as a nation in 1948, under very difficult circumstances. Israelis were not just satisfied with having a home of their own. They had a further vision: to be able to meet not only their immediate food and water requirements, but also those of the future. They wanted food and water security, in a place which was a desert. Water was scarce. They were surrounded by hostile nations, and had very little by way of natural resources. They were a small country too. Yet they not only had a vision for food security, but also aimed to become a leader in agro-food products and set standards in terms of productivity, yield or even in absolute production in many items of food, be it milk or fruit or other commodities. They did deploy a large amount of technology in this venture, leading to Israel being today a leader in agriculture and agro-food related technologies. Figure 2.3 compares the milk yield of different countries. For annual milk yield per head of cattle, Israel's figure for 1994 is about 9200 kg. The runner-up is the US with about 7000 kg per head of cattle per year. In India the figure is only about 500.

Israel did not stop merely at food security in food and agriculture. It needed defence. They have remarkable capability in defence and military equipment, including missiles. They sought nuclear, space and electronics capability, and now have several excellent products and technologies. Israel is globally acknowledged as a technological, military and economic power. That is due to its long-term vision and sustained action.

We are not alone in thinking of a vision for 2020. Many others are thinking of their future, and are striving hard to make a better future for themselves. One common feature is the greater emphasis on technological strengths in multiple areas such as manufacturing, advanced materials, electronics and information technologies. In addition, these countries share the concern for clean and environmentally friendly technologies. In China, USA and Europe there is a continued thrust for advancement of defence technologies. China's approach to agriculture has common features with that of India. USA, Europe and Japan place much greater emphasis on biotechnology with global markets in view. The vision that emerges for India is based on the perceptions of its security environment, its social and economic needs as well as an assessment of its core strengths. It is a vision for our people. Let us not leave millions of our sisters and brothers in poverty any longer. We should wipe out poverty by 2010 and become a developed nation by 2020.

Chapter 3

Evolution of Technology
Vision 2020

India's Core Competencies

Your country, brother, shall be your love!
Good unto better you shall improve!
Great deeds indeed are needed now!
Work hard, work long in farm and factory!
Let the land be abundant in milk and honey!
Flood the land with goods, all made at home!
Spread your handiwork all over the world!
Are you a patriot? Do not shout it aloud!
Bragging never did anybody any good!
Quietly, do a fine deed instead!
Let the people see it, it is they that decide!

—*Desha bhakti* by Gurajada
Translated from Telugu by Sri Sri Mahakavi

In the pre-independence days, India had many dreamers; many capable women and men thinking of a strong and modern India. Many of them took the initiative in various fields, political, social, economic, industrial, educational, literary, scientific, engineering and the religious. They enriched India by their actions, and reflected different facets of our independence struggle. Independent India was enriched by this inheritance.

Added to this was the fact that India had richer natural resources as compared to many other countries. These perceptions led to the passionate call for building a great nation.

After independence, India made simultaneous progress in many fields: agriculture, health, education, infrastructure, science and technology, among others. Her vibrant democracy was a wonder to the world, which thought India would be plunged into chaos after the British left.

About two decades after independence, despite our numerous achievements, doubts emerged about our ability to handle our system on our own. Many of our vital socio-economic and even military sectors began to have a greater dependence on foreign sources for innovation or technology. Self-reliance and commitment to science and technology were the declared policies, but often crucial economic and industrial decisions were based on technology imports or licensed production, both in the private and public sectors.

Space research and a few other areas developed more as islands of confidence rather than as movements for developing core industrial and technological competencies. Therefore, around the late '70s and the '80s, a diffidence to take major initiatives had begun to set in, though there are some remarkable examples of facing challenges too, be it by launching a missile programme or building a supercomputer or launching a few technology missions or in establishing institutions like C-DoT (Centre for Development of Telematics).

Faced with this unusual combination of growing dependency with a few bold successes, a unique institution called the Technology Information, Forecasting and Assessment Council (TIFAC) was born in 1988. Its major task was to look ahead at the technologies emerging worldwide, and pick those technology trajectories which were relevant for India and should be promoted. In its tasks, TIFAC networked various stakeholders: the government, industries, users, scientific and technological institutions, financial institutions and intellectuals.

TIFAC also studied the ideas of several Indian visionaries in the field of technology and the plans of various organizations. Over a period of years it produced several reports suggesting what India should do to assume leadership in areas like sugar, leather, steel, biotechnology or manufacturing. It did not stop merely at studies but also attempted to make the stakeholders take action. A few major government-supported technology missions with strong industry participation were an outcome of these activities.

All these were good initiatives successfully undertaken in exceptionally difficult situations. Though laudable, however, they did not go far enough in the context of a big country like India seeking to fulfil her true potential. This was uppermost in the minds of concerned Indians.

Technology Vision 2020

It is against this background that the TIFAC Governing Council met on 24 November 1993 with its forty members drawn from industry, R&D establishments, academic institutions, government departments and financial institutions and debated how TIFAC could contribute to national development. An intense discussion took place about India's past and present technological performance and what could be feasible in the future. In the midst of the discussion one of the TIFAC council members posed a very interesting question. 'Mr Chairman, we all have to address one issue: India today, almost fifty years since 1947, is branded a developing country. What will make the country a developed nation?'

Everyone present realized that therein lay the crux of the problem and to arrive at the answer to the question became the agenda. Two council meetings were held to discuss the means to arrive at the answer. It was realized that technology is the highest wealth generator in the shortest possible period if it is deployed in the right direction. Technology strengthens the political, economic and security structure of the nation. For India, technology had to be the vision for the future.

Technology can help transform multiple areas such as

education and training, agriculture and food processing, strategic industries and infrastructure in various fields. It is on this basis that the task forces and panels of the Technology Vision 2020 were constituted.

India's needs and core competencies

India's needs are very clear: to remove the poverty of our millions as speedily as possible, say before 2010; to provide health for all; to provide good education and skills for all; to provide employment opportunities for all; to be a net exporter; and to be self-reliant in national security and build up capabilities to sustain and improve on all these in the future. How can India meet these needs? To be able to chart out the possible paths towards this end, an assessment of India's core competencies is a prerequisite.

What is a core competency? Put simply, it means that in certain areas we have some inherent strengths whereby we can show a much better output and better results in a shorter time. In the final analysis, any given group of people in any given locale and under any conditions can accomplish what they really want to. But there are certain things which they can do much better given the same will and effort, either due to a more enabling environment or due to better experience. These, then, are a country's core competencies.

There have been a number of debates on the existence of core competencies in India: some backed by informed opinion and others charged with strong emotion. This is because India is a vast country with different regions having different strengths and weaknesses. There are also different types of people: some with the best of education, training, exposure and experience. There are many less fortunate ones with average educational opportunities and work experience. There are many unfortunate ones for whom survival on a day-to-day basis takes up all their attention; they have few skills and very little opportunity. Such problems need not overwhelm us. An objective appraisal shows that less fortunate Indians too have shown the ability to absorb new techniques and skills and also methods of functioning. In the early years after independence the rapid growth of the economy was due to our innate ability. Our people learnt new agricultural practices; many learnt to work in factories and various public service activities. An improved educational base helped them better absorb the new approaches and knowledge. Despite the appalling state of female illiteracy, it is also a fact that a large number of women from all walks of life rapidly adjusted to new forms of economic activity.

It is clear that the major technological and industrial achievements of our country have come about through the endeavours of thousands of young women and men who have studied in 'ordinary' schools and colleges in different parts of India. Not all of the few million persons of Indian origin who live and work in different parts of the world are from the Indian Institutes of Technology or other such prestigious institutes. They are from the 'ordinary' institutions of India. There are doctors, engineers, technicians, nurses, artists, writers, journalists, accountants, clerks, teachers, and various kinds of professionals and others in the work-force. Even the recent Indian software miracle is the making of a large number of 'ordinary' young women and men, who may not be able to talk fluently in English, but can understand instruction manuals and master computer operations well enough to enable them to stand up to global competition.

One thing then is crystal clear: India's human resource base is one of its greatest core competencies. It is India's strength. If we can train an unskilled Indian, if we can impart better skills to a skilled Indian and if we create a more challenging environment for the educated, as well as build avenues for economic activity in agriculture, industry and the service sectors, these Indians will not only meet the targets but excel them. The Technology Vision documents advocate the formation of a human resource cadre that will be the foundation of the action packages for the country in the near future. Such a cadre will lead us to economic achievement.

Indians not only have a great learning capability but most of them also have an entrepreneurial and competitive spirit. Today, there are not enough avenues to channelize this spirit constructively and productively. That is what we should aim for. Naturally the vision projects several elements that capitalize on this vital resource of India. The details of the emphasis vary from sector to sector, whether it is agro-food or materials or biotechnology or strategic industries, and take into account both socio-economic needs and the complexities of the technologies involved.

Another core strength of India is its natural resource base. Though India may not have rich deposits of all the ores and minerals, or of a uniformly high quality, it has abundant supplies of most of them. We have good ores for steel and aluminium. We have abundant supplies of ores of the wonder metal titanium and several rare earth materials, though we have not used them effectively. We have a vast coastline which stores many more resources and energy supplies. They are the strengths of our future as we use more of the land resources. Undersea resources are yet to be explored.

In addition to these, we have an excellent base for living resources: very rich biodiversity; abundant sunshine; varied agro-climatic conditions, almost a microcosm of the globe, from arctic cold to tropical green to bare deserts; and plenty of rainfall, though we do not tap it effectively. To illustrate: if the annual rainfall all over India were evenly spread over the country, the water would exceed one metre in depth. If only we could tap such largesse! India's Technology Vision 2020 is built around its natural resource base, its vast human resource base and the core competencies of the nation.

The generation of the vision—how was it done?

It is difficult to recapitulate all the details of the mammoth exercises done by the TIFAC task forces and panels. In Appendix 1 we list the names of chairpersons and co-chairpersons. There were about 500 persons active in the panels and task forces.

Many more—about 5000—participated through responses to questionnaires, or with written or oral inputs. Many others who did not respond to the questionnaires later said that it was an excellent exercise and the questions had set them thinking. They wished they had asked those questions themselves in the context of their business or other activities.

Keeping in mind India's needs, core strengths and competencies, the focus was on the crucial sectors. They were agro-food processing, road transportation, civil aviation, waterways, electric power, telecommunications, advanced sensors, engineering industries, electronics and communications, materials and processing, chemical processing industries, food and agriculture, life sciences and biotechnology, healthcare, strategic industries, and services. All these panels and task forces also considered the driving forces and impeding factors in their own areas and provided suggestions for speedy action. In addition, there was a special panel on Driving Forces and Impediments. The following paragraphs extracted and adapted from a few TIFAC documents describe both the objectives and methodology.

The objectives of the task forces and panels were to

(a) provide directions for national initiatives in science and technology to realize a vision for India upto 2020;
(b) provide a strong basis for policy framework and investment for R&D in the government and the private sector; and
(c) contribute to the development of an integrated S&T policy both at the state and national levels.

The major long-term national assessment and forecasting exercise was constituted into seventeen panels and task forces. Of these, ten were headed by experts from industry, five from R&D institutions and two from the government. Each task force had a chairperson, a co-chairperson and a coordinator.

The studies employed various techniques of forecasting like brainstorming sessions, preparation of perspective and scenario reports, Delphi rounds, nominal group technique in some cases, subsequent workshops, etc. (see fig 3.1). The task forces and panels addressed the following questions:

- Are there areas where India has a strong technology base?
- What are the technologies which can dramatically change Indian social or economic conditions or which have specific advantages?
- What are the spin-offs from the technologies developed?
- What is the focus on in-house and indigenous technological development?
- What should be the actions, strategies and policies which will be implemented in the future to secure a competitive advantage in the world market.
- Which are the technologies that would come into the future in a big way by 2010, 2015, 2020 and 2025 respectively?
- Which are the technologies that would become obsolete or disappear by 2000, 2005, 2010 and 2015 respectively?

The cross-linkages and input flow between various panels and task forces were maintained through chairpersons/coordination and the staff. At the subsequent TIFAC council meetings, several task forces and panels presented their findings from the reports. During the 23rd TIFAC council meeting held on 18 April 1996 in New Delhi, it was decided to widely disseminate the reports with the help of industry, industry-associations, government departments, agencies, organizations and other interested groups in these areas so as to formulate some action-oriented projects during the Ninth Five Year Plan (1997–2002) for realizing this Technology Vision for India.

The perspective and scenario reports of the panels, Delphi responses and Nominal Group Technique (NGT) rankings formed the basis on which the vision and action reports were finalized, and suggestions were also formulated for policy guidelines, strategies and action plans for the government, industry, R&D institutes and academic institutions to realize the vision for India up to 2020.

FIGURE 3.1

Methodology of Generating Technology Vision
for India up to 2020

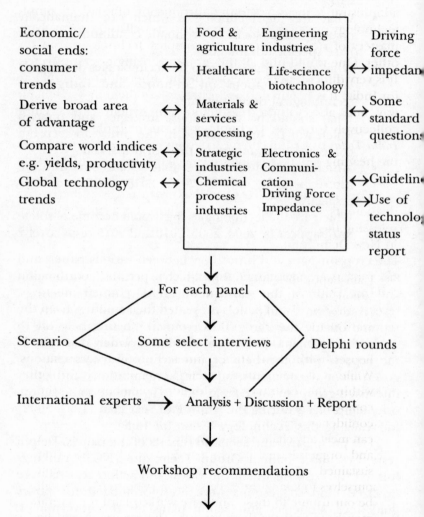

Source: TIFAC

Each vision report contains valuable information on the current status, forecasts, and assessment of a sector. One can see through these reports various outcomes and suggestions for action ranging from simple modification of policies and/or administrative measures to the introduction of relatively simple technology practices on the one hand, as well as those involving mastery of new and emerging complex technologies on the other. One would find all these options being interconnected. It is very difficult to choose one or the other alone as sufficient for India. It is essential to orchestrate all of them in a systematic way and also with a reasonable time-synchronism. These collectively form the Technology Vision for India up to 2020. *India Today* of 31 July 1996 carried an exclusive preview under the heading '50 Technologies That Will Change Our Lives' by Raj Chengappa.

The mammoth exercise has resulted in twenty-five documents. H.D. Deve Gowda, then the Prime Minister, releasing the Technology Vision 2020 reports on 2 August 1996 in New Delhi, said:

> I am happy to learn that the reports present not only a Vision in 2020 but also spell out the intermediary steps required to be taken by government, institutes, industry and others. The coming years require greater emphasis and investment, particularly by industry and business houses, for creating indigenous technological strengths. While it is not necessary that we develop everything within the country, we should remember that the competitive world respects technological strengths. I have confidence that our managers, experts and work force can meet any challenge—even the complex technological and organizational tasks—if we make dedicated and sustained efforts. I would suggest that we all commit ourselves to taking the necessary follow-up steps. This will be our tribute to those who have worked hard for several months to prepare these reports. The reports should be widely disseminated and become a source of inspiration to our younger generation.

The minister of state for science and technology, Prof Y.K. Alagh said:

> India is one of the very few countries which has produced such reports. This in itself illustrates the trend as technological strength built up in our institutions, industries and users.

Summing up, I said:

> I have presented the results in several forums to various persons: young and old. I find them uniformly enthused about the vision and they want to do something soon. Therein lies our strength. We have not really tapped the full potential of our multi-institutional networked strengths. I hope these documents will provide such an opportunity. I firmly believe that ignited minds are the power resources. Can we trigger the young minds in national development? Yes, we can.

A few chairpersons presented the key results. None of them had rehearsed or exchanged notes before the function; the smoothness of the presentation showed how well they had absorbed the findings.

Even though there are twenty-five documents for seventeen areas (see fig. 3.2), there are tremendous linkages across all of them. For example, when the near doubling of cereals is envisaged for 2020, it implies the crucial importance of post-harvesting processes, including storage, transportation, distribution and marketing. Similarly, if we are to become leaders in machine tool industries, the document calls for focussing our strength in software engineering. Through the wealth of our software engineering, we should enter into Computer-Aided-Design and Computer-Aided-Manufacturing (CAD-CAM), resulting in India assuming leadership in the key areas of machine tools and similar industries with value-added software. Our strengths in the conventional manufacturing of plants and machinery, the knowledge base in chemistry, the growth of computer simulation as well as rich biodiversity provide a new role for us in the modern clean chemicals

FIGURE 3.2

Linkages in Vision

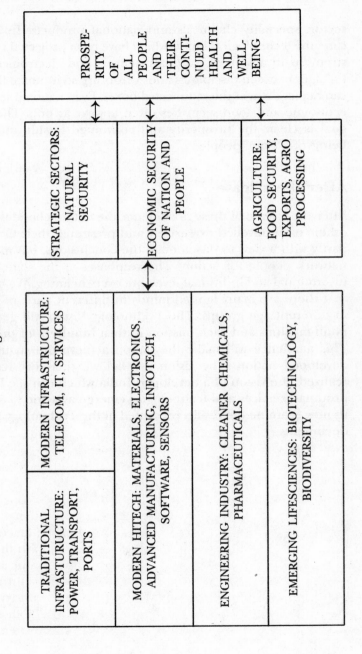

sector, speciality chemicals and national products. In health care, the technological inputs which have been projected require strengths in advanced materials, sensors and electronics. The linkages between disciplines and sectors are so intimate that we can depict them as interconnected boxes. Even national security, economic and food securities often appear as one. The final goal is clear: the prosperity and continued health and well-being of all our people.

After the release

After the release of these documents, the authors besides many others have travelled extensively and presented their findings, partly with a view to disseminate the conclusions, but more to network people for action. The responses at the state, local, institutional and individual levels are overwhelming. We believe that there are many ignited minds in different parts of India, in different age groups. The Technology Vision will generate multi-missions and each mission in turn hundreds of projects. This ambience will make the nation achieve the status of a developed nation. The vision, we believe therefore, can be realized: the vision of a developed India which can see Indian products, services and technologies emerge as world class! Let us now examine the results presented in the Technology Vision documents.

Chapter 4

Food, Agriculture and Processing

> *If the farmer's hands slacken*
> *even the ascetic's state will fail.*
> —Thirukkural, 104:6

About 40 per cent of our people live below the poverty line today. They face problems of day-to-day existence, with not enough money to buy simple food items, often not even for the next meal. Still, the situation is much better than what it was at many periods before independence and even during the 1960s. Today's teenagers would not know about the near famine conditions that prevailed in certain regions of the country before independence and even after, and particularly about our dependence on American wheat in the sixties.

The crisis and Indian food security

Prof S.K. Sinha, an eminent Indian agricultural scientist who led the food and agriculture panel of the Technology Vision is often fond of quoting the following:

> It is also important to recall the experience of
> C. Subramaniam, the then Union minister of agriculture

during the critical years of 1965–66 and 1966–67. He has stated that 'we had to import 10 million tonnes and 11 million tonnes during these two years—that was a danger signal, you can't be depending upon imported food-grains at that level, particularly when it came from 12000 miles away. During the second year of that critical period of drought, President Johnson, because of certain policies he had adopted, was releasing the foodgrains in driblets. At one point, we reached a stage where there were stocks for only two weeks and there was nothing in transit in the pipeline.'*

This crisis gave the country's leadership an opportunity to resolve to become self-sufficient in foodgrains. This period also coincided with a breakthrough in technology at international centres for improvement of rice and wheat strains. India took advantage of these technologies, experimented with them, and launched large-scale agricultural extension services, instead of viewing these technologies merely as research curiosities. Within three years the production of wheat doubled. This led to foodgrain self-sufficiency in the 1970s when we developed rice and wheat varieties acceptable to our people.

Later when two of the worst droughts of the century occurred in 1979 and 1987, the world did not take note of them because no food aid was asked for. The country now has a buffer stock of about 35 million tonnes of foodgrains. The 1990s have seen a certain degree of diversification of agriculture and exports of various agricultural products including wheat and rice. There is also a growth in the agriculture-based processing industry.

Future needs and capabilities

So can we rest on our oars, comfortable in the belief that there are no more problems on the food front? Will there be no

---

Wheat Revolution—A dialogue. Edited by Dr M.S. Swaminathan, Macmillan India Ltd., 1993.

possibility of a repeat of the humiliation and stress the country and our people had to go through from 1965 to 1967?

We may look at table 4.1 below, which is a prediction.

TABLE 4.1

Projected Grain Imports in 2000 and 2010

Countries	*Million Tonnes*	
	2000	*2010*
South Asia	9.2	12.8
East Asia	31.4	39.0
India	6.9	14.1
Pakistan	2.1	4.5
Indonesia	5.7	7.6
China	11.3	21.6

Source: TIFAC, Food and Agriculture: Technology Vision 2020

According to table 4.1, India may have to import about 14 million tonnes of foodgrains by 2010 and then imports will grow at the rate of 2 per cent every year! Can we draw comfort from the fact that Pakistan will have to import 4.5 million tonnes in 2010 and China 21.6 million tonnes? Along with many others who have studied these issues in depth and thought about possible solutions, we believe that we need not accept these conclusions at all since India has tremendous potential for increasing production. India either already has the necessary technologies or can develop them easily. Our people and our farmers are exceptionally entrepreneurial, and have proved it again and again. But we can belie the gloomy predictions only when we resolve to work hard with a long-term vision. We cannot afford to believe that we are far enough ahead in the race to go to sleep like the hare which lost to a tortoise.

Food demand and the Indian people

Let us pause for a moment and see how some of the doomsday predictions about availability of foodgrains in India or its import arise. Some of the reasons are:

(a) A growing population. India's population is projected at 1.3 billion by the year 2020.
(b) Economic growth is another factor. As the economy grows, people earn more and consumption rises. It will be a happy day when our poor have enough to eat.
(c) In addition, there is a definite change in lifestyle. There is a clear trend towards consumption of meat products with the increase in income. Consumption of non-vegetarian food tends to increase the consumption of cereals as well.

Based on many such factors and variables, several studies indicate the demand of foodgrains in the year 2000 to range from as low as 191 million tonnes to as high as 286 million tonnes! A scenario for domestic demand for foodgrains for different rates of economic growth is given in table 4.2.

Since we need at least a 7 per cent growth rate to reach developed country status, it is safe to assume a demand of 340 million tonnes of foodgrains by 2020. All these projected increases in demand place additional pressure on Indian agriculture. The optimum allocation of land and other resources for various crops will itself pose a challenge. Can we declare, consume less milk or oil or eat less vegetables? These are the new challenges before us in a not-too-distant future.

Challenges to Indian agriculture

Thus the growing demand for foodgrains, vegetables, fruits, milk, poultry and meat as well as cash crops is going to present greater and newer challenges to agriculture. Let us not forget that our existing food security has been mainly brought about by the increase in irrigated agriculture and the introduction of

TABLE 4.2

Projected Household Demand for Food in India at 7 per cent Income Growth

Commodity	Annual household demand (million metric tonnes)					
	1991	1995	2000	2010	2020	
Foodgrains	168.3	185.1	208.6	266.4	343.0	
Milk	48.8	62.0	83.8	153.1	271.0	
Edible oil	4.3	5.1	6.3	9.4	13.0	
Vegetables	56.0	65.7	80.0	117.2	168.0	
Fruits	12.5	16.1	22.2	42.9	81.0	
Meat, fish & eggs	3.4	4.4	6.2	12.7	27.0	
Sugar	9.6	10.9	12.8	17.3	22.0	

Source: TIFAC: Food and Agriculture: Technology Vision 2020

high-yielding varieties of crops. Current stability in production is through wheat, largely a winter crop. However, the rainfed areas, which account for 70 per cent of the net cultivated areas of the country, have not benefited from modern developments in agriculture. Of this 70 per cent, about 30 per cent area is under dryland agriculture where annual rainfall is up to 400 mm.

The problems in areas with rainfed agriculture need to be understood. The lesser the rain in an area, the greater the trouble for the farmers and villagers there. I recall my frequent visits to Suratgarh, Rajasthan, in the late 1960s and '70s, in connection with certain important projects, when sounding rockets of the Indian Space Research Organisation (ISRO) were being tested. I remember the pathetic situation which then prevailed. During many seasons, it was rare to find even blades of grass. Now when I visit some areas in Rajasthan for other programmes, I am struck by the change brought about by the irrigation waters of the Indira Gandhi Canal. The change in the quality of the people's lives is something that gives me immense satisfaction. I envisage an India with many such canals—big and small—connecting different river systems and waterbodies. I would like to see an India whose watersheds and rainwater are managed to benefit the poor people and to boost our agriculture.

What is to be done with the rainfed regions till then? Leave them to the centuries-old toil of their farmers? Or neglect them with the hope that we may be able to make a breakthrough in newer technologies so that we can achieve whatever we want from the 30 per cent irrigated, relatively affluent agricultural zones? There have been several successful small experiments in different parts of both the rainfed and dryland areas of our country. For example, there has been considerable success in some pockets of Maharashtra in conserving water, planting of trees, developing village-level grazing lands and regulating water use by the community. This has helped in raising suitable crops and livestock and in creating a viable market system. If we only recall how the Green Revolution took place: several farmers from the irrigated regions of India were given an opportunity to visit other parts of the world. Should we not as a country extend similar opportunities to the farmers in the rainfed and dryland regions of our country at least to visit other places in our country (and if possible to go abroad too) to observe for themselves the success of farmers there who have overcome similar conditions to increase productivity.

Our people and farmers are all integrated into one huge market. All those concerned need to be educated about another important scientific fact, through observation, discussions and mass contacts: that is, regarding agro-ecological considerations. Accordingly, the drylands of central India cannot have high productivity rates of rice and wheat (which are the major foodgrains relished by Indians). Therefore, agriculture in the central Indian drylands can be focussed on pulses, oilseeds, vegetables, fruits and livestock. Wheat and rice can be concentrated in more suitable regions. Each state should concentrate on agricultural products most suited to its agro-climatic conditions, as it cannot hope to be self-sufficient in all the essential commodities. Suitable marketing and transportation systems can be evolved to facilitate the exchange of commodities. In addition, special attention should be given to the agriculture in the eastern region of India, especially to increase productivity. Large parts of eastern India, though blessed by excellent agro-climatic and water resources, have a very low productivity. This situation has to change if India aims at food security and economic prosperity.

There is a need for multi-pronged action. Merely having better seeds or better irrigation will not suffice. The tasks involved today are much more complex than they were during the Green Revolution.

Environmental problems and international pressures

In the coming years we cannot address our agricultural problems in isolation. The General Agreement on Trade and Tariffs (GATT) and the obligations to the World Trade

Organization (WTO) have implications for the future course of agricultural research and development and other initiatives we may take. These relate to giving market access to other countries in selling their products in India. This will place a demand on quality and efficiency in our own agricultural operations. Limits will be also placed on how much domestic support we can give to our agriculture.

Restrictions in terms of sanitary and phyto-sanitary measures both for import and export of agricultural commodities will be imposed. This means there will be demands that residues of pesticides and chemicals be reduced to the internationally acceptable standards. Suppose we say that we will adopt these standards only for exports and that for our own domestic markets we may relax these conditions. Then our own people, starting with environmental activists, will insist that we should also adopt international standards as otherwise the health of our people will be in danger. Thanks to information technology, the demand for stiffer environmental standards in any one part of the world soon becomes a global issue. Thus, the use of agrochemicals and fertilizers has to often conform to international specifications. There are also other considerations of equal national treatment under the WTO. In other words, we cannot have one standard for Indian business and another for a foreign entity.

Serious implications arise from various international obligations for the protection of Intellectual Property Rights (IPR). This means far greater commercial restrictions in the use of technologies developed elsewhere in the world. Even our own research cannot be based on mere imitation of foreign technologies. For example, we cannot assume easy availability of better seeds as we had obtained through the Mexican high-yielding varieties at the beginning of our Green Revolution: witness the trend of foreign scientists and technologists attempting to patent an agriculture-related invention—new methods of growing basmati rice—as happened recently in the US.

Now let us go back to table 4.1 which projects possible

foodgrain imports by a number of countries with huge populations. If a number of them do import, many companies in developed countries will resort to selling foodgrains as a business. (Even now they do, though in ways that are not too obvious.) Once we have to depend on imports to provide food for our people, foreign companies and governments can use this issue politically to derive many trade and political advantages. It is also likely that they will resort to conditionalities which will perpetuate the dependence.

An environmental concern that is likely to have implications for Indian agriculture is the emission of gases like methane and carbon dioxide. These are calculated based on various models. India will be told that we contribute so much and there may be some penalties on those who emit more than an internationally established limit. Some of the concerns could be real but some could be an outcome of complex geopolitical motivations. The latter can assume various forms to mask pressures. In any case we have to learn to make our own models and counter geopolitically-motivated pressures. Further, since climatic changes will affect agriculture, we should also be able to filter out facts of scientific relevance and take advance action to protect our agriculture.

The technologies

In addition to representing the national will and organizing a large-scale national effort, technologies play a crucial role in achieving food security for the country.

We would naturally start with biotechnology as it deals with many aspects of basic inputs to agriculture: seeds, plants, soil treatment, etc. It is crucial to food security, if we take the right steps. One of the most important technologies is that which can lead to transgenic plants: that is, plants which are 'human-made' and are tailored to meet the desired objectives by transfer and expression of the desired type of gene to a target plant. Worldwide, a number of such developments are taking place. In 1994–95, of the total number of 482 transgenic plants that were produced, 30 per cent were field tested for herbicide resistance, 24 per cent for product quality, 21 per cent for insect resistance, 14 per cent for viral resistance, 3 per cent for fungal resistance and 8 per cent for other special traits. Targets of the developed world's biotechnology industry are given in table 4.3. Crops reported to have been transformed are vegetables, field crops, fruits and nuts besides others. Among the vegetables are: asparagus, carrot, cauliflower, cabbage, celery, cucumber, horseradish, lettuce, pea, potato and tomato. Among field crops: alfalfa, corn, cotton, flax, oilseed (rape), rice, rye, soyabean, sugarbeet and sunflower. And among fruits/nuts were apple, pear and walnut.

TABLE 4.3

Targets in Improvement for Selected Crops in North America and Europe Through Biotechnology

Tomato	:	Improved texture, increased solids, enhanced firmness
Potato	:	Increased solids, reduced browning, uniform starch distribution
Canola	:	Modified oil composition, improved oil quality, improved feed quality

Source: TIFAC Food and Agriculture: Technology Vision 2020

As of now it appears that the major benefits of biotechnology are focussed on the processing industry, e.g. tomato, potato. These are not the crops which can provide food security now or in the future.

In India, a certain amount of crop (transgenic) biotechnology is being put to use. Major efforts are being undertaken to make cotton pest-resistant. Most readers would be aware of the spate of suicides by cotton farmers recently. Let us hope there will be scientific and technological breakthroughs in pest-resistant transgenic cotton seeds. Till we achieve success in this on a commercial scale we cannot be sure that we will have enough supplies to plan large-scale operations. No doubt such researches should be encouraged, but we should look at other fronts too. It is necessary for research on crop biotechnology in India to be focussed on our important crops, especially those related to food security.

We have to bear in mind that the application of biotechnology may not have any major impact on food security in India in the next five years, though crops of industrial value and vegetables may benefit to some extent. Therefore, we will still need to depend upon conventional agricultural technologies even while we target biotechnology for future-oriented applications. Internationally, no major breakthrough in improvement of wheat strains has occurred lately. Hybrid rice is more productive. China had a few major initial successes in increasing the yield through large-scale use of hybrid rice. India has begun use of hybrid rice recently and there are plans to increase it. But it may be noted that in recent years there has been no further improvement in Chinese production of rice. Still, hybrid rice will play an important role in India, as we are yet to introduce it on a large scale.

There are a number of improvements in agricultural implements, machinery, plastics, water technologies, agro-chemicals and fertilizers which are possible and are well within the country's reach. There is an urgent need to conserve water in a number of ways: ranging from water harvesting to drip irrigation. There are a number of good examples in India of water harvesting though these are in isolated pockets. Israel has made water conservation a national policy and has achieved remarkable results. India with its size and with better endowments in water resources can make miracles happen. A major industry can grow around such agriculture support systems.

There are also other technologies which can contribute a great deal to agriculture. We need to use all available methods because the coming years are not going to be easy on the food front. Let us look at one, space technology.

Remote sensing or taking electronic pictures of the earth

from space is extensively used for assessing natural resources, land degradation and water resources as well as to predict crop yield and snow melt, among other things. Some developed countries monitor crop yields of other countries to help their own exports. India is strong in the area of remote sensing technologies. We have our own high resolution remote sensing satellites whose pictures are used all over the world commercially. We also have excellent capabilities in utilizing remotely sensed data for various applications: groundwater targeting, soil salinity assessment, crop yield estimates, and so on. In addition, space technology can be used very effectively to assist extension work: disseminate success stories to farmers, educate them on dos and dont's, and to help them ask questions through talk-back facilities that can be made available through satellite. A number of experiments conducted by ISRO in this regard in Haryana and Madhya Pradesh have to be taken up by other states in a major way. Our farmers should and can be given facilities to keep pace with advances in agricultural technology. Yes, it is a lot of effort. But we have plenty of talent and also the resources. As shown in the chapter on services, providing these facilities in different languages, partly with public support and partly through various business houses and private bodies, can become a good source of employment generation by itself.

Specific and urgent measures needed

Our country is and will continue to be a major producer and consumer of wheat and rice. The areas presently under wheat and rice are restricted and are becoming unsustainable in the face of growing demand. Therefore, several immediate steps that will ensure stability in production are:

(a) Broaden the production area of wheat in eastern UP, Bihar, Orissa, West Bengal and the North-East.
(b) Increase rice production in traditional areas by adopting hybrid rice.
(c) Increase production of coarse grains in central India and develop various products which can partly substitute

rice and wheat. Food technology should be developed as an important area for both domestic as well as export markets.

(d) Make central India the production centre of vegetables and fruits, and make efforts to make these commodities available at a lower price. This will have an effect on the consumption of wheat and rice. A similar effort is needed in a big way in the Indo-Gangetic plains in winter.

(e) Greater emphasis on tuberous crops such as potato, tapioca and sweet potato to make them available at cheaper rates.

(f) There is a shortage of pulses but not of protein in the country. On the basis of 50 gm protein per capita, 18 million tonnes of protein is needed for a one-billion-strong population. Milk, eggs, fish and meat alone provide 11 million tonnes of high quality protein and more than 25 million tonnes come from cereals, pulses, oilseeds, fruits, vegetables and other sources. However, meeting the demand of pulses will remain a priority because of dietary habits.

(g) Since vegetable and fruit consumption will increase in future, an appropriate choice considering agro-climate, input needs and economic returns should be arrived at for every region. Cold storage and long-distance transport will be essential requirements for this purpose.

(h) Animal products will be in great demand. Therefore, efforts to link production, processing and marketing have to be undertaken for each individual product. Involvement of the private sector may prove very advantageous.

(i) Land and water are most the important resources for agriculture, and we have them in adequate measure. India is one of the few countries where nearly 50 per cent of the geographical area is arable, a benefit not available to China or USA. However, per capita availability of land is continuing to decline, leading to still smaller, uneconomical holdings. Their size makes it nearly impossible to make sufficient investments in inputs, and increasing production from them is a difficult proposition. A strategy is needed whereby small farmers don't lose ownership and yet become a part of a larger area of cultivation. Could the private sector be involved in this effort? Different options/ models have to be considered on the issue.

(j) Water should be treated as a national resource and asset. Since the share of agriculture in water supply will decrease, it is essential that water-use efficiency improves. Sprinkle and drip irrigation are necessary in many areas, as also the recycling of water. The storage of water during floods or heavy rain, including ground storage, is a crucial national task. Wherever possible, particularly for horticultural crops, efforts should be made to introduce modern methods of irrigation. Multiple industries need to take part.

(k) Diseases and insect pests, loss of microbial flora from soils and other such factors add to the loss of crop production and cause unsustainability. The use of synthetic pesticides is considered a health hazard. In some areas even groundwater has been polluted. An approach which would consider host plants, climatic factors, use of biological agents and chemicals needs to be evolved. This would be region and season specific. Hence, it would have to be a highly knowledge-based approach.

The Indian approach to food security is not to be restricted or limited to just meeting our own demands. An analysis of table 4.1 reveals that it can be converted to our advantage. We should target exports as well, as an integral part of our strategy. Imagine the influence this would give the country, be it in geopolitics, business and in other strategic considerations.

Incidentally, Prof Sinha, who led the study and was helping with Vision 2020, developed serious eye problems in the course of his work. But he is a man with real vision and will. He went through the ordeals of an operation and medication and finished the report. He is now busy with organizing action packages.

In the course of finalizing action plans to realize the agriculture vision for India, we met interesting groups of persons in rural areas, in agricultural institutions and even in industry. We met an engineer-industrialist from eastern India who has made a lifetime commitment to providing appropriate India-made machines to rice farmers. He travels by road to talk to people himself to assess their needs. He has been successful in making a ploughing machine which can be operated by a kerosene engine of approximately three horsepower; it can also partly run on bio-gas. The ploughing machine weighs only about 100 kg. It has to be light not only because it has to be physically lifted, but also due to the high moisture content of our soils during the rains when rice is grown. Cost-wise it can replace a pair of bullocks with their maintenance requirements. It has a water pump attached to it to mitigate drought, as well as add-on facilities for transplanting and threshing. The industrialist, Ajit Mahapatra, has made it a mission to introduce these machines into farming. His slogan: 'The farmers and machines should grow together'. India has many such able people. There are many dedicated youths and NGOs. Let us build on their strengths.

Post-harvest technologies and agro-food processing

The authors are confident that India can excel and usher in a new era in agriculture. India can emerge as a global power in terms of agricultural produce, not as a diffident exporter but as one capable of meeting global standards. Above all, we should be able to grow plenty of food for our people. This agricultural prosperity will also largely help eliminate rural poverty.

But it is not enough or perhaps even possible to stop at agriculture alone if benefits from it are to accrue to the people and the country. We need to give much greater attention to post-harvest technologies. Today, losses in the food sector are large. Estimates of storage losses in foodgrains can be as high as 10 per cent by weight. In the fruit and vegetable sector the losses are estimated to be as high as 25 per cent. Losses in milk may be about 5 per cent.

Modernization of storage and processing facilities will not only reduce losses but also help in more efficient use of by-products.

We address four major items: cereals, milk, vegetables and fruits. These are critical for the food security of our country, and can also help establish us as an economic power. We are already first in milk and fruit production.

Our vision in agro-food processing can be categorized into three broad time periods: short term where the results can be seen soon; medium and long term where results can be seen only after seven or eight years or more. But our thinking and action should begin now!

Some glimpses of such a vision for India can be tabulated as under:

Issues & Vision	Action required immediately
Short-term Action: CEREALS	
High cost multi-crop harvesters not ideal for Indian conditions. It is possible to change the situation.	Develop harvesters capable of functioning on soil with high moisture content and in standing water. Make design changes to adapt harvesters to harvest grain at high moisture levels.
Increase use of manually operated mechanical devices for harvesting.	Provide government funding for development of low-cost manually operated mechanical devices. Review and revitalize extension services to educate farmers about associated benefits.

Issues & Vision	*Action required immediately*
Reduce glut in mandis during procurement. Reduce packaging and transportation losses.	Install automatic cleaners and graders at the mandis. Initiate use of plastic-lined jute gunnies. Machine-stitch all gunnies. Install 100 per cent weightment at all points of loading and unloading.
Modernization of mills and improved profitability is crucial for the value-addition chain. It is possible to do so with simple technologies.	Urge rice mills to modernize and upgrade operations such as: —using parboiling technologies that require less water and generate less effluent. —substituting rubber rollers with HDPE-reinforced rubber rollers. Facilitate formation of consortia of modern rice mills to fund research in order to: —develop continuous parboiling technologies to further reduce energy consumption and effluent generation —develop value-added secondary and tertiary rice products.
Improving secondary processing of rice as cottage industry is also possible and has to be stimulated.	Government to fund development of low-cost technology based on locally available fuel and non-conventional energy sources.

Issues & Vision	*Action required immediately*
Lack of initiatives to develop new secondary products from maize can be tackled with much more value-addition from maize.	Initiate closer interaction between wet maize millers and secondary product (specially modified starches) users for development, trials and commercialization.

Medium-term Action: CEREALS

Packaging and transportation losses can be brought to very low levels.	Facilitate formation of a consortium comprising modern rice mills to fund research in order to: —improve energy efficiency of mills —extract protein from rice bran.

Long-term Action: CEREALS

Shortage of bulk storage facilities to be made a thing of the past.	Explore the possible use of controlled atmosphere and vacuum storage systems.

Short-term Action: MILK

Poor cattle hygiene and health care practices lead to unhealthy cattle with low productivity. Learning to treat animals as important for our own health and also for economic benefits is an urgent necessity.	Improve availability of trained manpower for veterinary extension services and cross-breeding. Establishment of semen banks at the state/regional level. Development of cross-breeds through DNA markers. Develop feed and feed quality standards for cattle consistent with the breed and yield.

Issues & Vision	Action required immediately
	Upgradation of crop residues and other biodegradable wastes for use as cattle feed. Development of high-yield fodder seeds. Create awareness about veterinary drugs and antibiotics. Create awareness about hygiene standards for housing cattle.
Poor quality of milk processing leading to higher losses is the present status; this situation can be changed very rapidly.	Initiate innovative programmes for training farmers on hygienic methods of collection of milk. Ensure availability of funds for usage of bulk farm coolers/alternative technologies for longer life of raw milk.
Lack of availability of uninterrupted power in the milk production/processing belt is a major hindrance. Technological solutions are immediately available.	Fund research on use of non-conventional energy sources for primary processing. Review use of the LP system as a preservation technique of raw milk.

Medium-term Action: MILK

Medium and long-term vision for cattle management is to preferably treat them with care as they are the foundations of our wealth.	Programme for upgradation of quality of semen and availability of proven bulls. Design breeding policies according to agro-climatic zones. Development of transgenic animals.

Issues & Vision	*Action required immediately*
	Examine use of Rumen bacteria for improved feed absorption.
	Development of inoculants.
Lack of proper treatment of effluent leading to environmental hazards needs urgent attention and in the medium term we can envision them to be pollution-free.	Disseminate use of technology for processing effluent into by-products for small-scale industries.

Short-term Action: FRUIT & VEGETABLES

High level of post-harvest losses of about 30 per cent is a great national loss and especially to the poor growers. This can be brought down substantially.	Ensuring timely harvesting by educating growers regarding proper maturity indices for harvesting.
	Training and education to farmers to promote use of proper post-harvest treatment such as vapour-heat treatment, surface coating etc., at farm level.
Integrated approach to promote Indian horticulture products is needed and can inaugurate a major boom in the business.	Providing financial assistance to R&D institutes to initiate programmes for developing products with characteristics/ quality suited for specific markets.
	Educating the farmers and encouraging them to grow these varieties by entering into buy-back agreements, etc. (for fresh fruits and vegetables).

Issues & Vision	*Action required immediately*
	Disseminate information about specific characteristics of products desired by consumers in the target markets for Indian industry (for fresh and processed products).

Medium-term Action: FRUIT & VEGETABLES

Low yield has to become a thing of the past. This is possible with continual technological inputs.	Promote use of techniques such as tissue culture, grafting, etc. at farm level through effective extension programmes.
High level of harvest, post-harvest losses to be brought to acceptable levels in the medium term by using a multipronged approach.	Development of road infrastructure. Financial assistance to cooperative and private institutions to develop the cold chain infrastructure, CA/MA (controlled atmosphere/modified atmosphere) storage and transportation facilities. Continue promoting the processing of fruits and vegetables at farm level to reduce wastage by educating the farmers and providing desired financial assistance.

Long-term Action: FRUIT & VEGETABLES

Non-availability of good quality raw material for processing will become an issue in the medium	Continue to provide financial support to R&D institutes to initiate programmes for

Issues & Vision	*Action required immediately*
and long term as the food processing industry grows and consumers become more discriminatory. It is possible to meet their requirements.	development of new varieties of fruits and vegetables with characteristics suited for processing and promoting these varieties among farmers by entering into buy-back agreements, etc. It is possible to develop high quality Indian varieties if we focus on our efforts instead of relying on foreign companies.

Source: TIFAC Vision reports on Agro-Food Processing

The authors have often done presentations of these ideas, especially the core technologies which are required to realize the vision. They are given in figures 4.1, 4.2 and 4.3. More than the precise numbers, one should look at the possible growth expressed by the numbers.

The figures on the left hand side give a rough idea of the volume of business in the sector in rupee terms, for the year 1995; estimates of current losses; associated industries (in engineering, packaging, etc). The right hand side is the vision for 2020 for these businesses, with losses, etc. shown at present-day price levels. The middle portion lists some key core technologies required to realize the vision. These are given in the central box and are central to building the agro-processing industry in India.

Some of the requirements are very simple: educating our people in hygienic practices; showing them successes achieved elsewhere, through better practices that have borne fruit, for example, so that they can adopt these too. Our telecommunications and space technologies are well established. Let these be deployed in a major effort. Incidentally, it could become a major service industry and help boost rural economies. The other technologies are relatively simple: standardized chilled containers, or containers with controlled

FIGURE 4.1
Agro-Food: Milk

1995	*CORE TECHNOLOGIES*	2020
• Vol: 61 million tonnes	• COLD CHAINS	• Vol: 300 million tonnes
• BUSINESS:	• CRYO FLUIDS	• BUSINESS:
Rs. 61000 cr/yr	• CONTAINER	Rs. 300000 cr/yr
• LOSSES:	• ASEPTIC PACKING	• LOSSES:
Rs. 3050 cr/yr	• FODDERS	Rs. 3000 cr/yr
• RELATED INDUSTRIES:	• ELECTRONIC TESTING MACHINES	• RELATED INDUSTRIES:
Rs. 31000 cr/yr	• TRAINING TO BE 'CLEAN'	Rs. 310000 cr/yr
—CHILLING	• TO AVOID WASTAGE	—CHILLING
—PACKAGING		—PACKAGING
—VALUE ADDITION		—NEW PRODUCTS

FIGURE 4.2

Agro-Food: Cereals

1995

- Vol: 160 million tonnes

- BUSINESS:
  Rs. 90000 cr/yr

- LOSSES:
  Rs. 9000 cr/yr

- RELATED INDUSTRIES:
  Rs. 9000 cr/yr
  —PACKAGING
  —VALUE ADDITION

CORE TECHNOLOGIES

- PEST/RODENT CONTROL
- STORAGE
- PACKAGING
- HANDLING EQUIPMENT
- AUTOMATIC WEIGHING
- ELECTRONIC SENSORS (MOISTURE ETC.)

2020

- Vol: 270 million tonnes

- BUSINESS:
  Rs. 150000 cr/yr

- LOSSES
  Rs. 3000 cr/yr

- OTHER BUSINESS
  Rs. 86100 cr/yr

FIGURE 4.3

Agro-Food: Fruit & Vegetables

1995

Vol: 33 & 71 million tonnes

BUSINESS:
Rs. 10000 cr/yr &
Rs. 15000 cr/yr

LOSSES:
Rs. 6250 cr/yr

RELATED INDUSTRIES:
Rs. 2500 cr/yr
—CHILLING
—PACKAGING
—VALUE ADDITION

CORE TECHNOLOGIES

- COLD CHAINS
- PACKAGING
- PROCESSING
- ASEPTIC PACKING
- CA/MA CONTAINERS
- WEIGHING AND SENSING
  EQUIPMENT

2020

Vol: 90 & 150
million tonnes

BUSINESS:
Rs. 27000 cr/yr &
Rs. 32000 cr/yr

LOSSES
Rs. 5900 cr/yr

OTHER BUSINESS
Rs. 25200 cr/yr

or modified atmosphere to help preserve products, better packaging and so on.

These findings were presented to a high-powered scientific body. It was explained to them that while they may not appear exciting to top scientists, the steps proposed could bring prosperity to millions. The scientists were touched and affirmed that they would have to take an interest in such matters as well.

It is difficult to capture this vision and action in a few words or one or two catchy slogans. However, to focus on crucial issues, we have attempted to list a few important items below:

- India to aim to be a major player in the world in the agricultural sector and a leading exporter of grains and other agri-products.
- Eastern India to become a major producer of wheat.
- Rice-producing areas to use hybrid seeds on a large scale.
- Central India to be made a centre of vegetables, fruits, pulses and coarse grains.
- More emphasis on tuberous crops.
- Water as a national resource—water management as the key to agricultural prosperity.
- Core post-harvest technologies to be mastered and disseminated.
- Steps to educate farmers about what is happening elsewhere, if need be by providing them the opportunity to travel, and use of space technologies to facilitate interaction and encourage farmers to ask questions and share experiences.

How does one express the vision for agricultural prosperity, describe a vision which uses all the advantages of agro-climate and natural resources, with the use of right and continuous doses of modern technology? The vision naturally includes the fact that for all Indians the availability of food and worrying about where the next meal is coming from will no longer be a prime concern. They will have food in plenty compared to their situation today.

A vision for total production or per capita consumption or

export figures alone does not comprise the totality of what we envisage. The action taken to realize it is just as important. Achieving these projections is not at all impossible. Investments are not difficult. But there is a lot of hard work, synchronization of policies, administrative support and actual field work which includes taking people and farmers into confidence and reaching the benefits of technologies to them that is required.

I have often been questioned by people from diverse walks of life as to the actual realization of the vision. Scientists, technologists, managers or administrators ask, 'In your vision for agriculture, how do we place specific targets? Can we organize a programme like the missile programme?' School and college students ask, 'Sir, can we launch India into agricultural prosperity as you have done for national security with Agni?'

I explain the ideas in different ways. These are addressed in a later chapter. Generally, the answer is on these lines: 'A vision is not a project report or a plan target. It is an articulation of the desired end results in broader terms. For example, a vision for India in the 1980s was to have independent strengths in designing, developing, manufacturing and launching various missiles best suited to our strategic requirements. With the successful launch of SLV-3, with the strengths of DRDO and other potential strengths, such a vision was a realizable one, though difficult when looked at from the perspective of the '80s. But to define individual projects, their interlinkages and the teams required to implement such projects successfully took considerable work from many dedicated persons. Many years were spent in focussing on specific tasks and in defining specific work packages.

'Tasks involved in executing the vision for agriculture and agro-food processing will be equally and in fact more complex. The vision will have to be packaged in a large number of viable, focussed projects. Many of them will be executed by private individuals or groups out of their conviction and risks will be taken by them. A small group of people can be in touch with all of them to make an overall assessment of the direction in which we are going. If there are problems due to policy or perhaps adverse external environmental conditions (drought or pest or hailstorms or a slump in the export market, for example), efforts have to be made to mitigate the hardships of the farmers and entrepreneurs, so that they do not lose their will to pursue the harder tasks ahead.

'That is how a nation can realize its vision. If we tie ourselves into knots over everyday problems and project that attitude over 365 days, 730 days or 10,000 days, that cannot be the vision. A vision has to cut across the ordinary and aim at bigger things, but just take care that it is not impossible. At the time of articulating the vision, however, it should appear nearly impossible!'

So we have before us a whole range of simple technologies, a large set of needed organizational efforts and information exchange programmes, and above all a goal to attain food security for our country in a permament and sustainable manner. These efforts will usher in great prosperity to a large number of people in rural areas and small towns, through employment and wealth creation. Also for speedy economic growth, these are excellent avenues as the return on the invested capital is much higher and can be achieved in a short period. It is not like chasing the moon; the moon should come to us! There are some issues related to connecting hundreds of thousands of these new agricultural centres to the market place; this can be achieved by rural connectivity through roads and telephones. We address these issues in a later chapter.

Chapter 5

Materials and the Future

We will dig many mines,
And take out gold and other things,
And go eight directions to sell these,
And bring home many things.

—Subrahmanya Bharathi

Agricultural products come from biological resources. Other (non-living) natural resources give us energy (e.g. petroleum and natural gas), chemicals for daily use (e.g. salt), and various metallic products (e.g. steel, copper). If we were to pause for a moment to think about the growth of human civilization, we would find that the pace of social and economic growth has been closely linked to the proficiency with which people have been able to use and shape materials. Today this proficiency has become the bedrock of a country's development. Lightweight high-performance materials and alloys have helped us in building aircraft, satellites, launch vehicles and missiles. Our houses are full of modern materials: stainless steel vessels, shaving blades with special coatings, special non-sticking and slow-heating frying pans; plastic and fibre-glass products. Musical instruments and audiovisual equipment, including television, depend crucially on certain advanced materials.

What happens when somebody breaks a bone? Many implants to replace the broken bones are made of modern materials like titanium; the catheters used to save patients with blocked blood vessels are made of special metallic wires coated with plastic material. Many biomaterials are also now emerging.

Agni and disabled children

These illustrations give you an idea of how extensively and intensively advanced materials have penetrated every sphere of modern life. The subsequent chapters will show where we stand as a country with regard to materials, our strengths, our weaknesses and the vision for the future.

Before doing so let us look at a few touching incidents; at least for the authors they are illustrative of the human dimensions of modern advanced materials.

I quote from my address at a ten-day workshop on Indigenous Production and Distribution of Assistive Devices at Chennai on 5 September 1995.

A year back, an article appeared in the Press on 'Missiles for Medicine'. The article highlighted our experiment of adapting certain missile technologies into certain socially useful medical products primarily to bring them within the reach of the common man. Reading in the article about an ultra-light floor reaction orthosis which our scientists developed from a high specific strength material used to make radio-transparent heat shield of missiles, to assist polio affected children in walking, an ex-serviceman hailing from a middle class family in Karnataka wrote to us. He enquired whether something could be done for his twelve-year-old daughter who was suffering from residual polio of the lower limb and was forced to drag herself with a 4.5 kg calliper made out of wood, leather and metallic strips. Our scientists invited the father and the daughter to our laboratory in Hyderabad, and together with orthopaedic doctors at the Nizam's Institute of Medical Sciences there, designed a KAFO (Knee Ankle Foot Orthosis) weighing merely 400 gm. The child got a near normal gait while walking with this assistive device. The parent wrote to us a couple of months later that the

device breathed a new life in his daughter and she had
learned cycling and started going to school on her own.
The girl regained a near normal lifestyle . . . When I see
this enthusiastic gathering today with the focus to provide
support to the disabled, I realize that our dream to
provide similar devices in standard sizes to millions will
surely get transformed into reality.

Such devices can be sold at an affordable price, thus making
even a business venture to manufacture them not only
sustainable but also profitable. We believe that a chain of small-
scale industries can emerge in the industrial estates located in
various states.

India's material resources

Let us come back to the hurly-burly hardheaded industrial and
business world. Is it necessary to have good material resources—
base ores and minerals—to become a developed country?
America has a rich resource base; so does Russia; China's rich
mineral resource base is helping her in speedy economic
growth; Australia too is well off in this regard. Most of Africa
is endowed with some of the best mineral ores; many African
countries were colonized because of this. Now, even after
independence, a number of developed countries propped up
regimes in African countries which can assure them of these
mineral resources but which do not bother about local growth.
Therefore much of Africa is poor, despite having the richest of
mineral deposits. Japan, on the contrary, has practically no
mineral resource base of significance. Japan exports steel,
builds ships, and is avowedly the economic and technological
leader of this century. The Japanese mastered technologies to
use their minerals and materials for economic and practical
gains. High-cost products flow to the countries which supplied
the minerals as ships, cars, finished steel products and in
several other forms. That is how the economic strength of
nations which master technologies is built up.

There are also other interesting dimensions to these

technological strengths of deriving products out of ores. In some cases, developed and industrialized nations deny products derived from the ores to the very countries from which they got the ores in the first place, on the grounds that these products are of strategic use. I recall an experience during the seventies when I was developing SLV-3, India's first satellite launch vehicle. For making gyroscopes required for the guidance systems, the project required a few beryllium products. An American company making them declined to supply these. It was found that a Japanese company was making some parts of the product and therefore the project approached them. That company also declined. I now wanted to find out more about beryllium. It turned out that India has one of the richest stocks of beryllium ores, which it also supplies to developed countries. They have the technologies to convert this ore into metal and also to shape it according to the needs of the project. Beryllium is a toxic metal and requires a lot of care in handling, but as a metal it has many wonderful properties which makes it unique for gyroscopes or imaging cameras or other applications. The beryllium-copper combination creates products having several unique applications in electronics.

The denial of beryllium products was one of the early lessons for me: if you don't have the technology, your natural resource is of no value to you. Now, of course, India does not have to beg others for beryllium products. The technologists of ISRO and Bhabha Atomic Research Centre (BARC) have set up a beryllium machining facility at Vashi, Mumbai. Indian ore is finding its way to the Indian space, atomic energy and industrial projects! The project was guided by Dr C.V. Sundaram, an eminent material scientist, and was encouraged by Dr Raja Ramanna, the then director of BARC.

Fortunately, India has a number of excellent mineral resources. It has very good iron deposits; manganese ores, etc. As for the wonder modern metal titanium, India tops the list of countries having this resource. We have one of the best quality bauxite ores in the world. We also have several rare earth strategic and high value mineral resources; we have rich beryl ores to supply beryllium and abundant resources (about three million tonnes) of monozite, a source for many rare metals.

How are we using them? Much better than what was done before independence; Jamshyd N. Tata had to face many difficulties before setting up a steel plant in Jamshedpur about a hundred years ago, because those who colonized us wanted us to remain as merely exporters of ore. We have come a long way. We make our aluminium and aluminium alloys; we make our steel—but not all varieties, not still a quantity commensurate with our potential and capabilities. It is so with several other ores, minerals and materials.

When India built the Rourkela steel plant with German technology, its quality and cost competitiveness at that time, i.e. in the 1960s, was one of the best in the world. Did we build upon that strength—on the strength of many technologists, technicians and administrative personnel that made it happen? The answer, unfortunately, is no. We allowed things to slip. We were running between America and the then Soviet Union (now Russia) to build Bokaro. Even after that, we were generally slack. The steel research and development centre at Ranchi was not truly integrated with the steel technology of the country. The Steel Development Fund established by the Government of India played only a limited role in developing core competitive strength in the Indian steel industry. But we need not lament about the missed opportunities. As Henry Ford often used to say, 'Burn my factories but give me the people who were there; I will build a new business.' We still have a number of persons in our country in Steel Authority of India Ltd., (SAIL), Tata Iron and Steel Company (TISCO) and many other big and small steel plants who have the capabilities. They have the will to excel and transform the country, given a long-term vision.

If we now consider the case of alloys, we may ask if we have made an Indian one in recent times. We make use of steel alloys, designed by the US or France or sometimes Russia. When it comes to alloys like titanium aluminium alloys, our technologies are mostly of European or US origin. I have asked many Indian material scientists as to why such a situation exists whereby not even a single alloy has been created despite India's materials research. They reply: in our nation the golden triangle of R&D lab-academia-industry has not yet emerged. We will truly arrive as a country with advanced material technology when we create effective golden triangles to create new materials and new products from our own knowledge base.

Similarly, in other metallic and materials sectors as well, we have capabilities. Considering India's natural resources as well as industrial and R&D capabilities, we can narrow down thirteen areas for special attention. These are the areas in which India can excel and can have a long-term and sustainable competitive advantage over many decades, even beyond the year 2020. We know of many scientists in India who are committed to the development of these areas. They have the knowledge base. They itch for action. Many of them met with frustrations due to the slow decision-making process. Too little was given to them too late in their lives. But most of them still have hope alive in them.

These thirteen areas are: steel, titanium, aluminium, rare earths, composites, ceramics, building materials, photonic materials, superconducting materials, polymeric materials, nuclear materials, biomaterials as well as a generic technology area of surface engineering.

Materials to increase national strengths

Steel: With abundant iron ore resources (12000 million tonnes) and a well-established base for steel production in India, steel is poised for strong growth in the coming decades. Production will increase from the current 17 MT to 31 MT by 2001 and 66 MT by 2011. India will become an important global player, exporting about 5 to 8 MT by 2011. While steel will continue to have a strong hold in the traditional sectors such as construction, housing and ground transportation, special steels will be increasingly used in hi-tech engineering industries such as power generation, petrochemicals, fertilizers, etc. The blast furnace route for iron production will dominate in the future also. The share of continuously cast steel will increase to more than 75 per cent. Steel will continue to be the most popular, versatile and dominant material for wide-ranging industrial applications. While India may still not become a leader in the world steel market, it can become a powerful force. India can give strong competition to China and South Korea in the world markets.

S.L.N. Acharyulu of DRDO who heads the action team to realize the Vision 2020 for the materials sector has made several interesting observations. There are about thirty-five blast furnaces in various steel plants in our country with an installed capacity of approximately 18 million tonnes. The mini-steel sector accounts for the balance, which together constitute the total installed steel-making capacity of about 30 million tonnes. Despite the high installed capacity, the utilization is fairly low.

Although overall the cost of production of steel in India is low, our cost of processing hot metal to liquid steel is higher. In order to sustain this overall edge in the cost of production for a long time, attention should be paid to key factors constituting the cost of inputs such as labour, energy, raw material and so on. The labour component in the cost of production is two to three times lower than that of the developed countries and is close to China. But the energy costs are almost double that of the developed countries. Our raw materials costs are also higher, although marginally so, while the other indirect cost elements are nearly similar. Disturbingly, the pollution levels are very high in Indian steel plants and viewed in the context of the very low emission levels achieved in the plants operational globally, urgent action needs to be taken here as well.

In spite of the relative advantage of the lower cost of iron ore and lower labour costs accruable to the domestic steel industry, the long-term sustainability of the overall low cost of production is threatened primarily by higher coke rates in iron-making and higher total energy consumption. It is heartening to note that the blast furnace operations have progressively improved over the years. However, our steel plants have not yet reached world standards in the rates of coke consumption, a single most important index in iron-making and specific energy consumption. Some of them lag far behind. The current international standard of achievement of coke consumption is about 500 kg per tonne of hot metal. One Indian steel plant is close to it. Others are in the range of 550 kg to 600 kg and still others are in the range of even 700 kg of coke! Similarly, the international standard of achievement of energy consumption is about 6 gigacalories per tonne; the average Indian achievement is about 8.5 gigacalories per tonne. A few years ago it was in the range of 10–12 gigacalories per tonne. If the Indian steel industry is to be competitive, it has to tackle this energy consumption norm very vigorously. In the coming years energy prices are going to rise and hence the need to conserve more energy.

As we present this vision in 1998, some of the stalwarts in the steel sector, which is presently undergoing severe market problems and is marked by a downward trend in production and sales, may be cynical. However, most of the present problems are connected with a general slowdown in industrial demand during 1997–98. It is extremely unlikely that these trends will continue. India is continuing to show all the signs of a fast-growing economy. That means, consumption of steel and steel products will go up. Using this market base, we should be ready to compete in outside markets. We now have problems of competition with steel from China and South Korea in our domestic markets. If our steel industry gears up in about three to four years, Indian steel can be both in Indian and foreign markets. Our vision should be towards this.

Titanium: India occupies the top place in terms of global reserves, possessing 37 per cent of the world's illmenite ores. With the titanium industry on a sound footing and the growing application base for titanium and its alloys, our projection is that titanium will see a much larger and significant usage in the country. The production of mill products will go up from the present 100 to 5,000 tons/year by 2020. Titanium will penetrate into non-aerospace sectors like the naval, marine, oil and gas, power generation, etc. Titanium will also become popular in applications such as surgical tools, decorative items, building, architecture and jewellery. Development of cheaper alloys, e.g. Titanium-Aluminium-Iron (Ti-Al-Fe) will facilitate access into commercial markets. Development of alloys with higher temperature capability, near net shaping technologies and isothermal forging will pave the way for an increased role of titanium in aerospace. Titanium castings will be produced in India for extensive application in the aerospace, chemical, marine and mechanical engineering sectors.

A story about how our decision-making system failed to make good some great opportunities in relation to titanium may be told here. Prof M.M. Sharma, an eminent technologist and educationist, speaks with deep emotion as he lists several such missed opportunities. He narrates in detail how many committees were formed, reports generated and files created, often to lead to a massive non-action for decades. For him the case of the titanium industry tops the list of missed opportunities. He tells about a pilot plant to convert our titanium ore to sponge, which has been in a pilot plant stage for more than a decade now. Though we have ISRO, Defence Metallurgical Research Laboratory (DMRL), Mishra Dhatu Nigam (MIDHANI), BARC and many industries in the public and private sector which know how to use titanium for various applications, a titanium industry is struggling to be born. Yet, we feel, this is no reason to be overawed as some movement in the juggernaut is noticed. Now, the Department of Atomic Energy (DAE) in collaboration with the DRDO has initiated a joint project of titanium sponge production of 500-tonne capacity per year. We are confident that by the turn of the millennium, a titanium industry will start and grow into a major sector of our economy.

In addition to its excellent non-corrosive properties and several performance advantages over other metals and alloys, one feature of titanium is particularly attractive to both of us. It is bio-compatible. That is, it can be placed inside the human body without any adverse effects to the body or the material. Today many poor and less well-off people have bone or hip implants made out of some cheap local materials. Often, due to this, they suffer pain for a couple of years. They cannot keep changing the implants often. Many become handicapped. When titanium implantable parts are made available on a large scale, they will be affordable for many people. Not only would this reduce or eliminate pain, but since the lifetime of titanium implants such as hip joints or bone screws could be two decades or more, it is a lifetime cure for many, especially the aged.

Rare earths: India is in an advantageous position with reference to availability of raw materials (only next to China). With the advent of many high-technology products/applications based on rare earths, considerable effort will go into establishing large-scale production and application activities. Indigenous capabilities will be established to produce rare earth oxides, metals, alloys/compounds to the required degree of purity. The commercial production of Nd-Fe-B magnets, piezoelectric ceramics and other such products will be taken up and India will enter the export market. These products are not for esoteric applications. Miniature tape recorders or Walkman earphones, all these have been made possible on account of these wonder metals. If Indian engineering efforts can lead to manufacture of good agricultural motors of small size with these magnets, we may be able to provide each farmer with a pumpset powered by a solar array. It may appear difficult but it is a dream worth pursuing. Indian laboratories and industries, in particular agencies like Nuclear Fuel Complex (NFC), Indian Rare Earths Ltd (IREL) and Atomic Minerals Division (AMD), under the Department of Atomic Energy, have considerable knowledge and experience in this vital sector.

Aluminium: With excellent reserves of bauxite (India ranks fifth in world bauxite production), having a well-established production base for alumina and aluminium, and with a growing demand for the products, the industry is poised for major growth. The production of aluminium will increase from the current 0.5 to 1.5 MT/yr by 2000 and possibly 5 MT/yr by 2020. Bayer's and electrolytic processes will continue to be the route for extraction, but process efficiencies will be improved, particularly towards the reduction of power consumption for production of aluminium metal. Newer materials will be developed for high technology applications, for example, Aluminium-Lithium (Al-Li) alloys and aluminium-based Metal Matrix Composites (MMCs). Remelting requires only one-twentieth of the energy needed to produce primary metal—accordingly aluminium recycling will gain importance.

Aluminium alloys are essential because of their light weight in aeroplanes, for inexpensive household utensils and for power transmission lines. Aluminium alloys are likely to find a major place in furniture as wood substitutes, as we need to save the forests.

In the field of aluminium we have graduated from the ore-exporting stage to metal-making. According to some data provided by S.L.N. Acharyulu (in a private communication), a crucial problem with our aluminium industry is the large energy consumption which makes the cost of the product high and therefore less competitive. The theoretical energy consumption required in aluminium electrolysis is 6.34 kilowatt per hour per kg of the metal; early achievements of the industry were 20–25 kwh/kg. Presently, most levels worldwide are 13 kwh/kg. By 2000 the most advanced technology could reach 11.4 kwh/kg. In India the energy consumption of the aluminium industry ranges between 15–20 kwh/kg., which is higher than the globally accepted levels. But one of our aluminium companies, Hindalco, is among the low-cost producers of aluminium in the world. Recycling of the spent pot lining and recovery of by-products like gallium, vanadium and heavy metals such as lead, copper and tin would improve the economics of production.

Major advances have been made in near net shape processes such as the 'Full Mould' casting process of aluminium alloys, thereby permitting production of products with a degree of complexity and machinability unattainable in conventional permanent mould casting. This has enabled newer designs in automotives industry and aluminium components are fast replacing other materials.

Liquid forging technology offered pragmatic microstructural controls through the use of pressure to influence the solidification of a melt contained in a die. This ensured near forged properties with near net shape capability.

In order to enrich Indian industries technologically, newer alloys with high value addition are to be continuously developed and adopted. India is reported to be producing 20,000 T of plates/tubes and 10,000 T of foils. The semi-products manufacturing cost is only 10 per cent of the primary metal and hence the capital cost of setting up a semi-fabrication plant is just 10 per cent that of a smelter. This makes growth and expansion easily achievable. The downstream products would include special aluminium cables, domestic products, aluminium products in the house-building sector and various transport applications. Particularly in India, the base for the semi-fabrication and fabrication of these downstream aluminium products should be considerably widened. Greater inputs in design, development and application engineering should be enabled for supporting this downstream aluminium industry. Capacity enhancement should be associated with quality improvements.

As a country we have plenty of scope to market many high value-added products based on aluminium and its alloys. That is the vision we have for the Indian aluminium industry.

Composite materials: There will be a substantially increased usage of composites in many sectors by 2020. The major volume of growth will be contributed by the transportation and construction sectors. Glass fibre-reinforced polymers (GRP) will see a major expansion in the civilian sector. Production/processing technologies suitable for mass production will be established, bringing down the cost. Production of metal matrix composites (MMCs) will be established by 2010 for hi-tech applications—e.g., space structure, aero engine components, and landing gear for aircraft. Ceramic metal composites will be developed by 2020 for application in reciprocating engines, gas turbine engines and wear-resistant parts. Repair/maintenance schemes for composites will be standardized.

I have a great deal of interest in both rocketry and composites. When the fibre-reinforced plastics (FRP) division was established in the late sixties at the Space Science and Technology Centre (SSTC) at Trivandrum (which is now a part of Vikram Sarabhai Space Centre—VSSC), I had a number of projects aimed at the civilian commercial uses of FRP and composites. These ranged from fishing boats to foodgrain storage silos. Due to the demands on my time from the sounding rocket projects and India's first satellite launch vehicle (SLV-3) project which was in the formulation stages then, it was not possible for me to pursue these projects then. My efforts towards application engineering using advanced composite materials went into the design of rocket motor cases and other structures required by the launch vehicle and satellite project. A centre, called Reinforced Plastics Centre (REPLACE), was created to meet these demands. Today REPLACE, in addition to meeting ISRO's requirements of composites products, is developing prototypes for other commercial civilian products.

When I left ISRO to head India's first Missile Development Programme, I did not forget the role of advanced composites. Under the Defence Research & Development Laboratory (DRDL) and the Research Centre Imarat (RCI), I nurtured a Composite Production Centre called COMPROC (now Composite Products Development Centre). This centre was to provide the missile programme with composite parts. It also produced composite devices like FROs for disabled persons. In addition, the ideas created under the aegis of RCI and COMPROC have led to a major Advanced Composites Mission supported by the government. This mission is to catalyze a number of advanced composites products which can be commercialized in the civilian sector—doors, tables, pushcarts for vegetable vendors, brake-drums for automobiles, and so on.

In the coming decade there will be major application of

this technology to railway sleepers. While wood is a well-proven material, we need to avoid its use to save our forests. We are importing wooden sleepers now. In addition to costs there are other operational problems. Concrete-iron sleepers have been tried on a large-scale; they break too often. FRP (Fibre Reinforced Plastic) based sleepers would be a major substitute. Trials are underway now.

India is way down in the use of composites; this itself is partly an indicator of the low status of industrial technologies. Our vision is that this will change drastically in the near future. This vision is not merely because we like composites technology but because it is an important 'performance material' of the future. It will improve energy efficiency in the transport sector as it reduces the dead weight to be carried. Composite materials give much better strengths than conventional materials with much lesser weight. A composite product can be designed directly. This is an important property which brings down weight with additional strength for any application. Its light weight coupled with high strength has made it a favourite choice for today's sports goods. Industrial operational efficiency would also increase with selective use of composites. And, of course, for the disabled it is a wonder material to mitigate several of their physical handicaps. Today composite materials are also helping in providing lightweight bone-setting bandages as against the bulky plaster-of-paris casts normally used.

We have no doubt that Indian industries and other users will soon 'taste' the technologies available in multiple laboratories and will join the world leaders in the use and production of composite materials.

There is an interesting observation in a book published by Westview Press entitled *The International Missile Bazaar*, edited by William C. Potter and Harlan W. Jencks. 'The RCI recently joined with the Technology Information Forecasting and Assessment Council of the Department of Science and Technology to market advanced composites, such as carbon-carbon fiber. Composites will be produced at the Composite Production Centre (COMPROC) at RCI, which will be operated jointly with Indian industry. Finally, many private industries supplying materials and technologies to the IGMDP could export their products.'

Ceramic materials: When we stand before a wash basin, or have a bath in a tiled bathroom or sip tea in a cup, we take for granted the ubiquitous presence of ceramics in our life. They have been with us in some form or another for centuries. We also note that their quality has improved over the years. With the Total Quality Movement gripping the Indian industry over the past several years, one industrialist recently commented to us: 'With improvement in quality and the practice of International Standards Organization (ISO) 9000 systems, my business volume is going down as there are less breakages after sales!' Therefore, he has been looking for diversification into newer ceramics applications. He is a wise person. Because, even while the sale of traditional ceramic products will greatly increase in our country, with the growing demand for ceramic-ware of better quality and appearance, there would be many more entrants into the field. Soon foreign products will also come to India and compete with the local products.

It is thus time for the Indian industry to enter into other areas of advanced ceramics as well. Ceramics are now entering into automobile aircraft engines; with the newer requirements for fuel efficiency, not only for economic reasons but for environmental reasons, internal combustion engines and other energy conversion systems are likely to operate at higher and higher temperatures. They have a unique advantage of heat resistance at these kinds of temperatures. Ceramics have also started competing with traditional machine tools. The cutting capability of ceramics is good for a number of applications. Ceramics can also be engineered to be biocompatible and are being used as replacements for broken bones. Some of the readers may already be having ceramic caps on their teeth. Many may not be aware of the crucial role of ceramics in the electronics industry. They form the base, called substrate, for a number of miniature electronics devices which are coated or etched on such substrates, keeping up with the trends of micro-miniaturization. Many ceramic materials are crucial for advanced sensors. The tiny microphones in your tape-recorders or in a collar mike have elements of ceramic in the form of piezoelectric crystals.

Indian industry or the laboratories are not new to these materials or their application. Any future vision of a developed India will thus naturally include a vibrant advanced ceramics industry and also many new innovative products designed, developed and manufactured in India. India has to be a global player in this area.

Advanced ceramics are poised for impressive growth in the country. The Indian market for functional ceramics, which in 1995 was about Rs. 170 crores, will grow to about Rs. 1400 crores by the year 2000. The market for structural ceramics will double from the present Rs. 190 crores over the same period. India will enter the export market for advanced ceramics by 2000–05. Structural ceramics will find application in high-technology sectors both as components (e.g. turbine blades) and coatings. Advanced sensors based on functional ceramics will be extensively used in many fields in India, for example, agriculture, automobiles, pollution detection and control and security systems. There is good scope in the domestic market for advanced ceramics as well as for their export to other countries.

Building materials: The dream of most middle class and lower income families is to have houses or flats of their own. In Kerala, for example, the Gulf employment boom was most visible in the flood of house-building activity. The employment boom in the Gulf countries which was spearheaded by the talented people of Kerala, has resulted in their having greater earnings. They have money to save after spending on food and clothing. These savings have led to a rapid growth of construction activities all around Kerala. This attitude of investing first in a house and, of course, jewellery is common to all Indians. Such investments, if directed towards industries, will have a good impact on national wealth.

Still, we have to remember that most Indians do not have proper habitation. Most of them live in houses made of earth and biomass. They naturally desire to have stronger and more durable dwellings. In the India of our vision, we would like to see all Indians not only well-fed, well-clothed and with access to affordable health care systems (preventive and curative), but we would also like to see that all of them have durable habitation with good sanitation facilities. Using cost-effective bricks with local cementing material could be the answer.

The buildings of the future will have many new features of aesthetics and convenience. Many houses may have built-in flat panel displays for entertainment, business or educational information. Their energy sources will be cleaner, based on solar power or hydrogen. The glass panes of windows and doors may have conducting polymers to regulate transmission of solar rays into the room. The leakages during the monsoon may be a thing of the past due to improved design and construction methods. Above all, the time taken for construction of houses and buildings may be cut down to several weeks or a few months, instead of years. This would be achieved through the use of prefabricated structures and various other factory-manufactured parts like advanced composites doors.

Cement will continue to be a dominating building material. Its consumption will go up from 75 MT in 1995 to 115 MT in 2005. Natural aggregates are likely to predominate even beyond 2020 due to their easy availability. Concrete will continue to be an indispensable material of construction. Steel, too, will continue to be used as one of the major structural materials as well as for reinforcement in concrete. Fly ash produced by burning coal in electric power stations will be increasingly used along with cement as there is a need to conserve cement. The basic raw materials that go to make cement are not going to last long. Presently limestone, the principal input for making cement, is easily available with little effort required to mine it. However, such limestone reserves may last only a century. Then we may have to dig deeper, which means more cost. Therefore, the use of fly ash is required not only as an environmental protection measure but for conserving natural resources.

The Government of India has mounted a major technology demonstration project for fly ash utilization. This mission mode project was the result of earlier work by TIFAC and is now being implemented by it along with many national and state government agencies as well as industries and institutions. In many parts of India, there are successful examples of the use of fly ash. The first was for the Okhla flyover bridge which is operating successfully. This success led to its use for another bridge, the Hanuman Setu. The central and Delhi governments have also cleared the construction of a 1.7 km approach road, connecting a new bridge at Nizamuddin, New Delhi to NOIDA, which uses fly ash. Another project for construction of a 1 km road using fly ash has started at Panipat. The construction of four dwelling units at the abandoned fly ash pond of the National Fertilizers Ltd (NFL) at Panipat has been successful, and they have been tested through a monsoon season. The results indicate that a structure up to four storeys high can be safely and economically erected at abandoned ash ponds. However, initial testing of the site is required as is usually done for regular soils as well.

Among other successes with fly ash is a 1 km road near Raichur which is operating well, and a road in New Bhuj, Gujarat. Road building through the use of fly ash has been standardized with these experiments, and draft specifications have been prepared for submission to the Indian Road Congress. There are other uses of fly ash, as in the underground mine fill demonstrated at Ramagundam. Several other projects aimed at agricultural applications are underway.

Photonic materials: The development of electronics in India is recent and has marked a revolution in industrialization and economic growth, besides adding to human comforts. Most of the modern technological 'miracles' are due to electronics, that is, controlling the flow of electrons. The growth of electronics has led to newer and greater demands: of the amount of data to be transferred; much higher resolutions of transmitted pictures; many more parameters to be measured, and so on. These demands have led to the mastery of 'control of photons', that is, the 'particles of light'. Lasers and fibre optics fall in the category of photonics. While there is considerable knowledge of electronics, optics and software are involved in the applications of photonics, and the basic devices and assemblies need very advanced engineering of materials, process engineering and design methods.

Photonics will dominate all walks of life in the twenty-first century. It will penetrate into several areas traditionally covered by electronics such as communication, computation, memories etc. It will have far-reaching effects in several critical areas such as information technology, fibre optics-based telecommunication, diagnostics and therapeutic applications in health care, pollution control, life sciences, besides others.

Developments in photonic materials will accordingly keep pace. There will be new developments in laser materials. Newer compounds and rare earths will assume great importance for electro-luminescence applications. India's missile programme uses many of these materials for missile guidance. They are also used in aircraft transport systems and satellites. A new class of phosphors may revolutionize display technology. Opto-electronic systems will increasingly use polymers. While it is difficult to describe these technological scenarios in simple terms, consumers can expect better and larger TV pictures, new lighting sources, new medical diagnostic devices, while communication facilities will be more easily accessible than present-day India's water taps!

Superconducting materials: We all know that the cost of generating electricity is high. In India, a policy of subsidizing electricity has kept the rates down. There is an increasing tendency, for sound economic reasons, to reduce such subsidies and let the price of electricity be market-determined. But the consumers naturally would not like to pay for the inefficiencies in generation of electricity nor for the losses in transmission. There are increasing pressures to introduce better and well-proven technologies to improve efficiency in power generation. We have, overall, one of the lowest indicators of power generation efficiency in the world.

In addition, our transmission and distribution losses are high. Some, called 'non-technical', is pilferage of power. But a good part of it is also due to use of poor technologies in transmission line materials and transformer materials. Not that earlier there weren't people with knowledge, or that there were no technologies to overcome this problem. But somehow, most of these avenues were callously ignored. Now sheer economics is taking over with pressure on the power sector to perform. So it is likely that most of the new well-proven technologies will be used in transmission lines and transformers to reduce losses.

In advanced countries, the emphasis on efficiency and cutting down losses has led to the experimental use of superconducting materials as wires. These can be considered the ultimate in the use of electrons, with practically no hindrance to their flow, meaning practically no losses. India has invested a considerable amount in building up a scientific base. Now it is a question of orienting this scientific work to commercial products of the future. As is true with most generic high technologies, there are applications of superconductors in the medical and industrial sectors as well.

Low-temperature superconductors (LTSC) with improved performance will have to be developed. Indigenous development of superconducting cyclotron and X-ray synchrotron would take place. These equipments are useful for medical and industrial applications. Superconducting generators with 5MVA field, magnetic separators with field strengths greater than 3.5T would be commercially built in India. Multi SQUID arrays will be developed for medical diagnostics.

SQUIDs based on high-temperature superconductors (HTSC) will be developed and used for non-invasive diagnosis of diseases, biomedical investigations, Non-Destructive Testing (NDT) of oil pipes, bridges, etc. HTSCs will work their way into microwave communication, energy storage devices, sensing and electro-magnetic devices for space exploration, high-speed computers, etc. HTSCs will facilitate the building of smaller and less energy-consuming Magnetic Resonance Imaging (MRI) devices. Yet another dream is a superconducting train.

Polymeric materials: Just as electronics and photonics are the marvels of modern physics and materials technology, modern chemistry has given birth to a whole range of polymers. For a simple understanding we may look at the range of plastic products. The solid propellants used in launch vehicles and missiles are also a type of polymer, as also the foam beds we sleep on or the special soles in our footwear. Polymers are an integral part of modern life. The polymer industry in India will grow at 15–20 per cent up to the year 2000 and at 10 per cent thereafter. Commodity plastic production will increase from current 1.7 MT to 4.5 MT by the year 2000. Elastomers and synthetic rubber will grow at the expense of natural rubber. There will be a large usage of ecofriendly (biodegradable, non-toxic) polymers. Recycling/reprocessing of waste plastics will assume great significance. Newer inventions in polymers such as conducting polymers are knocking at the doors of bio-electric devices and systems. The future will see many exciting applications of polymers.

Nuclear materials: Most of us have tended to associate anything nuclear with the bomb and to a certain extent with power generation. Use of nuclear energy has placed considerable demands on advanced materials technologies and spin-offs from them are very many.

Let us review the future of nuclear materials. The Nuclear Power Corporation plans to set up seven more plants of 2100 MW by the year 2000 and seventeen more by 2020 to raise the total installed capacity to about 20000 MW. There could be other entities setting up nuclear power plants as well. The requirement of nuclear material will accordingly go up. Monozite production would increase to 8000/9000 TPY at Manavalakurichi, Tamil Nadu, alone. There will be demands to enhance the facilities to meet the increased requirements of zirconium alloy and uranium dioxide (UO_2) fuel. The large-scale production of reactor grade hafnium oxide and its conversion to hafnium (Hf) metal will be taken up to keep pace with increasing demands. Newer zirconium alloys would be designed for fuel cladding applications with better corrosion/radiation resistance. The spin-off from nuclear technologies could form the basis of the emergence of major industries. Let us see one example of such a spin-off. Zirconium is an important material used in nuclear reactors. One of its compounds used along with another material called Yttirium and processed in a special manner, results in a product called cubic zirconia. This is nothing but the artificial diamond, popularly known as 'American diamond', and is used in jewellery.

Biomaterials and devices: India can be truly proud of having made at affordable costs some very demanding biomedical products: blood bags, heart valves and Kalam-Raju stents, to name a few. However, the advancement in biomedical R&D or industry has not fully kept pace with the ever-growing demands. Therefore, several industries will be set up in the country with imported technology for the manufacture of medical devices. Polymers, ceramics and metal alloy industries would upgrade themselves to produce the required biomaterials.

Medical and health care sectors will undergo a major transformation with increased availability of artificial organs, blood and improved diagnostic devices. For example, implantation of artificial human parts will be possible—the heart, the pancreas, the lungs, and kidneys. Artificial blood will be available for transfusion to leukaemia patients. Bone, hip and tissue replacements will be possible for accident victims. Heart patients can receive heart valves, artificial hearts and other implants. The requirement of biomaterials would accordingly go up. Tissue engineering will aim at replacing the affected tissue in a natural way.

The challenge is to shape products, devices and systems in order to make them affordable to a large number of Indians. It is not merely a matter of cost engineering. Innovative technological inputs are called for.

Surface engineering: So far we discussed materials, alloys and composites. A new generic area of technology is emerging in a major way during the past decade. This involves treatment of a metal or material with an extremely thin layer of another material to get the benefits of both materials! The Teflon coating of a frying pan is a simple example. More sophisticated atomic level coatings are used to reduce the wear and tear of tools and moving parts of machinery. Diamond coatings can be made on some materials. Simply stated, the future holds a promise of a customer demanding and getting a specific combination of various, often contradictory performance parameters: of light weight, least corrosivity, biocompatibility or least cost.

There are several technologies like thermal spraying or plasma spraying or laser treatment. A laser surface engineering centre has been established at the Defence Metallurgical Research Laboratory (DMRL) campus at Hyderabad. New methods are being invented. It is fortunate that India has good R&D strengths in this area. A few Indian industries have forged partnerships with global technology leaders and Indian institutions, to take a leading role commercially. We believe India can emerge as an important player at the commercial level in the use and generation of surface engineering technologies.

Investments

In the earlier chapter on agriculture and agro-food processing, there are suggestions for many measures ranging from education and sensitization of farmers to successes within the country itself to bringing in new agricultural practices, new hybrid seeds and establishment of cold chain and food processing units. What about investments? We believe that much of the government-level investment (such as public information, awareness generation and covering risks for the early experiments) can be done within the existing budgets of the Central and state governments. Perhaps a seed fund to catalyze actions can be specially created to break the 'ice'. Much of the other investments can be from farmers, banks and industries. When the right climate is created, these investments will flow as they involve several small- to medium-level decentralized actions. For items like cold chains and carriers even foreign investment could be attracted. The main effort is to shed the present state of lethargy and cynicism that 'nothing can be done in India, nothing can change Bihar or UP'. We have to combat this trend and transform the neglected areas.

Investment levels required for the materials sector are of a different class. As described earlier, many decentralized, small and medium levels of investments would be the dominant pattern in the agricultural sector. But for production of steel or aluminium or titanium, huge investments running to several hundred of crores of rupees for a single plant would be required. To set up a carbon fibre plant may cost a few hundred crores of rupees. The gestation period for return on investments is longer. However, for the downstream products from these materials, which have been described earlier, investment levels would be much less and the return on investments would be much quicker. For material processing technologies like surface engineering, there can be dramatic return on investments even for investments under ten crores of rupees. India has to find methods of attracting large-scale investments for production of steel, aluminium and titanium as well.

For example, the annual world production in steel is now 750 million tonnes and is expected to be 980 million tonnes by 2010. It may perhaps rise to 1200 million tonnes by 2020. India's current steel production is 24 million tonnes and is likely to be 60 million tonnes by 2010. Compare this with China's present production of around 100 million tonnes and South Korea's 30 million tonnes! Japan, the USA and Russia are there too as giant steel producers. The investment required for a one-million-tonne steel plant on a greenfield site is about Rs. 3000 crores. Besides, none of the Indian steel industry or steel R&D outfits have produced something very unique, which would not just make us proud but would make steel better and cheaper.

However, when we consider some of the details about the types of talent in the business and technological areas, we believe we do not need to be pessimistic. The Indian business and technological community has to learn to think innovatively:

for example, avoid greenfield sites, upgrade the existing ones, scrap obsolete ones, learn the relevant foreign technologies, go in for foreign investment or preferably joint ventures in the country or abroad, concentrate on giving better products to the growing domestic and world consumers.

While doing all these in the short term, we should not stop at the first success and stagnate thereafter as we did after our initial successes in steel plants, especially after Rourkela. Our technological community in industry and institutions can be activated to help this process to introduce continuous new additions to help the big and small-sized steel producers: all actions to improve the efficiency of operations, all actions to introduce new products; new performance features. Even amidst the fierce competition between our companies, they can evolve consortia mode to share their knowledge base to enhance India's business abroad.

In addition to the total volume of production, India can also make its mark in certain special niche markets where value addition is more. India, with all the above actions, has to aim to be a top steel producer in the world by 2020. Its status can be much higher than what it is today. I continue to hope that Indian material scientists shall introduce an Indian alloy to the world.

The picture concerning titanium may appear much bleaker. Present annual world production is around 0.1 million tonnes (USA—20 per cent, Russian and CIS countries—52 per cent, Japan—26 per cent). India is just about 100 tonnes per year, mostly of the milled products based on imported sponge in a country which is tops in titanium ores! Some estimates are that India can target for an annual production of 5000 tonnes. After about a decade of discussions and delays, a new plant to produce 400 tonnes titanium sponge from our own ore is being planned to be set up at Palayakayal in south India. It may cost about Rs. 100 crores. There are many potential users in India for titanium in the private sector as well. We believe this situation concerning titanium has to change. We understand that the Department of Atomic Energy and DRDO are planning to set up a titanium sponge production plant. Many others may follow suit. These are detailed technological and business decisions which we would like to leave to adventurous and entrepreneurial Indians. But our strengths in titanium can help us in many other businesses as well. For example, it can make India a preferred production base for several world chemical plants. Imagine the level of new employment such possibilities can bring in! Let us learn to think big.

What is the government's role in this? First of all to provide an enabling environment and remove a number of bureaucratic hindrances. Allow new entities to come in without 'apply-wait' mode. Free the technical agencies to loan their experts on a long-term basis to Indian industries. Help industry-oriented research out with various developmental funds which are marginally utilized or used for purchase of equipment.

The vision and actions

To avoid too much of technical discussion, we have only provided glimpses of possibilities in thirteen areas of modern materials. To further facilitate understanding we have tried to encapsulate the vision in four figures for steel, aluminium, titanium, and rare earth (Figures 5.1, 5.2, 5.3, 5.4). The left side gives the present scenario and the right side gives the future one. The centre box highlights a few core technologies that need to mastered. India can be one of the key leaders in all these sectors commercially and technologically. It will generate lots of wealth for the nation and employment of highly skilled personnel. Export earnings will be substantial. Indian companies may set up ventures abroad in many of these areas and export technologies as well. Some short-term actions require investments by the government and private sector. To attract the private sector, certain policy changes are required such as providing the sector with long-term developmental and commercial contracts in strategic sectors and allowing it the use of expertise available in the national laboratories in a speedy manner and on easy terms.

FIGURE 5.1

STEEL—The Dominant Structural Material

Present Scenario
(1997)

Future Scenario
(2010)

* **Production**
  World 750 MT
  (China 100,
  S. Korea 30)
  India 24 MT

CORE TECHNOLOGIES

* Modernization
  of existing plants
  (higher productivity,
  energy efficiency,
  secondary refining)

* Alternative routes
  using non-coking
  coal

  (COREX, ROMELT,
  Iron carbide)

* Compact strip
  production
  and rheocasting
  technologies

* **Production**
  World 1000 MT

  India 60 MT
  (why not 120
  MT?)

* **Export 7 MT or
  more**

* **Energy
  Consumption**
  India: 5–6 G cal/
  tcs

* **Coke Rate**
  India 400 kg/thm
  (with auxillary
  fuel)

* **Continuous
  Casting** 100%

* **Products**
  'Tailor made'—
  special steels
  designed for
  customer

* **Very high degree**
  of "cleanliness"
  (ultra low, S.P.
  gases)

* **Export 1.5 MT**

* **Energy
  Consumption**
  World 5–6 G cal/
  tcs
  India 7–11 G cal/
  tcs

* **Coke Rate**
  World 400 kg/thm
  India 550–800 kg/
  thm

* **Continuous casting**
  50–60%

* **Production focus**
  Structurals

* **Cost Competitiveness**
  India $415/t
  (US 505, Japan 625)

(Compiled by Deepak Bhatnagar, TIFAC)

FIGURE 5.2

ALUMINIUM—The 'Lightweight' Wonder

Present Scenario
(1997)

Future Scenario
(2010)

* **Production**
  World 26 MT
  India 0.6 MT

* **Per Capita Consumption**
  India 0.5 kg
  (US 28 kg,
  Mexico 3 kg)

* **Power Consumption**
  World 12–13 kwh/Kg
  India 14–17 kwh/Kg

CORE TECHNOLOGIES

* Modern Smelter designs (pots of >300 KA), heat recovery, optimum inter-anode distance.

* Modern Processing techniques like Liquid forging, rapid solidification, premium casting, etc., for high performance products.

* Eco-friendly disposal/utilization of red-mud (recovery of vanadium, gallium)

---

* India's production would be doubled to 1.3 MT; may attempt more

* Special alloys (Al-Li) and composites (e.g. MMCs) for automobiles & aircrafts, etc., high strength alloys for electrical conduction

* Asia projected to become largest consumer of Al, India a major supplier

* Power consumption by world standards

* Increased recycling (from present 20% to 50%)

India—highly cost competitive
World average $1230/t
India $1055/t

(Compiled by Deepak Bhatnagar, TIFAC)

FIGURE 5.3

TITANIUM—A Material of the Future

Present Scenario
(1997)

Future Scenario
(2010)

World Prodn
100,000 T
(CIS 52%,
US 20%,
Japan 26%)
India 100 T

**Power
Consumption**
Conventional
process
37000 kWh/t
Combined
process
17000 kWh/t

**Alloy Develop-
ment** with Al,
Mo, Sn, Si, V

**CORE
TECHNOLOGIES**

* Productionize
'combined
process' techn-
ology at 400 tpy
plant—Palayakayal
(reduction and
vacuum separation
of Krolls process)

* Improved
melting techno-
logies (cold
hearth, plasma arc
and electron beam
welding)

* Develop cheaper
alloys using Al, Fe

* Alloy development
& downstream
products for
non-aerospace
(e.g. medical,
golf clubs)

* **India's Production**
5000 T
(aim at 20,000-T
capacity build-up)
— India has 37%
of world's resou-
rces)

* Extensive use of
near-net-shape
technologies like
super plastic
forming, isother-
mal forging.

* Development and
use of titanium
aluminides, com-
posites and inter-
metallics

(Compiled by Deepak Bhatnagar, TIFAC)

FIGURE 5.4

RARE EARTHS—Great Potential for India

Present Scenario
(1997)

Future Scenario
(2010)

Resources
Global 62 MT
(China 80%
US 11%,
rest India & EU)
Production India
5000 Tpy
India 2.7 MT
(largest thorium
deposits)

Global Market $400
million of Nd-Fe-B
(high energy
magnets); Indian
production limited

Demand (India)
7 tonnes/year

**Nd-Fe-B upto 35
MGOe developed**

**CORE
TECHNOLOGIES**

* Recovery of
  metals (Nd, Sm)
  (mineral →
  oxide → metal

* Value addition of
  RE materials

* Application
  Engineering for
  use of Rare Earths
  in high tech areas
  like, catalysts,
  phosphors,
  magnets,
  special ceramics
  and metallurgy

* Applications
  to sensors,
  guidance,
  automation
  etc.

**Production of
Rare Earths**
India 15000
tonnes per year
(India could have
an export niche)
High growth
expected: 12–15%
Thorium applica-
tions in a major
way—India's lead-
ership Nd-Fe-B

Global Market
$900 million;
India to have
good share of
production

Demand (India)
15 T/year

**Nd-Fe-B Magnets
of 85 MGOe**

(Compiled by Deepak Bhatnagar, TIFAC)

We require the will to take action and to commit ourselves to be one of the key world leaders at least in these thirteen materials areas within a decade. Once there is a will, missions can be launched. Projects can be mounted. There are persons of Indian origin who have set up or run giant metal companies around the world. India can generate many more such entrepreneurs and help them to establish such endeavours on their native soil. The vision can be easily within our reach. Materials are crucial to several other sectors that follow: engineering industries; electronics and communication; chemicals; biotechnology; and strategic industries. Strengths in material technologies are crucial for the agro-food processing and agriculture sectors covered earlier. If India loses out on this crucial materials front, then the future of many sectors would be doubtful. If we master it, we have a bright future for our people.

Chapter 6

Chemical Industries and Our Biological Wealth

Deliverance? Where is this
deliverance to be found?
Our Master himself has joyfully
taken upon Him the bonds of creation;
He is bound with us all for ever.

—Rabindranath Tagore

The use of chemicals and chemical products affects our lives in several ways, direct and indirect. Fertilizers and pesticides are needed for food security. Drugs and pharmaceuticals relieve pain and save millions of lives. Petrol, diesel, natural gas and plastics have become an essential part of modern living. There are several other household items we take for granted: salt, soaps, detergents, cosmetics, beverages, packed foods, paints, textiles, leather goods, books, newspapers, and so on. Modern chemical engineering facilitates these comforts and tools for knowledge which keep improving the quality of life. At the same time, the manufacture of these chemicals also creates the challenge of ensuring a clean and healthy environment.

Chemicals—modern demons?

Well, what about air pollution? What about soils degraded by salination? What about the chemical effluents which have polluted our beautiful rivers and lakes, and endangered marine life? What about carcinogenic chemicals and the ban on these by developed countries (to be followed later by the developing countries)? In view of the Bhopal gas tragedy, we need to remember how chemical pollution can be responsible for enormous loss of human life.

Aside from the damage caused by such accidents is the deliberate use of chemical engineering to wreak destruction. It was modern chemical engineering that gave us the napalm bomb, used extensively in the Vietnam war. The threat of more dreadful chemical weapons has been looming over humanity for a long time: it is only recently that a treaty for banning chemical weapons has been signed. India has the ability to make chemical weapons. However we spearheaded a movement to eliminate such weapons and India is the pioneering signatory to a treaty to this purpose. We are with the international community on this where there is no discrimination between nations, in contrast to the case of nuclear weapons. Let us also not forget that the deadly bombs used by terrorists are the products of modern chemistry assisted by multi-disciplinary technologies of packaging, electronics and communications, among others.

Yes, we want to repeat this again: just as in every other field of human activity, science and technology also can be used for wrong purposes. Accidents can occur as our knowledge is an outcome of trials and corrected errors. But, barring the occasional case of lack of ethics on the part of a scientist or business group, if the ill effects are known at the time of development of a product or a process, that activity will be abandoned. Present-day technologies allow for many accelerated and simulated tests. The fact of the matter is that at no time in human history have the benefits of knowledge been as widely available to a large number of persons as in the second half of the twentieth century. When we look back at previous centuries, it is striking that the benefits of new creations, inventions and therapies (in art, literature, science, medicine, in techniques and technologies) were available only to a privileged few. There were several economic constraints: production levels and production techniques were such that the amount of 'surplus' wealth created was not great. Therefore, the good things of life were confined to the rich and powerful. A vast majority of people worked unceasingly to create the small surplus. This was true not only for India, but all over the world.

In early times the artisans' skills were preserved by their guilds or held as a family secret. The products that they manufactured were, however, sold over a large geographic region. A cross-fertilization of various skills and disciplines took place. It is this rich heritage built up over several centuries, that has led to the modern technological revolution. Building on past successes and failures, humanity entered the twentieth century with a greatly enhanced knowledge pool. It was the age of the internal combustion engine. This invention marked a major step towards mass production. Newer inventions involved more complex technologies, processes and production methods. They required mass production to derive the advantages of economies of scale. The 'surplus' wealth created was great enough to share with more and more people who were involved in the production process. The mass-produced goods could reach the people at an affordable price; the rapid growth also created more jobs, salaries enabled people to buy more commodities. For example, affordable bicycles improved the mobility of rural people. People could sell and buy goods with greater ease, thus creating economic opportunities. Many villagers go to work by cycle. The transistor radio provides information and entertainment to millions. At an even more prosaic level, mass-produced cups and saucers enable many thousands to set up small tea shops in every nook of the country. This, in short, is a glimpse of how improved technologies have helped and are helping large masses of people.

Chemical technology is one such means to improve the quality of life. Knowledge in this field has increased to the point where chemical technologies can be made 'clean'.

Against this background, let us look at the chemical sector of Technology Vision 2020.

Chemical industry-economy linkages

The development pattern of the chemical process industry can be divided into three phases: penetration, consolidation, and speciality.

In the penetration phase, the chemical products which protect crops and improve health (agro-products, fertilizers and pharmaceuticals), contributed to economic and social advances. In the consolidation phase, resource-rich countries geared up to meet domestic demand as well as exports. Poor countries imported basic foodstock and converted it into finished goods, instead of importing the latter. In the specialization phase, emphasis was placed on the manufacture and marketing of speciality chemicals.

It is natural that, given the technology involved in their manufacture, the maximum value addition occurs in these.

The inter-linkages between technology, economy, environment, society and policies have never been more intimate than they are today. Technological demands have changed rapidly due to changes in the market, the availability of raw materials, environmental concerns, energy requirements and major changes in the policy framework. Existing production technologies have often to be upgraded. No industrial process/ production system can ever completely transform the input resources into the desired product. Owing to the inexpensive and abundant availability of raw materials, the emphasis in the past was to isolate the desired product of the purest quality without paying much attention to the waste generated in the process. For example, in the early years of the sugar industry the focus was on maximizing sugar output. The waste products, except for molasses, were not used. Even bagasse was burnt. Nowadays, bagasse is used for making paper or for co-generation of electricity. There are about a dozen chemicals from other wastes such as oxalic acid. Action is under way to recover these by-products as well.

The world chemical industry is one of the most basic and important manufacturing businesses globally. Its total turnover approaches $1000 billion, giving it a size comparable to that of other large international industries such as automotive, steel, mechanical engineering and electronic industries. The industry's activities are linked to a large number of other industries to which it provides both products and services. Typically, in most countries the chemical industry sells roughly half its turnover to other manufacturing operations rather than directly to the consumer. These commercial areas include other branches of the chemical industry itself, as well as important parts of industries such as consumer products, engineering, defence, automobiles, packaging and construction. This interdependence with so many other industrial branches makes the structure of the industry inherently complex, and underlines its general importance to economic development.

The chemical industry has its most important components in the developed world, with western Europe, Japan, and North America accounting for roughly 70 per cent of the world chemicals production and consumption. The world chemicals market is shown in table 6.1. The Indian share in this is small. However, Indian industries are present in all those sectors, as is apparent from table 6.2, and we also have R&D capabilities in these areas.

The Indian chemicals industry

The Indian chemicals industry has come a long way since the establishment of the first petroleum refinery in the country in 1954, and has gained considerable momentum in the last thirty years. Its pattern of development has been similar to that of the global chemicals industry. The 1980s in fact witnessed the Indian chemicals sector entering a phase of consolidation. But in the course of its development, the industry has displayed several unique features. For example, a bulk of the chemicals in India are still produced in the small sector, a phenomenon not found anywhere else in the world. The co-existence of a number of different feedstocks for manufacture is yet another phenomenon, almost unique to India.

TABLE 6.1

The World Chemicals Market

Total Sales: $1.2 trillion	
Sector	**Percentage of total sales**
Petrochemicals	39.0 per cent
Pharmaceutical chemicals	16.4 per cent
Performance chemicals	16.0 per cent
Agrochemicals	11.0 per cent
Textiles	9.9 per cent
Inorganic chemicals	6.7 per cent
Other fine chemicals	1.0 per cent

Source: TIFAC, Chemical Process Industries: Technology Vision 2020

At present the Indian chemical industry occupies a premier position in India's industrial set-up. It accounts for nearly 7 per cent of the total number of factories in the country, about 12 per cent of the fixed capital, 13 per cent of the gross output and 12 per cent of the net value added in the manufacturing sector. Table 6.2 gives the status of different sectors of the chemical industry. The chemical industry has witnessed the fluctuations of various sectors, as is shown in table 6.3 which gives the sectoral growth pattern of the Indian chemical industry since 1991. The fluctuations are partly due to market forces and partly due to changes in tax structures. However, the Indian chemical industry and R&D is robust enough to survive these vicissitudes and emerge as an important player at the global level.

The turnover of the Indian chemical industry between the years 1989 and 1994 increased by 158 per cent. During 1994–1997 the growth was about 80.5 per cent. India is entering into the polymer sector in a major way and has made beginnings in speciality chemicals. The chemical industry is usually subdivided

TABLE 6.2

Status of Different Sectors of the Chemical Industry (1989-90)

Characteristics	Basic industrial chemicals	Fertilizers & pesticides	Paints & varnishes	Drugs & pharmls	Cosmetics & toiletries
No. of factories	1264	556	820	1699	787
No. of workers	58847	62535	24335	82985	43769
No. of employees	85664	94072	39592	138220	55015
Gross output	450933	830049	235290	527925	305567
Net value added	93496	96892	47863	119485	44981

Source: TIFAC Technology Vision 2020 Report on Chemical Process Industries

TABLE 6.3

Indian Chemical Industry: Sector Growth Pattern

Annual Growth in Total Turnover (per cent)

S.No.	Sectors	1991–92	1992–93	1993–94	1994–95	1995–96	1996–97
i)	Chemicals & plastics	28.5	12.2	11.7	29.6	21.8	8.5
ii)	Inorganic	26.2	36.7	10.1	42.3	20.1	11.8
iii)	Alkalies	24.1	18.2	11.0	27.3	59.7	4.4
iv)	Fertilizers	32.4	3.7	1.7	30.3	15.0	3.6
v)	Paints & varnishes	21.4	6.3	10.3	20.5	18.7	4.1
vi)	Drugs & pharmls	24.2	23.5	20.2	24.6	21.8	21.1
vii)	Soaps & detergents	22.0	2.0	15.5	25.2	18.9	26.8
viii)	Polymers	42.6	17.0	8.6	37.0	21.5	– 2.7
ix)	Plastic products	35.4	15.8	32.0	43.6	33.7	5.6
x)	Petroleum products	8.8	16.5	5.4	33.6	19.6	28.0

Source: CMIE Report on Indian Corporate Sector, April 1998

in terms of generic product-user segments or characterized by functional areas like dyestuffs, pesticides and so on. But broader divisions like bulk chemicals and specialities are also used. Based on projections of basic indices like population, per capita income, industry, agriculture and services, the growth indicators for the Indian chemical industry can be envisioned as in table 6.4. If we add a component of vigorous action for exports, the growth would be much higher than what is indicated in here.

TABLE 6.4

Growth Indicators for the Chemical Industry

Sector	1995 (million tonnes)	2020 (million tonnes)	Growth
Petroleum products	70	240–250	3.5 times
Fertilizers	9	>20	8.5 times
Polymers	1.7	>15	8.5 times
Fibres	0.8	>5	6.0 times
Organic chemicals	3	20	6.0 times
Dyestuffs & pigments	0.1	0.21	2.0 times
Leather chemicals	0.1	0.5–1.0	5.0 times
Surface active agents	0.3	0.7	2.5 times
Surface coatings	0.5	1.5	3.0 times
Speciality chemicals	0.1	2.0	20 times

Source: TIFAC, Technology Vision 2020, Chemical Process Industry

Table 6.4 indicates areas which are likely to provide major opportunities for innovation. Speciality chemicals stands out, followed by polymers and fertilizers. The basic domestic demand would stabilize the minimum demand, thus enabling investments in R&D. With good R&D, these industries can venture into the export market.

What is the chemicals technology vision?

So far, the industry's growth has been based on imported process technology. However, the strong capabilities established in R&D, engineering and equipment manufacturing have led not only to the assimilation of imported technology but also to the development of indigenous technology. We have reached a level in certain areas (particularly in batch processes) where we are not only competitive but have achieved excellence. The capabilities in equipment manufacture and plant construction have made India a choice for certain chemical manufacturing facilities.

The combination of a base of imported technology and capabilities built up indigenously led initially to product and process improvement. Equipment and engineering developments also contributed towards continuous improvements in process technology and engineering to optimize efficiency and reduce emissions and waste products.

Despite remarkable growth and diversification in the chemical industry, our technological strengths in process design and engineering have been poor. We have and are depending upon imported process technologies to a very large extent.

The demands are now for cleaner processes with total recycling and recovery; for highly energy-efficient, tailor-made products; a shift from batch to continuous processes and for increased automation.

The target for Indian industry and institutions is to achieve their own processing technologies for most of their products by 2020. A mastery of the science and engineering of catalysts is imperative. The country should be capable of designing higher capacity and low energy consumption processing machines, and exporting them as well.

Indian chemical technology can also aspire to be one of the leaders in generating environmentally clean and safe products, which would mean zero waste technologies in addition to total recycling capabilities. We should also seek to innovate newer applications.

A new area is emerging which draws on the convergence of chemistry and biology in some sectors. India should prepare to reap rich benefits from this development.

Biologically catalyzed processes for production of fine organic chemicals and pharmaceuticals will be a force to reckon with by the turn of the century. Bioengineering systems will be used to dispose of hazardous waste and also to generate valuable by-products. The technologies involved are biocatalysis, bioengineering systems, biomolecular materials and biomaterials.

Engineering bacteria and other organisms to synthesize monomers, polymers, pharmaceuticals and other chemicals is now possible, as is synthesis of polyphenylenes using bacteria and benzene.

Bio-organisms will be utilized to carry out the elaborate sequences of organic reactions that convert simple building blocks into complex natural products in aqueous environments close to room temperature. Many natural products which were replaced with synthetic substitutes would reappear as a result of genetic engineering and other biotechnology techniques for higher efficiency and cleaner process conditions.

Some of the areas indicated above provide India with the opportunity to play a leading role in this industry. That is the vision we need to capture for action.

As can be seen from the earlier parts, the field covered by the chemical industry is very large. It offers many opportunities but is at the same time subject to restrictions placed by environmental considerations. It is vulnerable to constraints imposed by intellectual property rights regimes. If action is taken in advance, the threats can be converted into opportunities. Figures 6.1, 6.2 and 6.3 attempt to encapsulate the vision for this vast sector. A few elements such as petroleum and natural gas, speciality chemicals, polymers and petrochemicals are addressed in these figures. The left side describes the current scenario and the right side gives the vision for 2010.

Biodiversity and national wealth

We have just seen how biotechnology is going to affect future chemical technologies, and how much it can help in agriculture

FIGURE 6.1

Chemicals & Petrochemicals: Gearing up for the New Millenium

Petroleum & Natural Gas

Current Scenario (1997)	*Core Technologies*	*Future Scenario (2010)*
• Demand for natural gas : 80 million cubic meters/day	Hydro-processing techniques such as hydrotreating, hydro-cracking, reforming, hydro-isomerization for reducing heavy ends & also for lube oil base stocks (LOBS)	• Demand for natural gas: 275 million cubic meters/day
• Demand for petroleum products: 81 million tons		• New sources found offshore
• High demand for natural gas in power, fertilizer, sponge iron and LPG production	Gasification for generation of hydrogen & syn. gas from refinery residues	• Demand for petroleum products: 149 million tons
• Demand for petroleum products to rise to 120 million tons (conservative estimate) to 160 million tons (optimistic estimate) by turn of this century	Computerized process optimization & equipment monitoring system.	• An investment of Rs. 12500 crores in creating additional refining capacity
• 2600 km of pipeline for transportation of crude and refinery products		• A network of approx. 8000 – 10,000 km of pipelines to be laid for oil transportation

Source: Compiled by TIFAC from CMIE report on 'Corporate Sector, April 1998'; TIFAC report on 'Chemical Process Industry: Technology Vision 2020'; 'Survey of Indian Industry 1997'—The Hindu
(Courtesy: S. Biswas TIFAC)

FIGURE 6.2

Chemicals & Petrochemicals: Gearing up for the New Millenium

Speciality Chemicals

Current Scenario (1996–97)	*Core Technologies*	*Future Scenario (2010)*
• Demand for rubber processing chemicals (accelerators, antioxidants & others) : 20000 tons • Demand for polymer additives (antioxidants, heat & UV stabilizers, lubricants & flow improvers, plasticizers, slip agents, antistatic agents, fire retardants etc.): 120000 tons	Development of potent non-staining antiozonants New rubber to metal bonding agent Improving the green strength of rubber & reversion resistance, tear resistance and viscosity modification Development of antidegradant for high temperature applications of rubber Indigenous production of UV stabilizers & antioxidants for polymers Development of plasticizers such as phosphates, adipates, isophthalates etc. with consistent properties Development of colorants & pigments	• Estimated demand for rubber chemicals: 75000 tons • Estimated demand for polymer additives: 440000 tons • New applications invented by Indian researchers and industry

(Courtesy: S. Biswas, TIFAC)

FIGURE 6.3

Chemicals & Petrochemicals: Gearing up for the New Millenium

Polymers & Petrochemicals

Current Scenario (1996–97)	*Core Technologies*	*Future Scenario (2010)*
• Current demand for polymers (LDPE, LLDPE, HDPE, PP, PVC etc.): 1.8 million tons • Demand for synthetic fibres & fibre intermediates: 2.0 million tons • Demand for synthetic detergents: 0.23 million tons	Use of paraffins instead of olefins for polymer manufacture like ethane to polyethylene, propane to polypropylene, ethane to ethylene oxide & vinyl chloride etc. Carbonylation of ethylene or methyl acetylene or oxidation of iso-butylene to methyl-methacrylate Bio-processes for succinic acid from glucose, hydro-xylation of aromatics, acrylonitrile to acrylamide etc. Bio-synthesis of polyphenylene, polymers & co-polymers of lactic acid Development of intelligent polymers for electronics, robotics & bio-medical applications	• Estimated demand for polymers: 10.5 million tons • Estimated demand for fibres & fibre intermediates: 6.25 million tons • Estimated demand for synthetic detergents: 0.90 million tons • Recycling in a major way

(Courtesy: S. Biswas TIFAC)

and the agro-food processing sectors. Much more is in store.

In our search for a developed India our rich biodiversity appears to be one of our significant research bases. Let us look at figure 6.4, which is the Biodiversity-Technology Matrix.

It is somewhat ironic that in human history most countries which are rich in biodiversity have been by and large poor, while affluent and technologically advanced countries are poor in bioresources! India is in a unique position. We are rich in bioresources and have a sound technological and industrial base, but this has to be further strengthened. If only we could capture the wealth of these biological resources through the assiduous application of technology, we could easily become an economic power to reckon with. If we do not capitalize on our technological and industrial strengths to tap our rich biodiversity, and depend on the West for technological inputs, as we have done in the past, the benefits of our biodiversity will flow to the developed world. We may end up deriving only marginal benefits. Also India can easily reach quadrant 2 in the figure 6.4 as with the wealth so generated from our eco resources, it can invest in other areas of technologies as well.

The applications drawn from the life sciences are going to affect almost all walks of economic and social life in the coming years. Biosensors are likely to be used to monitor environmental pollution or in the analysis of blood or to judge a fruit's ripeness. Computational systems closer to the operation of the human brain are likely to emerge in future. These apart, there are a number of potentially significant applications in agriculture, health care, marine and industrial sectors. Herbal medicines and marine products are likely to emerge as huge areas of income generation and employment.

The rediscovery of traditional knowledge bases

The benefits of modern science may not have reached all parts of the world but there is a far greater awareness of these among people. People are now demanding more equitable share of the fruits of modern knowledge and skills.

In India too the benefits of scientific and technological

FIGURE 6.4

Biodiversity—Technology Matrix

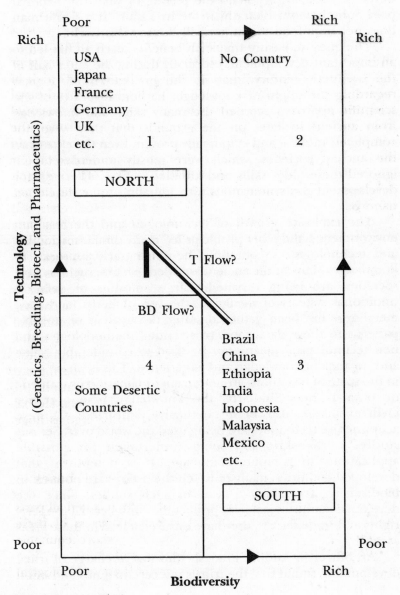

Source: *Dr T.N. Khoshoo*

breakthroughs have not reached all segments of our society. Until this happens, we cannot claim that India is truly a developed society. We echo the feeling of what the national poet Subrahmanya Bharathi wrote in Tamil: 'If a single man does not have food to eat, we will destroy this world.'

The quest to ensure that such benefits reach all has led to an important development, especially during the latter half of the twentieth century: that is, the breakdown of dogmas regarding the origin of knowledge. Earlier, advocates of the scientific approach scorned the many skills and knowledge from ancient societies on the grounds that they were not completely rational and empirically proven. Even the elite from the ancient societies, which were mostly underdeveloped, ignored these older skills and knowledge base. The rush for development was synonymous with imitating some developed nations.

The explosive growth of technologies and the resultant environmental and other problems led many thinkers, scientists and technologists to question the single-track approach to knowledge. Many of the ancient knowledge bases, such as tribal societies, are being revisited. Large amounts of data on traditional systems of medicine, the use of herbs, and even metallurgy has been gathered. After the analysis of possible patterns in these data, modern scientific methodologies and new technological means can be used to considerably 'value add' to ancient knowledge and experience. This is what we see in the spate of inventions around neem or tamarind or turmeric or basmati rice. Similarly, the knowledge base of other civilizations is also being extensively utilized: Chinese acupuncture techniques are being used the world over. Serious studies of Sanskrit are being undertaken for possible applications to computer language. It is noteworthy that developed countries, many of which themselves are not rich in biodiversity, are taking a lead in such studies. Since the developed countries jealously protect their intellectual property rights and trade secrets, they have ensured a lead in these areas as well.

An officer in Andhra Pradesh who was in charge of tribal development found that the tribals put certain gums and wood materials in turbid water to make the water clear. Apparently some chemical or physical action takes place which absorbs the materials that make the water turbid. Being curious, this officer asked some scientists he knew to study the materials. After experimentation they found that the materials used by the tribals even had the property of absorbing heavy minerals such as nuclear metals. The officer wanted to pursue the investigation further. As often happens in our system, he faced resistance. He tried to approach a few laboratories which did not respond. A foreign university showed interest. What the officer established was that a new technology based on tribal knowledge was a viable proposition. The case of sarpagandhi is another example. The ancient knowledge of this plant led to the invention of Serpasil, which is used for controlling blood pressure.

We are aware of many foreign companies which are funding academics from Indian universities to record such ancient knowledge. These companies can pay research scholars handsomely to recover this knowledge for them.

What should India's response be? Just to vent our moral indignation and talk about exploitation by the developers? We believe that the most crucial action India has to take is to step up our technology to chart out and understand our biodiversity, to protect it, and above all to forge new technologies out of our rich biodiversity. If we have to play the game of converting materials into intellectual products or actual products to be protected legally, let us do so. Let us use these not merely to enrich a few in our country but to create sustainable wealth for all people. Let us also attempt global leadership in the production of such commodities.

We believe that the newer turns in modern technological advances, be they studies of natural products, biotechnology or information technology, offer a new set of opportunities for us to not only catch up with the developed nations but also to surpass many of them.

How to achieve it?

Technology Vision 2020 documents on life sciences and biotechnology contain details of efforts to realize the benefits of India's biological wealth and to channel these for the general good.

We want to share with the readers some of the excitement and opportunities that lie ahead of us in fulfilling this major task. Even those familiar with basic Indian geography will be aware of the rich flora and fauna of the Himalayas, of the North-East, the coastal region, and central India. Even the desert regions of Rajasthan have their own special plants and animals. If we, as a nation, will it, we can organize a systematic campaign to utilize the talents of colleges, schools and several other local institutions to record the availability of various bioresources. Thanks to our survey organizations and several other research institutions, considerable information has already been collected. This can be updated and oriented towards an action plan: of protection and conservation; of systematic study and utilization; then of protecting various rights relating to intellectual property or similar rights; and of economic utilization. In addition to these physical surveys, the local knowledge of biodiversity can be documented. This is where the involvement of others from the disciplines of linguistics, sociology and so on also comes into the picture. If the teams are resourceful enough, they should not stop at collecting such information alone. They can collect information on local arts, music, crafts and other skills. Modern technology, with its video cameras, laptop computers and tape recorders has made this task easier than ever before. This will also help to identify those sources of knowledge which hold economic potential. People in different parts of the country can share the sights and sounds of a particular region.

Another rich bioresource is our long coast. We have more than 3500 km of coastline on the mainland, including that of Lakshadweep and the Andaman and Nicobar islands this increases to 7516 km. India has the unique privilege of an ocean being named after it. Still, many Indians are landlocked. We look forward to a day when all Indian children can happily enjoy a swim in our sea waters. Our neglect of the ocean leads not merely to a loss of enjoyment but to an economic loss. We only minimally harvest our fish. There are many varieties of seaweed which could be used for food or medicinal purposes. In addition, certain marine plants, animals and micro-organisms hold the key to growing plants in saline regions. For example, their genes can be isolated and crossed with the genes of land-growing plants to make them resistant to salinity. There are many active ingredients in marine resources which hold good promise as drugs and pharmaceuticals. Already there are some drugs for cancer treatment which are derived from marine sources. This is another rich bioresource India should learn to understand and to use, without, of course, being rapacious.

Himalayan medicinal plants—an example

India is rich in medicinal plants which are available all across the subcontinent. Many 'folk' medicines and practices are prevalent even today. There have been several systematic studies about these, though they cannot claim to be complete or adequate.

Here we will quote a few examples of such studies being conducted in some of the remotest parts of India, in the Leh and Nubra valleys. These are documented in the volumes on *Cold Desert Plants* by Om Prakash Chaurasia and Brahma Singh of the Field Research Laboratory, DRDO at Leh. Here one may add that almost all the climatic regions in the world are represented in India—roughly in the same ratio as the global distribution of such geographical zones. Cold deserts, for example, are found in the interior of Asia and in the inter-montane zone of North America. Of the total world land mass 16 per cent is under cold deserts. In India cold deserts come under the trans-Himalayan zone, and are confined to Ladakh in Jammu and Kashmir and Lahaul and Spiti in Himachal Pradesh.

In India, the history of medicinal plants can be traced back to the Vedic period (4500–1500 BC). The identity of several plants, viz. semal, pithuan and pipal referred to in the Suktas of the Rig Veda can be fixed with reasonable certainty. While the Rig Veda contains only minor references to medicinal plants, the Atharva Veda contains more detailed information, describing about 2000 species and their uses.

After the Vedic era, the works of the renowned physicians Charaka and Susruta, namely the *Charaka Samhita* and *Susruta Samhita*, deal with about 700 drugs of daily and specific uses. Between the sixteenth and seventeenth centuries India witnessed great upheavals in the development of medical botany and some of the most widely used herbal drugs came to light in this period. For this reason the period is also called the Age of Herbal Medicine.

It has been estimated that out of about 2000 drugs that have been used extensively in India, only 200 each are of animal and mineral origin while the rest are of plant origin.

Since time immemorial, Himalayan flora has been a major source of medicinal plants, and the cold desert is not an exception to this. The people of the cold desert still prefer herbal prescriptions based on the Tibetan system of medicine. Herbal medicine is practised by specialized local doctors called Amchis. Herbal plants available in this region have been found useful in the treatment of diarrhoea, cold, cough, stomach complaints, headache and skin diseases. Besides certain plant species found in this area such as Peganum harmala and Artemisia spp. have been found useful in controlling problems associated with menstruation and as aphrodisiacs.

Information about the growth areas, growth patterns and usefulness of medicinal plants has been gathered. This has been done with the help of Amchis, local tribals and by scanning of available literature.

These examples are only illustrative of the immense potential by way of medicinal plants in India. Imagine the possibilities if a detailed survey is done in each village or taluk of our country, and, above all, if we use this knowledge to make concrete value addition, and for commercialization. Can we rise up to this challenge? We believe we can, and with relatively modest investment. Let our vision be charged with the desire to extract the best out of our biological wealth.

Chapter 7

Manufacturing for the Future

If the three ranges of time, it is naturally hardest to get people to think about the long term vision of a more sustainable world, but it is vital that we overcome our reluctance to make concrete images of such a world.

—Murray Gell-Mann

The presence of traditional Indian skills in medicine, metallurgy, construction, textiles, hydraulics or early shipbuilding was an integral part of our innovativeness in ancient and medieval times. Witness the splendid metal icons and monuments like the Taj Mahal which were created employing intricate human skills and human/animal power. India was renowned for her prowess in skills as diverse as surgery and muslin weaving. We were advanced in the use of fire and in metallurgy. Still, the invention of machines that generate their own locomotive power by burning external fuels eluded medieval India. The internal combustion engine, the cornerstone of the industrial revolution in Europe, reached India only in the colonial period. India was a latecomer in learning the new manufacturing techniques invented in Europe. It was only in the late nineteenth and the first half of the twentieth century that India established a few sugar factories, steel and textile mills and began to think in terms of ambitious projects like shipbuilding and aircraft and automobile manufacture thanks to visionaries like Walchand Hirachand.

The modern face of manufacturing

Mankind has seen rapid transformation in the last 150 years because of the mass manufacturing techniques perfected in western nations and later taken to new levels of efficiency by Japan. Mass production and production for the masses became the bases of new business strategies. Large-scale consumption by all with the social benefit of removing poverty became the dominant economic strategy.

The advent of electricity and its large-scale application to lighting, heating and operating machines added a fresh dimension to manufacturing. By the 1950s came inventions in electronics and transistor devices to be followed by innovations in microelectronics, computers and various forms of sensors, all of which irreversibly altered the manufacturing scene. It is now no longer necessary to make prototypes in a factory or a laboratory to study a new product. Many new products can be designed on computers, and their behaviour simulated on them. By choosing an optimum design through such simulations, computer programmes can directly drive the manufacturing processes. These processes are generally called Computer Aided Design (CAD) and Computer Assisted Manufacturing (CAM). These capabilities are leading to newer forms of demands by customers. Each customer can be offered several special options. Customized product design or flexible manufacturing are other popular techniques currently in vogue in many developed countries.

The tools used in manufacturing today have multiplied greatly: lasers and waterjets are in increasing use. It is no longer specialized steels or even ceramics which monopolize the cutting tool industry. It is hard to believe that lasers can be used to cut heavy steel plates as also for delicate eye surgery. Can you imagine that the plain water you use at home can be used to cut steel? Water pumped at high pressures and focussed as a jet cuts cleanly. This technology holds a promise for use underwater, for example for off-shore installations.

To digress, anything focussed, and focussed sharply, becomes a good cutting edge or a welding source. A laser is a focussed and coherent source of light. A waterjet is a sharply directed high pressure jet. If we also, as a country and as a people, focus our efforts to eradicate poverty and to develop in a sustained manner, we don't think any obstacle could withstand the force of that collective, coherent, and focussed will!

Manufacturing in India

According to the TIFAC Task Forces on Technology Vision 2020, India stands to gain enormously by the coupling of computers and the manufacturing process. Here we have many success stories, albeit small compared to the potential, which encourage us to share this vision.

What are these? First and foremost is, of course, the fact that India is being looked at as a source of software the world over. Bangalore has become synonymous with the software prowess of India. Now Hyderabad is also being called Cyberabad to symbolize its emergence as a software and information technology city. In fact, it is not only these two cities but all of India which contributes to software export. How does this happen? The fullest credit goes to the many youngsters from Indian schools and colleges. To earn a livelihood, they have adapted their skills to suit the demands that have arisen, and performed splendidly.

The real issue before us is how to draw out the great potential of our people, their ability to work hard, and their motivation to learn more in order to excel. We will address this aspect elsewhere too. But suffice it to say that Indians have to be triggered by a vision, a supportive environment and some personal benefits to them and to their families. Many of those who left the country in the past fifty years were motivated by these requirements. When our own country did not offer a challenge or an opportunity for a better life, they sought it elsewhere.

Let us come back to the discussion of our software strengths.

There are some in our country who casually dismiss it as mere 'data entry' strength. This is taking a very narrow view of things. No big economy can survive *only* with activities which demand highly intellectual inputs. The economies of America, Germany, Japan or China will bear this out. But, in the long term, there is one element which should make us feel concerned. Can this boom of software export and application last for decades, merely based on software developed in other advanced countries which is operated by our people, as application support personnel, data analysts and market developers? Also, as it happens nowadays, those who create the original design very often reap most of the benefits, due to the nature of technology and often because of various forms of protection—trade contracts or intellectual property rights. Microsoft's success is a classic example of these trends. Microsoft has world rights to many software packages. Therefore, there is a definite need for India not only to derive benefits from the present software boom and demands, but also to prepare itself for the higher end of the market. India should dream of becoming a software business bidder in a decade.

What is the nature of this higher end software? Here we may quote from the Report of the National Critical Technologies Panel, USA in March 1991:

> Software is the basis of countless applications in information handling, manufacturing, communications, health care, defence, and in research and development . . .
>
> Increasingly, the development of advanced software is an important limiting factor in the introduction and reliability of new military and commercial systems. Software requirements, . . . expand at a dramatic pace as automated systems proliferate and increase in sophistication. Despite these growing demands, the generation of advanced software programmes remains largely a painstaking, labour-intensive market. As a result, the ability of US industry to provide high quality, reliable software is in jeopardy . . .
>
> In 1990, a 'minor' programming flaw resulted in a nine-hour shutdown of the major US long-distance telephone network . . . Advanced software therefore poses

a paradox: a fundamental source of technological progress, it is also going to be a growing source of technological vulnerability.

It is this labour-intensive phase in software which has created an immense opportunity for India. But advanced economies would not like to live with a vulnerable prosperity.

The US report quoted above describes many efforts required as well as those under way to resolve these problems. 'The essence of software is in its design. . . software requires no extensive fabrication or assembly. . . However, it is frequently difficult for the programmes to anticipate all of the circumstances that may arise when the programme is executed . . .' Innovative concepts being developed are software-based design tools as well as new management concepts for software design development.

The report concludes that these new approaches 'have strong potential to transform software development from labour-intensive craft to a more highly automated production process. With such advances, the writing of the software can give way to the manufacturing of software.' Thus, one can see that not only has the face of manufacturing physical products changed beyond recognition, but the computer software which has made this revolution possible is itself in the process of radical revolution.

Technology vision for software

India should start making a concerted effort to capture a share of the market in the newly emerging processes of reliable software for manufacturing, healthcare and other applications. We have certain innate strengths: CAD/CAM packages developed by the Aeronautical Development Agency (ADA), and required for the LCA (Light Combat Aircraft) project have found applications in major civilian markets and are now being marketed worldwide by a US company. There are a number of instances where Indian software has found applications in Europe and the USA, in tasks ranging from airport applications to manufacturing. Also, certain types of software from the academic sector are being tapped by a few global giants, eventually to be integrated by them in value-added packages. The targets for India's software export are projected as: $ 10 billion by 2002 and approximately $ 38 billion by 2008. Even these projected levels of achievement can be greatly surpassed by encouraging entrepreneurship. Experts also believe that by 2020 India could capture about 10 to 15 per cent of the total world market for upper end manufacturing software, emerging as an important supplier of software to companies of the developed world. This will be in addition to a large business in lower end software. Since by 2020 the language barriers for software would have been reduced considerably, most Indians would be using Indian languages for domestic and local applications. It is likely that 30 per cent of those in employment would be using various kinds of software.

The nature of business in the manufacturing sector is such that a few companies dominate the world scene due to the superiority of their technological base and organizational strengths. However, the demands of modern technologies and customer preferences are such that even these global giants cannot do everything on their own. They need several sources for software, design practices, applications development and so on. India's manufacturing sector can align with some of these giants to provide at least part of their value-added software and designs. These efforts will bring in considerable earnings and also place India in a position of strength as the software industry becomes more sophisticated in the coming years.

In return, Indian industry can also benefit by acquiring the most modern manufacturing equipment and practices required to meet rigorous quality and time schedule standards in modern business. These new manufacturing practices will also give a fillip to overall economic growth because each sector, be it agro-food or chemicals or biotechnology or electronics or packaging, will benefit from these new capabilities. Even though technologies and knowhow may be imported, the Indian machine tool and engineering sectors could well aim to manufacture the most sophisticated and automated systems in the world. Eventually, India can acquire a leadership position in a few areas of advanced machine systems. It will require a concerted effort involving people from industry, research laboratories, designers, consultants, exporters and marketing persons. The management of several such teams in a highly competitive and business-like environment requires new skills, capabilities and commitment. It cannot be achieved in the older style of central coordination and delay-prone hierarchical systems. In fact, the managerial tasks involved are going to be as demanding as the professional skills of software or manufacturing systems design.

Other manufacturing sectors

We have discussed the upper end of the manufacturing sector which is emerging in a major way in the developed countries because it is most likely to be the model for the future globally. We believe that Indian industry cannot escape this route and in fact, if we are alert enough and 'get our act together', we can take major advantage of the newly emerging opportunities and even make up for the ones missed earlier. Therefore, we need to act on this front speedily.

Yet we cannot afford to forget a large number of small and tiny manufacturing units which are in the organized and the so-called informal sector. They range from the level of artisanal craft to those with obsolete machinery and equipment, surviving mostly because of their low wage-costs. Of course a number of them have people with great innovative capabilities and basic skills. Some of the smaller units have come up to meet the demands for equipment arising out of import substitution, or because of the local sourcing requirements of industries using imported equipment and knowhow. The automotive sector is a good example of this. Many plastic products, textiles, leather and electrical goods are also manufactured by small and medium-sized industries. The problems facing them are not merely automated manufacturing or availability of software. Eventually, say in a decade or even earlier, this sector will also face competition from more efficient units using advanced technology. It is imperative that we prepare the tiny, small, medium and even bigger (not so advanced) Indian industries to face a more competitive future. That would mean a systematic upgradation of human skills in most of these industries and also large-scale modernization of many of them by continuous injection of newer (albeit incremental) technologies. Many of these industries have to be helped to re-orient themselves speedily for different product ranges and production processes, keeping in mind future demands in the domestic and export sectors. A redeeming feature of the newly emerging advanced manufacturing methods is that there is no longer going to be a centralized and monolithic mass manufacturing base. The factories of the future will be a network of highly specialized design, development and production bases, spread over the globe. If we have a collective will we can transform most of our existing industries along these lines and thereby also create enough space for totally new techno-entrepreneur-based units to come up.

We do not envision an India which gives up manufacturing in favour of agriculture and services. A country of a billion-plus people has to excel in many crucial sectors; manufacturing is one of them.

Engineering industries

Some of the elements envisaged in the TIFAC Technology Vision report for engineering industries are:

- By 2010, 60 per cent of the machine tools produced will be Computer and Numerically Controlled (CNC).
- By 2020, 80 per cent of the machine tools produced will be CNC.
- By 2000–05, Indian industries will go in for flexible manufacturing systems (FMS), artificial intelligence (AI) applications, processing using laser, waterjet, etc., cold forming/extrusion, near net shape manufacturing, high speed machining, intelligent manufacturing using sensors, continuous forming, reduced set-up times, virtual reality applications and hard machining.

- Boiler designs for many alternate fuels will be available by 2005. Fluidized bed combustion technology will be in wide use by 2000–05.
- By 2000–05, technological upgradation covering materials design, manufacturing, quality, reliability, packaging, marketing and servicing will take place. These will include Computer Aided Design (CAD), Computer Aided Manufacturing (CAM), FMS, ISO 9000, ISO 14000, R&D in new materials, modular design, casting and forging, mechatronics, precision manufacturing and automation.
- Design and development of high-precision machine tools, high-speed spindles, linear motor slides, diamond tuning machines, etc. will also come up.
- India will become a net exporter of technologies by 2010.
- Software development for processes and systems will take place.
- By 2020 India will be a leading producer of quality castings and forgings and will be a large exporter of these items. India will be self-sufficient in advanced machine tools and boilers using state-of-the-art technologies. Exports of these items will progressively increase.
- Employment generation will be on the rise.

The select areas of strength are automobile parts, casting, forging and CNC machine tools. A few more could be added after close evaluation. Urgent action is needed to realize this vision. Among these manifold tasks are:

— Gradation of processes—CAM, robotics, welding, near net shape manufacturing, precision manufacturing, automation, tooling, improving quality, delivery and cost, and state of the art technology adoption.
— Improving the supplier base for components and sub-assemblies as well as evolving modular designs; flexible manufacturing and agile systems are crucial.
— In the foundry sector, the increased accent has to be

on control of dimension/surface finish, value addition through machined casting, forging and mechanization and automation with increased scale of production.

— In the forging sector we need to develop better tooling capabilities—CAD, adopt cold forging and near net shape technologies and resort to mechanization and automation with large-volume production.

— In boiler and pressure vessels manufacture, urgent action is required for the upgradation of welding systems, automation in welding, use of robotics for improvement in radiography, controls, reliability and safety.

— Further advanced boiler technologies that are required to be mastered are development of fluidized bed technologies, once through boiler designs, improvement of boiler tubes, thermal efficiencies and design for alternate fuels.

In addition to the above, advanced manufacturing technologies would crucially depend upon improved precision manufacturing capabilities. This demands considerable investment in research and development in areas such as:

- Fundamental research in machining including micro-machining
- Development of advanced automation systems including software
- Development of robotics
- Development of sensors and adaptive control
- Mechatronic development
- Development of measuring and testing equipment for quality and reliability as well as
- Development of proper standards

The above will require all-round upgradation of skills and their continuous enhancement. The workforce at all levels has to be readied for mechatronics through multi-skill training. Most of the updated curricula in ITIs, polytechnics and engineering colleges will require drastic revision. Their facilities will need to be modernized. In the transitional period, innovative teaching methods for the use of the advanced facilities existing in industries and national laboratories have to be adopted. As depicted briefly in the earlier chapters, we have attempted to present the transformation of the present status to the vision for 2020 for engineering industries through figure 7.1. In the centre core technologies to be mastered are highlighted.

Vision for textile machinery

The textiles sector is crucial for India to meet its domestic needs and more important to provide the major share of its export earnings. While there are a number of strengths in this area, there are also several technological weaknesses. For example, we depend upon imported machinery for quality production. The TIFAC Task Force teams which have looked at these aspects in totality are confident that India can be a leading textile producing country and become a top player in the global market.

This is how they envision the steps (assuming that corresponding action is taken well in advance):

- By 2000, technology upgradation, productivity improvement, energy conservation and environmental protection aspects and quality improvement will take place. This will include use of CAD/CAM, robotics, high-speed machines, material handling systems, auto doffing and high-speed ring frames, electronic instrumentation and computerized automation, airjet looms, spinning and preparatory-autoleveller cards and draw frames.
- Agricultural research will result in better cotton yield. Organic cotton and coloured cotton will be available.
- There will be a reduction in the cost of hank yarn, use of cone yarn by handlooms, development of high-value yarn, production of industrial filter fabrics, medical textiles and use of micro fibres.
- By 2010 eco-friendly textile exports and domestic use will start. Production of geo and technical textiles will begin in a major way.

FIGURE 7.1

Vision 2020 for Engineering Industries

1997

- Limited CNC machines
- Experimental laser, waterjet cutting
- Modernize forging and casting industry
- Mix of imported technologies and limited capability in machine tools and state of the art boilers
- India emerging as software producer
- Import dependency

Core Technologies

- Advance machining
- Micro machining
- Advanced automation
- Sysems including software
- Sensors and adaptive controls
- Robotics and artificial intelligence
- Mechatronics
- Development of measuring and testing equipment for quality and reliability
- Fluidized bed technologies
- Materials technologies
- Design capability
- Virtual reality

2020

- 80 per cent of machines produced will be CNC
- Intelligent manufacturing
- High speed machining
- India leading producer and exporter of casting and forging

- Self-sufficient in advanced machine tools and boilers

- About 10–15 per cent advanced software in the world will be of Indian origin

- Net exporter of technologies by 2010

- Machinery modernization will be achieved and there will be development of advanced machines with electronic controls. New weft insertion techniques and a continuous rotating system for weaving will be developed.
- High-tech knitting technologies, multiface weaving, meltspinning of microfilament yarn, eco-friendly processing, improvement in indoor air quality and recycling of waste will all be done.
- Fibre inputs like jute, linen, polyester, acrylics and polypropylene will find a place in yarn manufacture.
- Large-scale units with assembly line plants will diversify into high-value garments, jackets, industrial wear and sports wear; integrated textile mills will enter garment manufacture by 2010-20.
- Fashion changes will be faster by 2000 than at present.
- Employment of women will be on the increase, especially in garment making.

Figure 7.2 attempts to capture these details in a simple form with the left-hand side presenting highlights of the current status, the right side being the vision for 2020, and the centre portion highlighting core technologies to be mastered.

Vision for the electrical machines industry

This industry is poised for a quantum jump with excellent growth opportunities. Multinational corporations are likely to base their manufacturing units in India. R&D focus will be on materials, electromagnetics, mechanical engineering, manufacture, thermal engineering and power electronics. By 2000 CAD/CAM and automated production lines will be used by Indian companies. Maintenance-free machines will be produced in India. Direct torque control technology, automatic winding, use of pressure die castings, trickle impregnation, manufacture and use of CRGO/CRNGO sheet steels will all be available. Inputs for production will undergo a change. Aluminium foil will replace wires. Use of new materials like samarium, ferrite and laser-etched magnetic material sheets

FIGURE 7.2

Vision 2020 for Textile Industry

1997

- Limited number of large scale units and limited products range

- Limited automation
- Environmental aspects beginning to be addressed
- Limited geo and technical textiles

- Synthetic dyes
- Poor horizontal integration within various elements in the value-added chain

Core Technologies

- High speed machines
- Computerized automation CAD/CAM/robotics

- Agricultural research: better yield of cotton; coloured cotton
- Eco-friendly processing techniques and recycling of wastes

- Design capability
  —machine to fashions design

2020

- Integrated textile mills for garments
- Manufacture with diversification into high value-garments beginning 2010
- Highly automated
- Eco-friendly textiles for domestic use and exports
- Large scale geo and technical textiles

- New cottons
- India a world leader of natural dyes
- India a leader in fashion design

and use of polyestermide and polyamide as alternative enamel will be on the increase.

By 2000–10 designs for better heat dissipation, better bearing design and development of 11 kVHT motors will be prevalent. Large-scale flexible manufacturing facilities will come up. Better magnetic materials, insulation and high-current density conductors will be used.

By 2015-20 development of power-conditioned motors will be taken up and organic conductors will replace metallic conductors. Applications of superconductivity, linear motors and single-chip controller will be widely available.

Vision for the manufacture of transport equipment

India will follow the world trend in transport equipment with a reduced time lag. Commercial vehicles will have a higher power to weight ratio and two-wheelers will use four stroke engines with electronic controls. More diesel engines with direct injection and electronic control will come up. Indian industry will become one of the preferred suppliers to world markets. It is essential that the new vehicles are eco-friendly.

Anything uniquely Indian?

As we look at the developments in the various sectors, we may ask whether they are uniquely Indian or are we merely following the trends of the developed world, and whether India is merely adapting itself faster than in the past. These are not easy questions though posing them is easy!

What if the country develops very well, the well-being of all Indians is taken care of, and the country's security needs are fully met, and yet we have not done something 'uniquely' Indian? We don't think the great majority of Indians will be particularly worried about this. The most important tasks confronting us are to remove poverty altogether from our midst, to provide considerable social and economic opportunities to all Indians and also to provide for the security of their quality of life. In real terms, aspects other than these are of secondary importance. Of course, geopolitics and other geo-commercial realities dictate that we achieve these with a basic core strength of our own, even while we strike many strategic partnerships with others in the world, in terms of technology, trade or business development.

However, the aspiration to find something unique still remains alive in a number of Indians, specially those, perhaps, with an intellectual bent of mind. They often look at their own capabilities and wonder why India has not done something exceptional. There is some legitimacy to such aspirations as well. In fact, it is only such aspirations or such dreams that can propel a nation in the long run. The India of the past has had many unique inventions and discoveries which have had a great impact on human thought and civilization. These have not merely been in the fields of philosophy, art, trade or statecraft but in terms of technological artefacts as well. However, in the recent past, there are not many obvious examples that one can be proud of except in missiles, space or in atomic energy. The name of Bose has become synonymous with the most modern sound systems. But Bose did not achieve this when he was in India.

During the five decades after independence we had so many major problems to solve. Looking back we have also not had the type of resolve that is required to wipe out the centuries of stagnation and emerge as a vibrant society. We have let go many opportunities presented by technologies, as well as by trade and business. Missed opportunities do not usually recur in the same form. In a competitive world, there are others waiting to seize these opportunities. Much more than the blows to national pride or that of the intellectuals, the worst outcome of such missed opportunities is the loss to the nation. Slow economic growth hits the poor the most. Our utmost attention during the next quarter century should be to attend to these problems of growth and removal of poverty. In order to do so, we may have to adapt many things from the world, as also prepare ourselves for future creative adventures.

Having looked at some of these macro issues relating to our being unique, let us address each of the earlier sectors to see what the possibilities are of such accomplishment. In the agriculture sector, let us not forget that our Green Revolution was based on research done elsewhere in the world. It was later adapted to Indian conditions. The way the farmers adapted these techniques is remarkable. In the coming years, India faces the challenge of having to find her own solution for higher yields. Indian agriculture has its own specific features relating to land holdings, terrains and agro-climatic conditions. Many techniques and practices will call for newer and novel solutions, though they may not all be flashy. There are possibilities of unique applications of biotechnology or newer forms of agricultural management providing examples of ecologically sustainable practices. There are good possibilities that India, with its biodiversity, may develop a few new varieties of crops with a broad genetic base.

In the chemical sector by and large, it would be a question of catching up, adapting newer inventions made elsewhere speedily and also producing our own innovations. There are immense possibilities for Indian contributions in specific areas of the chemicals sector: catalytic sciences and their applications, new clean chemical processes, and new inventions for medicinal applications.

In the field of natural products, given India's rich biodiversity and immense base of ancient knowledge still extant, we may be able to make several contributions. Further, as this is a virgin area worldwide, the success rate for India's efforts is likely to be very high.

In the manufacturing sector our uniqueness can manifest itself in terms of applications. If we take up applications of advanced software for manufacturing, as described earlier seriously, there are possibilities that some modules or approaches may emerge with a novel thrust for which India will be known on the world scene. While this itself cannot be the end goal for society as a whole in the coming years, a determined group of Indians could steadfastly work towards such possibilities and make a mark in the world.

In the pursuit of all-round economic growth, the physical and social well-being of all our people and national security, we may have to ensure the creation of an enabling environment to try something uniquely Indian. Such an inventive spirit will be useful for the long-term sustainability of our gains.

Chapter 8

Services As People's Wealth

We are what we think
All that we are arises
With our thoughts
With our thoughts
We make our world.

— The Buddha

The services sector has come to be considered a major part of the economy only in recent times. It generally subsumes all economic activities other than those related to agriculture or manufacturing (including mining). Trading, marketing, repairing and, of course, service in public organizations including various forms of government service, the postal services, teaching and so on come under this sector. Changes in agriculture and manufacturing have propelled the growth of the services sector.

Modern agriculture with its improved inputs and greater mechanization has led to decreased agricultural employment and migration of farm workers to urban areas in search of better living standards which the manufacturing sector is expected to offer. In India 60-70 per cent of the workforce is in agriculture. But slow economic growth does not allow a greater absorption of the rural poor in other activities and many Indians still survive as marginal farmers or marginal landless labourers. This problem requires special attention, partly by helping some with better inputs in agriculture and also by finding avenues for many of them in related or other professions so that they do not depend on land alone. There have been attempts to build rural roads or other employment generation schemes. But more creative and economically sustainable options are available in the agro-food sectors, in exploitation of biodiversity, water conservation programmes, tourism, value added crafts and other activities.

In the manufacturing sector, as seen in the previous chapter, there are higher demands of skills and knowledge. Increased economic activity is definitely going to increase employment in manufacturing but the rate may not be as much as it was, say, two or three decades ago.

There is, as elsewhere in the developed world, a search for new employment, namely, for a shift to a sector loosely defined as the services sector. One way to define this sector is to include anything other than direct agriculture or manufacturing. The emergence of modern information technologies has made the demarcations even more fuzzy. How do you treat the activity of generation of computer simulations of several potential products? Or regular monitoring of soil conditions and weather forecasts with the help of satellites and other data, in order to provide advisories to the farmers? Or monitoring of global markets of agricultural products and the possible global yields to analyse and advise farmers on possible sales strategies? Or monitoring of the coasts through satellite sensors to advise fishermen about potential areas of high yield of fish? The examples we quote are in regular commercial operation in advanced countries and successful experiments have taken place in India as well. Tourism, testing and calibration, technical and management consultancy, training, security services, banking, financial services, real estate, marketing, media and advertising, to name a few, are a part of the services sector.

Can a country survive on services?

There are some who would like to believe in simplistic statements about post-industrial society and the revolution of information technology whereby societies can be sustained through the services sector alone. This may be true for smaller countries. A country like India cannot hope to build its future on the services sector alone though it can be and will be a major component of the economy. India cannot afford not to build its strengths in agriculture for reasons of food and nutritional security. Nor can it afford to ignore manufacturing strengths for reasons of economic and national security. Based on the strengths of these two sectors, it can build a major economic infrastructure for the services sector and use it to generate great wealth and employment for her people.

Thus, the services sector, if properly developed along with the other two important and basic sectors, can really be considered a sector in the service of the people, to find new jobs and individual prosperity. In our Technology Vision 2020 documents we have given great importance to the services sector as it covers multiple sectors of technology and manufacture.

Technologies and employment

We remember the amount of paper work we had to do to get government permission for purchase of computers by the Indian Space Research Organisation (ISRO). For procuring each computer, there was a long series of notes, meetings, questions and answers!

The country has come a long way since then. In fact, the opening up of the computer front since the mid-'80s has resulted in India's one-billion-dollar software exports today. Computers have increased efficiency and service, the computerization of railway ticketing being a notable example. There is of course specific displacement of workers in the real or virtual sense; for example, a type of clerical staff may not be further recruited because computerization has helped streamline the paperwork. The existing workforce thus needs to be trained in new skills.

So far the transition has been relatively smooth, but to sustain this process it is essential for the government, the organized sector, and even trade and labour unions to anticipate such changes and prepare our workforce. We have the success story of Japan before us as an example.

In the coming years, requirements for rapid changes in the skills of a large number of people in periods of say three to five years may become a continuous feature when newer technologies are introduced into the economy. Such rapid changes will occur in all sectors, underlining how the agriculture, manufacturing and service sectors are intertwined. In the agriculture sector there will be better optimization of input resources like seeds, soil conditioning, fertilizer-micronutrient mixes, pesticides and so on, as well as changes in the overall agricultural management. The agriculture sector may also use information technology much more intensely than it does now, be it in the use of remote sensing through satellites for regular monitoring of crops and soil conditions or water resources, or for better weather forecasts through satellites and ground-borne systems, or in the use of modern communications to be in closer touch with old or new markets. Water quality may be monitored more carefully in the future whether for human or animal consumption. Rapid improvements in advanced sensors would make it possible to have such sensing systems at affordable prices in many of our agricultural sectors.

In the industrial and manufacturing sector, of course, the use of sensors, and modern electronics and information technology will be a continual feature requiring rapid reorientation of the skills of not only the workforce but also the entire management including board level operations.

Installation of IT systems for all these sectors, training persons at all levels and maintaining and improving their skills would be a major service industry.

India and the services sector

The agricultural sector in India accounts for 32.7 per cent of GDP and has an annual rate of increase of about 3.5 per cent. The secondary sector consists of manufacturing, power, etc., and forms 25.8 per cent or the GDP with a growth rate of 5.9

per cent. Services like trade, storage, transport, communication and finance are the traditional components of the tertiary or services sector. Among the newer services that have emerged are advertising, marketing management, and various consultancies. The services sector provides essential inputs to the other two sectors and so they are dependent on the efficient operation of this sector which in India is now about 40 per cent of the GDP. Employment in the services sector covers a large range of occupations involving relatively little investment in capital equipment. There is also a great potential for exporting services.

Some of the sectors considered to be of great value for India in the TIFAC reports are:

— Financial services
— Marketing communication services (i.e. advertising, media, consultancy and infotainment)
— Marketing logistics, trading and distribution
— Trade promotion services
— Human resources development
— Technical and management consultancy
— Testing, certification and calibration services
— Government administration
— Security services

There are also other important activities. To name a few:

— Repair and maintenance
— Tourism and hotels
— Leisure and sports resorts
— Cultural activities
— Old age care services
— Preventive health care services

We shall examine a few sectors to assess future requirements.

Financial services

The financial sector includes a large number of institutions such as commercial banks, financial term lending banks, insurance companies, capital markets like the stock exchanges, and so on. In the last twenty-five years the number of branches of commercial banks increased sevenfold, to about 65000 in 1995. Aggregate deposits of commercial banks have increased by two and a half times in the last six years, to Rs. 4500 billion in January 1996.

The gross value added to GDP by insurance services increased at the rate of 7.5 per cent during 1980–81 and 1993–94, but only 22 per cent of all insurable persons are covered by life insurance. The number of persons covered will increase significantly due to population increase, economic growth and the rise in the magnitude of risks due to rapid urbanization. Currently less than 1 per cent of the population has any dealings with non-life insurance business, but the demand on these services is bound to increase as manufacturing, trade and other activities grow. Additionally more and more people will go in for personal accident insurance, medical coverage and other such forms of protection. The business in non-life insurance even currently is increasing at the rate of 20 per cent per annum and is expected to accelerate to 30 per cent in the next decade.

Despite voluminous growth in the banking and insurance sectors, processing and transactions have been carried out by largely manual means. A national network of banking and the insurance business has to emerge. This lack has adversely affected efficiency and is a major cause of the high rates charged for financial services. The introduction of IT for various operations at the earliest has become a necessity. This means use of computers for near total electronic data management and the use of telecommunications and multimedia data, adopting a total systems approach. Some modern technologies like Automated Teller Machines (ATM), automatic cheque clearing systems, telephonic banking, credit cards, and electronic fund transfers are being introduced in a small way and will be prevalent in most of the banks in the coming years.

In other financial services, including insurance services, very little computerization has taken place. This lack of IT resources has resulted in poor services to customers and inadequate controls leading to delinquency in loans. In capital markets, both primary and secondary, only low levels of technology are in use. In primary markets the lack of computerization and communication facilities results in long delays in the finalization of subscription of new issues. The Bombay and National Stock Exchanges have recently adopted screen based trading.

At the lower end of banking, that is, rural banking, many of these technologies may not have relevance except for the wealthy, at least for a decade or more. The problem in the bulk of our village communities is to generate money and make it available to workers, not merely for their subsistence but to carry out some economic activities of their own with small investments. Financial or lending systems for such poor rural folk could be patterned on the 'grameen bank systems', successfully operated in Bangladesh. Rural telephone access either through RAX (Rural Exchanges) systems developed by C-DoT or through wireless in the loop systems, will be useful in extending the range of operations.

Marketing communication services

Marketing communication which comprises services such as advertising, market research and entertainment, depends primarily on the stage of economic development and the nature of the target groups. The Indian economy has been growing at an average rate of 5 per cent from 1980–81 resulting in a middle class population of 200–250 million. Though currently 70 per cent of the population is rural, by the year 2020 this figure should decline to 55 per cent; the literacy rate is expected to rise to 80 per cent. Because of these trends there would be major shifts in marketing communication. The strategy now is to focus on innovation and to create new needs.

Market research and market communication have so far been confined to a handful of consumer goods like soaps, cosmetics, toothpastes, beverages, and select food products.

They are now being applied to white goods like television sets, refrigerators, and washing machines. In rural areas too the purchase of these goods is on the increase. Marketing of agricultural inputs and appliances is also going up. It is estimated that nearly 50 per cent of the purchase of consumer durables will be in rural India against less than 30 per cent today. Also in the agricultural sector, many private entities are likely to enter into the marketing of seeds, fertilizer mixes, pesticides, and a variety of agricultural tools and implements. The demand for India-specific domestic appliances like idli-mixers and chapati-making appliances or packed foods and sweets is likely to increase and these will be sold at competitive prices. Foreign products may soon be competing with Indian goods just as our goods will be exported to a number of countries.

Demand for quality and standards

The sale of an increased volume of products would also create a trend of market segmentation for high quality products. People would demand newer features, like greater user-friendliness or greater portability or better aesthetics or looks.

There are also other demands which are of a technical nature. They are: greater reliability, tending towards zero repair over the products' lifetime, or lower energy consumption, or lesser noise or radiation emissions, or lower levels of environmental pollution, etc. These demand new standards of performance and greater technological inputs. Companies themselves would introduce improved features to maintain a competitive edge. In India too, such trends will be on the increase and local businesses and industries will have to learn to adjust to them. Marketing communications by foreign companies even through satellite-based TV and other information services will also affect Indian consumer preferences—even in rural India. Presently, Indian industries or markets or consumers follow trends which are often a decade or more old in the developed world. This has to change.

Value systems in marketing communication

A question that arises is regarding the place of value systems in marketing communication. Is it necessary to pursue this 'one-upmanship', characteristic of consumerism? Why not promote those changes related to energy conservation or environmental protection or safety, and not encourage trends which are addressed to the mere looks of a product or to some vague concept of user-friendliness? Should we encourage this kind of marketing communication? Most Indian companies spend about 1 per cent or more of their turnover on advertisement, often more than what they spend on research and development. Is this necessary? Can we not rid ourselves of the advertisement culture? If the social or commercial purpose of advertisement is only to provide technical and commercial information to the people, why not give this information freely on demand or display it in suitable public places in an inexpensive manner, as the advertisement costs are really finally borne by the consumer himself.

On the face of it, many of these ideas are wonderful. But in real life the behaviour patterns of people are very complex and there are many individual variations. Not everybody has the patience to thumb through a directory to search out different products. Therefore, advertising becomes a useful source of information. Rural and urban dwellers, poor and rich, literate and illiterate, all require a flow of information in various forms to know, to choose and to feel that they are not being left behind. Besides they help people save time which would be used in searching out information. Regarding the contents and the ethics of these messages, most healthy societies learn how to come to a dynamic equilibrium.

It is very interesting to note that as the physical production in the agriculture and manufacturing sectors expands, the demands on marketing communication grow, thus providing people additional employment opportunities. This is an area which can be given a thrust.

The future scenario of marketing communication

Among the newer technologies which are likely to enter this area are: composing; multi-addition; portable IT technologies; automatic language translation; hand-held terminals; satellite digital audio-broadcasting; three-dimensional workstations; exemption for access control; systems for viewer censoring; stereo music broadcast; three-dimensional animation; multilingual audio and interactive random data graphical user interface.

It is essential that Indian industries work in advance to acquire or develop technologies in these areas so that they can be market leaders in India and possibly export to other countries as well. If they do not take action now, it is likely that those in need of providing such services will import products. The business volumes in many of these areas range from a few tens of crores to several thousand crores per year. Table 8.1 provides a brief picture.

TABLE 8.1

Projected Volume of Communications Business 2020

		(Annual turnover Rs. Crores)
1995	Activity	2020
	Marketing services	
60	Market research	800–1000
3500	Advertising	18000–20000
	Mass media:	
1500	Press (Circulation/Sale)	6500–7000
1500	TV (Software)	7000–8000
200	Cable operations	8000–1000

		(Annual turnover Rs. Crores)
	Entertainment media:	
1000	Cinema (Production & collections)	4000–5000
300	Music	2500–3000
35	**Multimedia**	1000–1200
35000	Telecom Telephone & Data	600000–700000

Notes: *(1)*   *All estimates are at 1995 prices.*
        (2)   *Cinema includes production meant for Cable and TV.*
            There is some overlap between media and entertainment.

(Source: TIFAC Technology Vision 2020 : Services)

Marketing logistics, trading and distribution

Having communicated information about products and goods, it is necessary to reach them to the consumer. Trading has been the important service activity that fulfilled this need.

Services like wholesale and retail trade, warehousing, transportation and distribution which link producers/manufacturers with the consumers are the components of marketing logistics. These services accounted for 21.5 per cent of GDP in 1993-94. Marketing logistics are required for three broad categories, namely agro-based food products, major materials and intermediate goods like coal, steel, cement, etc. and consumer goods like durables, textiles, and so on.

The trading and distribution of the above categories is done by traditional methods of commissioning wholesale distributors at selected centres and a large number of retailers. Due to increase in GDP, a large volume of product changes are expected within a decade in trade and marketing logistics.

Future scenario in trading

Some of the traditional outlets in villages and small towns are one-stop shops. Though options may be limited, they can meet a range of requirements. In most of the advanced countries this feature has taken the shape of big retail channels and shopping malls which are now catching on in the bigger Indian cities. By going to one place, one can get almost any item of domestic consumption. As the production of goods and their consumption grows, which is definitely envisioned for our country, these shopping malls and big retail stores will be in position. Let our technologists and industrialists dream and think of business opportunities in equipping such big malls and maintaining them. There is no reason why many of these accessories and fittings cannot be made in India. We emphasize this because at present several items for our five-star hotels are imported since those of comparable quality are not available in the country. It is essential that a country that can tame atomic energy or produce complex metallurgical products, should be able to make relatively simpler products using Indian knowhow and designs.

Coming to packaging, wherever possible we can avoid the older route of plastics, though they are necessary for some products. Bio-degradable tapioca-lined paper packages have been developed in our country. Why not try many such innovations instead of adopting mere imitations of other advanced countries?

Another important technological input in marketing logistics, trading and distribution is going to be satellite communication and computer networks. We often forget we are a vast country of about 3.2 million sq. km, where goods move by trucks or railways. A fast-growing, high-volume economy cannot sustain its distribution channels without a first-rate computer network and satellite communication channels. Why satellite? Computer networks are possible even with fibres. But a truck, goods train or a ship each requires different links. Mobile communication can be established. Satellite navigational systems help in pinpointing the position as well. Mobility of businesspersons and traders is also crucial. The way they have taken to cellular or mobile phones is remarkable. Once we provide good computer networks as well as regular and mobile communications, we ourselves will be surprised by the ingenious use people can put them to. The barrier between rural and urban areas will be broken by the service sector in communications.

Future scenario in marketing logistics

Greater speed in transportation will be a key demand, as also the demand for larger loads having greater reach. Specialized containers, often with controlled atmospheric conditions (for example cooling to a certain temperature and with moisture control, etc.) will be required. Modular and bulk containers will be in demand. In addition there will arise demand for a single container that can be sent by air, road, rail or ship. This is called capability for multimodal transportation. Internationally many such standardized containers are used. It will be advantageous if Indian industries begin acquiring such a capability now and adapt it to our conditions. There will be a great demand for such containers in about five to ten years.

With larger cargoes, requirements for better cargo handling facilities, modernized packaging systems and loading and unloading systems will increase. A natural requirement would then be for large modern warehouses. Once these are built and since there will be pressure at the time of delivery, the connectivity between farms, factories, godowns, warehouses, head offices, field offices, supermarkets and other retail outlets will be crucial. These connectivities will be by road, rail or waterways as well as through data/voice communication.

An important point needs to be emphasized here which applies to all areas, and particularly to this area of services. Simple training with visuals and in the workers' languages is what is required to ensure that people perform well. If we do not invest in our workforce and treat them as unskilled labour which can be drawn on merely for manual labour, their performance will also be similar.

There is a great scope for educating people to maximize efficient use of resources. For instance, 5 per cent of fuel used for vehicles can be saved if drivers are given proper training in correct and energy-efficient driving habits: don't press the accelerator unnecessarily, avoid braking suddenly, slow down earlier, etc. But does a normal driver know that these factors are connected with the thermodynamics of engines and fuel burning? Similarly, if the stove's flame is kept at a level that will prevent it lapping around the sides of the vessel and just be under the pot, though it may take a few minutes more to cook food, there will be a considerable saving of precious gas. Such wastage exacts a heavy price on the economy. Marketing communication skills can be deployed very effectively to impart continual training to our workforce and curb such wastage. That will be an excellent service industry itself.

Trade promotion services

New global trade arrangements are expected to add US$ 213–274 billion annually to world income. The GATT secretariat projects the largest increase at 60 per cent of world trade in the area of textiles and clothing followed by agriculture, forestry and fishery products. The potential gain of Indian exports is estimated at $2.7 billion (the current export is $20 billion). Effective trade promotion services would be required to tap new markets and increase our exports.

Short-term activities (five years) should include strengthening IT for trade and building necessary infrastructure for meeting customer requirements. Medium/long-term activities (ten to twenty years) should include large global databases, communication links and improved transportation and banking facilities.

Tourism

Most people are familiar with the traditional concepts of

tourism: hotels, access to easy transport, special places to visit, starting from the Taj Mahal, Goa, Kanyakumari, the beautiful North-East, coastal India and the islands, the deserts and the Himalayas. But the modern-day tourist expects something more and different. He comes here not merely to eat, drink and make merry. Many want to learn more about the people they meet and the places they visit. We can call it 'cultural' or 'knowledge oriented' tourism. There is plenty of scope for meeting such a requirement through the help of information technology. Multimedia presentations can be made available in most tourist spots on the music, culture, history, biodiversity and other features of that place and nearby areas. Or imagine the possibilities that could open up by giving foreign tourists glimpses of such information, including local maps, by electronic mail even as they are planning their trips! The possibilities are many, it only remains to try them.

Human resources development

As must have become self-evident, the services sector is dominated by human needs, comforts and convenience. Naturally, development of human resources becomes an important requirement for having a services sector. We have shown a few examples in earlier sections. The very activity of human resource development and continuous skill upgradation in the face of changing technologies or preferably in advance preparation of likely changes in technologies and consumption styles is going to be another major component of the services sector. All of us have to unlearn a lot, learn a lot, continue to learn a lot, use new aids in learning, teach others and so on.

As the UN Human Development Report of 1995 makes clear, massive investments in human capital and development of managerial and technological skills are needed in developing countries if they are to improve their peoples' living standards. India itself is ranked very low, at 134th place out of 175 countries, below countries like Malaysia, Thailand and Sri Lanka. As much as 73 per cent of our population has no proper sanitation, and 21 per cent lack access to drinking water.

The following table sets out the future challenges and priorities.

TABLE 8.2

HRD : Future Challenges and Priorities

Serial No	Activity	Time-frame for completion (in years)
1	**Improvement in primary and secondary education**	
	Quality and competence of teachers	5–10
	Entrepreneurship oriented education	5–10
	Use of multimedia and other mass media technologies	10–15
2	**Empowerment of women**	
	Social engineering with widespread social awareness and campaign	5–10
	Technological interventions for improved women's education	5–15
3	**Investment in science and technology**	
	Reorientation of R&D activities more focussed	5–10

Serial No	Activity	Time-frame for completion (in years)
	Leadership training and skills development for institution building for national laboratories and institutions	5–10
	Devising HRD programmes and strategies for national laboratories and institutions	5–10
4	**Entrepreneurship development**	
	Development of entrepreneurial skills and employment generation by the Government NGOs and financial institutions	5–10
	Creation of entrepreneurial attitude and spirit, achievement motivation etc.	5–10
	Improved availability and management of credit facilities	5–10
5	**Human resources development Role of private agencies and NGOs**	
	Development of entrepreneurial skills and institution building capabilities of NGOs	5–15
6	**Improvement of performance by government agencies and institutions**	
	HRD programmes related to bringing in attitudinal and behavioural changes of government personnel	5–10

Serial No	Activity	Time-frame for completion (in years)
	Infusing professionalism in government services	5–10
	Deployment of less manpower and improved mechanization in Government services	5–15
7	**Concern for the environment**	
	Improved environmental awareness and education among common people through mass communication technologies and contact programmes	5–10

Source: TIFAC Report—Technology Vision 2020: Services

It needs also to be realized that if we are to effectively develop our human resources we must decentralize the HRD function so that self-correcting learning systems develop at the local level. Modern technologies including IT help the process very greatly and provide new opportunities.

Technical and management consultancy services

HRD is itself a knowledge and skill based activity in great demand in the technological society of today. But the complex technologies in operation and the continual demands for them in day-to-day life ranging from domestic operations to defence, require that there are no critical failures. In fact, the objective of most manufacturers and service providers is to provide maintenance-free systems. Earlier, rigorous demands for quality assurance and reliability were restricted mainly to the areas of defence systems, space applications and for devices implanted in human bodies. Nowadays, the highest specifications of quality standards are demanded in several civilian applications. On the one hand, technological progress is reducing the product life-cycle to a few years. Earlier, people were happy with a mean time between failures (MTBF) of a few or several thousand hours. That means any equipment once delivered or repaired would perform without any major problem for a few or several thousand hours, which was specified as the MTBF. The present-day trend is not to have a failure during the entire product life-cycle, which may be only a few years because of constant updating. Those who buy personal computers in India will know the rate of change of models with substantive performance changes. How does one assure these rigorous standards? Naturally by incorporating many of the design, technological, and management features used in defence or space systems.

Earlier we used to purchase military standard or space quality components at specially high prices and call other components for ground equipment as the 'garden variety'. Now the standards and reliability figures of these garden variety components have increased manifold. This is one reason why military procurement in developed countries is nowadays sourced from common civilian sources as well because there is an all-round increase in reliability and quality. In this way, by spreading the market-base and their own production volumes, both sectors gain.

All this means greater and greater emphasis on design, rigorous review of production systems even before hardware is procured, severe control of standards and specifications of inputs to production, continuous monitoring and testing of processes, and various tests and checks on products. Thus the modern demands on technical consultancy, testing, calibration, and certification of processes as well as various management consultancies required to handle these complexities, are ever on the increase. Skills demanded for such tasks range from technical knowledge to data entry to meticulous analysis of data, to having good managerial systems. India has a whole set of capabilities in all these areas thanks to its human resources base. This whole area of services can emerge as a major source of employment and wealth generation. Indians can offer such services not only to the Indian industry but can become a global platform for providing services in various aspects of testing, calibration and technical consultancy. In order to realize this natural potential, we need to provide all-round avenues for our people to upgrade their knowledge base and skills. Information technology provides just one element in the whole chain of skills and infrastructure requirements.

Some of the projections can be seen in tables 8.3 and 8.4.

TABLE 8.3

Consultancy: Technical and Management Strategies and Priorities for the Future

Serial No	Scenario	Likely Timeframe (in years)
1	With the increasing level of specialized knowledge, organizations will seek more and more assistance from external sources(technical consultants) rather than depending only on 'in-house' capabilities, retraining, redeployment, re-engineering	5–10
2	Technical consultancy functions will be greatly supported by information collated from specialized databases; creation and marketing of databases as a lucrative business	5–15
3	The focus will shift from pedagogy to more specific and specialized training right from undergraduate levels in education and in management education	10–15
4	The key sectors like infrastructure (power, ports, water management, telecom, housing etc.), natural resources (mining, oil and gas exploration, water resources, etc.) and services will record high growth and call for technical consultancy support	5–10

Serial No	Scenario	Likely Timeframe *(in years)*
5	Technical consultancy will be sought for application-oriented new materials development suitable for high temperature, corrosion, erosion and wear resistance	10–15
6	Consultancy related to computer technologies will be increasingly related to systems integration and application-specific package development with the involvement of area experts	5–10
7	Safety, health and environment will emerge as important areas for consultancy inputs	5–10
8	The technical consultancy sector may be accorded industry status in view of financial assistance etc and promoted with adequate fiscal incentives	5–10
9	An efficient and unified coding and classification system will have to be evolved for an effective assimilation of the vast knowledge base	5–10

Source: TIFAC, Technology Vision 2020: Services

TABLE 8.4

**Management Consultancy:
Strategies and Priorities for the Future**

Serial No	Activities	Likely Timeframe *(in years)*
1	Consultancy for retraining, redeployment and business process re-engineering of client organization	5–10

Serial No	Activities	Likely Timeframe (in years)
2	Consultancy for diversification, joint ventures and business alliances for client organizations	5–10
3	Consultancy, in mergers and acquisitions, divestments, downsizing of client organizations	10–15
4	Consultancy in outsourcing, franchising, strategic business unit concept for client organizations	5–10
5	Use of proprietary and public domain databases by the consultants	5–10
6	Increased application of modelling and simulation techniques in problem solving by the consultants	5–10
7	A shift from pedagogy to practical problem solving and experience sharing in management education	5–10
8	International business, strategic management technology and R&D management, quality management, environmental management will be future thrust areas in consultancy	5–15
9	Training and skills development based on self-training system, multimedia devices for client organizations	5–10
10	Agribusiness, biotech applications, consumer products, infrastructure (power, telecom, roads, transportation, ports etc), IT strategy will dominate the consultancy business in future	5–10

Source: TIFAC, Technology Vision 2020: Services

Testing, certification and calibration services: strategies and priorities for the future

These are very important areas with rapid technological growth. They are vital in international transactions as well. The projections are as in table 8.5.

TABLE 8.5

Testing, Certification and Calibration Services: Strategies and Priorities for the Future

Serial No	Activities	Timeframe for completion (in years)
1	Accreditation bodies for qualifying various calibration/testing agencies to conform to international norms themselves	5
2	Accreditation systems to be initiated for inspection/certification agencies	5–7
3	Financial incentives and infrastructural support to quality assurance, testing and certification as an important business entity for its fast proliferation across the country	5–8
4	Facilitation of technical cooperation and MoUs between India and international accrediting agencies for quality business	5–8
5	Improved awareness for insurance companies towards calculation of premium, etc. based on product quality, safety norms, preservation needs and other environmental regulations	8–10

Serial No	Activities	Timeframe for completion (in years)
6	Testing and certification for gems and jewellery for the international market	5–10
7	Establishment of voluntary, non-profit organizations for accreditation in various areas of specialization	5–10
8	Privatization and autonomy in maintaining calibration facilities, test houses, inspection agencies and accreditation authorities governed by the market economy	15–20

Source: TIFAC, *Technology Vision 2020: Services*

Government administration

Traditionally the role of the government administration was confined to certain essential services like defence, law and order, etc. With independence, the Indian government has launched a process of planned economic and social development towards improvement of living standards. In this process private sector activities in a large number of areas were regulated, and the government itself became one of the economic agents by establishing many commercial and industrial enterprises.

Such activities widened the scope of government administration for policy formulation, framing of rules and regulations and implementation of policy. The proliferation of government agencies has meant a rising cost of administration. This enormous strain on the system and the change in the global economic environment has led to economic reforms.

The economic policy reforms aimed at redefining the role of government administration through dismantling the regulatory framework in many economic sectors. The purpose is to integrate the Indian economy with the global economy for efficient use of available natural and human resources. The Panchayati Raj systems offer a new dimension.

The strategies to be adopted are shown in table 8.6.

TABLE 8.6

Strategies and Priorities for the Future

Serial No	Scenario	Likely Timeframe (in years)
1	Government administration to undergo a radical change towards service orientation for 'facilitation', from action as 'administrators' to 'managers' and 'team players'	10–15
2	Instead of exercising controls and curbs, the government will function by regulation and adopt a promotional role	5–15
3	There will be a greater transparency in government functioning	5–10
4	The government will need improved access to information for an effective decision making process	5–15
5	The decision making and planning processes in the government to involve more and more area specialists inducted from major segments of society like R&D, industry, consultancy, academia, NGOs, sociologists and others	5–10
6	Towards an effective integration of the Indian economy with the global one, the government has to keep abreast with international developments and reorient its policies and practices	5–10

Serial No	Scenario	Likely Timeframe (in years)
7	In tandem with the developments and demands in the international area, the government has to forge close and cohesive linkages in the decision making process from federal to state and grassroot level aspirations	10–15
8	International trade practices like IPR, pesticides residue, product quality, etc. and other crucial issues like employment of child labour, violation of human rights, etc. would have significant influence in government policies and the planning process	5–10
9	Keeping in view the single most important agenda of the Indian economic reforms and a better quality of life, the government has to accord top priority to infrastructure (port, roads, power, telecom, etc.) development	5–10
10	The radical changes in the government functioning will warrant specialized training, retraining and skills development of the personnel employed	5–15

Source: TIFAC Technology Vision 2020: Services

Security services

Security services cover national internal security, internal security of commerce and industry and security of the civil sector.

Traditionally, national security used intensive manpower rather than technology. But it is currently essential that security services acquire state-of-the-art technology and all R&D efforts must be pursued to effect the change. Also technically trained personnel should be recruited in large numbers.

Internal security's main role lies in protecting the people

against attacks by terrorists and criminals. The security forces need sophisticated instruments for early detection and neutralization of bombs. Electronics, computers, databases, etc. are essential for tracing criminals, the detection of white-collar crime, prevention of industrial espionage, etc. To face all these new challenges, security services have to be modernized through large-scale adoption of science and technology.

The implementation in various areas except defence are shown in table 8.7.

TABLE 8.7

Security Services

Serial No	Area		Technological Implications
1.	Border security	1.	Sensors of all types: seismic, thermal, infra-red and electronic are needed
		2.	Optical equipment for long range surveillance
		3.	Satellite surveillance
		4.	Tamper-proof documentation, infra-red, ultra-violet and radiography examination of passports and visas
		5.	Computerized access control systems including portable radio computer terminals
2.	Prevention of entry of harmful substances into the country	1. 2. 3. 4.	Metal detectors Explosive detectors Drug detectors Poison, gas, etc. detectors
3.	Explosive detection and neutralization	1. 2.	Explosive detectors Explosive neutralization/ disruption detection equipment

Serial No	Area	Technological Implications
4.	Prevention of sabotage	1. Access control systems 2. Detectors of various types 3. Arson control systems
5.	Prevention of industrial espionage	1. Data protection equipment 2. Sophisticated access control systems 3. Behavioural science capabilities to detect 'moles' and 'unfaithfuls' 4. Anti-eavesdropping devices to prevent bugging, telephone tapping, fax interception, etc. 5. Sweeping devices and direction finders
6.	Prevention of white collar crime	1. Tamper proof systems 2. Built-in safeguards in credit cards, account transfers etc. 3. Technical inspection to detect malfunctioning of mechanical devices dealing with money
7.	Protection of common people and VIPs	1. Alarm systems 2. Electronic fence systems 3. Bullet-proof cars 4. Systems to neutralize electronically and radio controlled explosive devices 5. Detection of incendiary devices

Source: TIFAC, Technology Vision 2020: Services

Other services

We have seen only a few major possibilities in the above

descriptions. This is an area which can grow depending on the imagination and enterprise of our people. For example by 2010, India will have a large number of old persons, who are well-to-do and staying alone because their children may be in different parts of India and the world. The whole set of services required for them will be an essential social concern. It can also be a good business.

The services sector can also be used to earn considerable foreign exchange. In all these there are a number of enabling technologies and information technology which play a key role. We need to master them.

Role of IT in services sector

As an example of role of IT in the services sector, we give the following table:

TABLE 8.8

IT Applications in the Services Sector: Future Scenario for India

Serial No	Future Technologies	Likely Timeframe of introduction (in years)
1	Networked Automative Teller Machine (ATMs) for banking and other transactions	5–10
2	Smart phones for home banking operations	10–15
3	'Virtual' branches of bank operating from Customer Activated Terminals (CAT) or a kiosk	10–15
4	Debit cards for Electronic Fund Transfer at Point of Sale (EFTPOS)	10–15
5	Smart cards with built-in microchips for electronic cash, pay phones etc	5–10
6	Electronic Data Interchange (EDI) for paperless banking transactions	5–10

Serial No	Future Technologies	Likely Timeframe of introduction (in years)
7	Image processing	5–10
8	Expert systems and neural networks for credit risk appraisal, monitoring/prediction of stock price movement, detection of credit card fraud	10–15
9	Business process re-engineering, training and skills development for absorption of new technologies	5–15
10	Information security for confidentiality, prevention of data corruption and fraudulent practices	5–10
11	Legal aspects for paperless and electronic financial transactions	5–10
12	Single optical fibre connection to homes to blur the differences between communication and infotainment cables offering a whole range of services like home shopping, music and movies on demand, interactive TV	10–15
13	Telemarketing and visual shopping will be in great demand	5–10
14	Online electronic newspapers and magazines will dominate the print media	5–10
15	Multimedia technology and virtual reality to emerge as the major medium of advertisement	5–10
16	Availability of interactive television and user controlled on-demand interactive advertising	10–15
17	Direct broadcast satellites, PCs for reading electronic books, digital cameras for storing, viewing and editing still photographs on discs to be available	5–10

Serial No	Future Technologies	Likely Timeframe of introduction (in years)
18	Barcoding to emerge as an important device for payment processing, accounting and inventory management.	5–10
19	Decentralized warehouses to act as hubs for rural distribution to be networked to manufacturers, material suppliers, etc.	10–15
20	Complete networking of supply chain viz. retailers, distributors, warehouses, transporters, manufacturers, material suppliers etc.	10–15
21	Use of demographic database for age and sex composition, income levels and distribution, regional disparities, fertility and mortality rates, incidence of diseases, life expectancy, etc. will come in handy for designing new insurance products and services	10–15

Courtesy: S. Biswas
Source: Information Today & Tomorrow, Vol. 16, No 3, 1997

As a country of one billion, we should gear ourselves to take up the opportunities offered by the services sector in our march towards an India where every Indian will have wealth and well-being.

Chapter 9

Strategic Industries

Strategy means generalship or the art of conducting a campaign and maneouvring an army or execution of a plan of action in business or politics. In modern usage, however, it has come to denote the means used to gain a position of decisive advantage. The word strategy is also used when speaking of planning for the long term; that which is done on a short term basis becomes 'tactical'. Thus, when we use the term strategic industries, we are thinking in the context of industries which give India a decisive advantage over a broad range of areas, and not merely in military terms. In the period following the Second World War, as nations have focussed on the development of their economies, security has come to mean more than just protecting borders with military forces. Other forms of security have come to be of as much importance.

Food security

The availability of food is a critical factor in the well-being of any nation, one that even developed countries cannot afford to ignore. For a country like India with a large population the task of maintaining a regular supply of food in a stable, consistent and a viable manner to its people, irrespective of the vagaries of the weather and other natural calamities, is itself a stupendous task. Measures aimed at ensuring such unhindered supply fall under steps aimed towards 'food security'.

Economic security

Economic security or, simply stated, the security of a steady rate of economic growth along with a continual spread of benefits to the people is becoming important. It is a complex phenomenon which not merely concerns the fiscal policy or behaviour of financial institutions but also touches upon the very structure of the economy and polity. In the search for economic growth, seek to continuously expand the market for their products. Developed countries achieve this by expanding their activities in several parts of the globe through multinational or transnational companies. They also form visible or invisible cartels to have preferred access to many markets. In addition, they also continually improve their technological strengths and provide machinery and knowhow to others at a very high price. Their knowledge-intensive and technology-intensive activities are called 'high value-added products'. Much of the more routine activities are transferred by these multinationals to developing countries in order to derive the advantage of their locations, cheap labour and various other tax incentives. But whenever developing countries have to import technology and knowhow from the developed countries, they often have to pay a huge sum because of the value addition to the already exploited knowledge. There is no easy method of working out this value addition because often data on how this is calculated, or how various costs are apportioned by different multinational companies is confidential.

Thus, developing countries often pay a very high price for old technological inputs and in return have to sell much more goods and services to balance the high price of technology imports. This exerts a continuous pressure to export more, often at lower and lower prices, since the import bills are constantly rising because of the continual input of technological upgradations flowing from the developed countries. This is what is generally called an export-led economy. Some of the foreign exchange required to maintain this import-export balance comes through foreign investors who invest in physical assets in the country such as factories, plants, offices and laboratories, or through investments in stocks and companies. There are also special developmental loans given by bodies like the World Bank or the International Monetary Fund. If for some period the imports greatly exceed the exports or if during the period some withdrawals of foreign investment takes place, fear of a currency crisis ensues. In other words, most developing countries which are basing their strategy of growth on an export-led economy often find themselves maintaining a precarious economic balance. We are witnessing this in Far Eastern countries, where recent events show how a single developed nation, which has tremendous investment and business in a developing country, can cause its economy to collapse in a matter of weeks.

If transactions were conducted purely on economic and market considerations, even such a tight-rope walk might be possible. One would learn to cope with the rapid changes that such a situation creates. But the reality is far more complicated. There are various commercial pressures and interests, geopolitical considerations besides other disturbances over and above the inherent instabilities of such a situation. A crucial stabilizing factor to tackle such situations is for a country to possess the necessary technological strengths. That is the main insurance against global pressures. Real economic security is assured through technology strengths in areas which are important to the economy.

Critical technologies for India

A country takes a long time to develop technological strengths. What is important is that it concentrates on a few crucial or critical technologies which can give it a decisive advantage in meeting the kind of economic instability described above. It is interesting to note the list of critical technologies in the report of the USA's National Critical Technologies Panel in March 1991. The criteria used for the selection are given in table 9.1.

TABLE 9.1

	Criteria	Description
NATIONAL NEEDS	Industrial competitiveness	Technologies that improve US competitiveness in world markets through new products, introduction and improvements in the cost, quality and performance of existing products
	National Defence	Technologies that have an important impact on US national defence through improvements in performance, needs cost, reliability or producibility of defence systems
	National Security	Technologies that reduce dependence on foreign sources, lower energy costs, or improve energy efficiency
IMPORTANCE/CRITICALITY	Quality of life	Ability to make strong contributions to health, human welfare and the environment, both domestically and worldwide
	Opportunity to lead markets	Ability to exert and sustain national leadership in a technology that is of paramount importance to the economy or national defence

	Criteria	Description
	Performance/ quality/ productivity improvement	Ability to cause revolutionary or evolutionary improvements over current products or processes in turn leading to economic or national defence benefits
	Leverage	Potential that Government R&D investment will stimulate private sector investment in commercialization or likelihood that success in the technology will stimulate success in other technologies, products or markets
MARKET SIZE/DIVERSITY	Vulnerability	Potentially serious damage may be caused if a technology is held exclusively by the other countries and not the United States
	Enabling/ pervasive	Technology forms the foundation for many other technologies or exhibits size/ strong linkages to many segments of the economy
	Size of ultimate market	Ability to exert a major economic impact through the expansion of existing markets, creation of new industries, generation of capital or creation of employment opportunities

Source: Report of the National Critical Technologies Panel, March 1991

It can be seen from the above that the criteria for selection of critical technologies mentions national defence only as one element. Other criteria include their ability to enhance the quality of life for the American people, industrial competitiveness and energy security. Americans are acutely aware of their dependence for oil on the Gulf countries.

What would be the critical technologies in the Indian context? Would it mean defence technologies alone? Definitely not! Would it mean space or atomic energy alone? Definitely not! Elements related to these areas would be certainly included, but there should be much more. Besides, even in the sectors of defence, space or atomic energy there are a number of items which are not that critical in the sense that they would be available relatively easily from several sources. Many of the items would not involve numerous complex operations or be very costly; other items could be relatively easily stockpiled for future consumption. We should then be selective in what we term as critical technologies.

Defence supplies in India

Let us look at some facts and figures about the nature of the defence equipment and supplies in India. The indigenous production is about 30 per cent and there is a general feeling that this figure ought to be brought up to 70 per cent in the long-term interest of our defence needs. In order to achieve this we need to take several steps towards developing certain technological processes in our industries. However, most of these activities would not really qualify as critical technologies. The absence of certain processes in India so far has often been due to the same reasons as it is in the commercial sector: insufficient attention to absorb, adapt and to upgrade imported knowhow and equipment. In the process, we have become stagnant technologically and industrially, and have missed out on indigenous improvements to imported systems. In most of these areas, it is possible for us to achieve self-reliance in a relatively short period provided defence R&D, industries, the defence forces and other policy makers work together as a mission. This will not be a cakewalk, but with a concerted effort to build a few prototypes, modify them and subsequently go into production we can meet our needs. We have experience in most of the industries of this sector. There is a tendency even in advanced countries to source out defence equipment and products from many assemblies and sub-assemblies drawn from the civilian sector making other similar products. Such an approach can also be adopted to speedily achieve the goal of self-reliance in at least 70 per cent of products and systems for the defence forces.

Is that enough? Even while this target is important, there are some critical areas in which India will not be given technologies easily by other countries, irrespective of whether or not India signs some of the existing unequal treaties. That is because they are critical technologies not only for defence, but also for several other purposes, as shown in table 9.1. Some examples would be submicron level microelectronics or advanced transgenic biotechnology. The countries which possess submicron technologies, for example, can gain a top position globally. Advanced transgenic biotechnology can lead to global markets in agriculture, food products and medicines.

The Indian space programme

Let us look at the Indian space programme. Several elements required for launch vehicles including the materials, propellants, guidance and control and so on have been indigenously developed and are manufactured here. India has faced difficulties in achieving all this, as for example, when it attempted to speed up the schedule for the launch of the Geosynchronized Satellite Launch Vehicle (GSLV) through import of cryogenic technology. Some countries were willing to sell it to us. But when one of them agreed to the sale of a full engine, other countries pressurized them into not selling it to India. In a few years India should acquire capability in this field. Nevertheless, as far as satellites are concerned, many of the electronic components and some materials are still sourced outside the country, though India has successfully made many of the assemblies: control system components, guidance systems, sensors, various other electro-mechanical and electronic parts.

The dependence for many of the space/special quality electronic components can, however, still be a problem for the Indian satellite programme, especially when it must be competitive internationally.

The end of the Cold War has led to shrinkage of markets for aerospace and defence industries in the developed world. They are in stiff competition with each other and do not want other countries or companies to emerge as suppliers of satellites as their own market shares would be further reduced. It is in this context, in our endeavour to achieve the commercialization of our strengths in satellite technology, that many components required for Indian satellites may still have to be considered critical.

The nuclear programmes

Atomic energy programmes have been subject to severe restrictions for very obvious reasons as the Department of Atomic Energy in becoming self-reliant in areas in which only a few countries have such capability. There are a number of items in the atomic energy programme which are being made indigenously. However, commercial aspects of exploiting nuclear capabilities, especially for power-generation programmes, have been recently given high priority. Given the overall energy situation in India, the use of nuclear power in some measure is inescapable even while thermal and hydro power continue to be the dominant elements. Even to meet these nuclear power requirements, India critically requires a commercial-level power-generation capability, with its commensurate safety and nuclear waste management arrangements. Thus in the Indian context energy security is also crucial, perhaps much more than it is for the USA, because India imports a good part of its crude oil requirements, paying for it with precious foreign exchange. The growth of nuclear technology indeed has become a trendsetter for many high technologists in India.

Dual-use technology

This discussion of strategic industries mainly concerns defence, space, atomic energy and also critical technology areas which have the potential of multiple uses in the defence and civilian commercial sector in the future. Not that other areas do not have multiple uses. For example, canning or processing of food or preservation of food is equally applicable to the civilian sector, to the export sector or for supplies to the defence forces. But since these are relatively well-stabilized technologies which can be handled by inputs from several sources, including, often, imports in the first instance, we are not covering such dual-use items.

Newly emerging technologies such as robotics or artificial intelligence, which would have a crucial impact on future defence operations and also on many industrial sectors if they have are to be really competitive, merit a closer look. As we look at the emerging manufacturing scenario, it will contain many elements of artificial intelligence and robotics in the medium-term future. If Indian products have to be competitive worldwide and if we aim to earn substantially through value-added products and services, India has to master these technologies. To import them fully from others will often not be cost-effective since the competing foreign companies would not like to part with their best technologies. Often enough not even the better ones will be sold. Thus, even if we do manage to purchase some technologies from them, they will be at a point of technological obsolescence where one has to struggle with very low profit margins which is not good for any business.

The technology areas critical for growth of strategic industries for India, given the above broad considerations, are in the aviation and propulsion sector, high-end electronics, sensors, space communication and remote sensing, critical materials and processing, robotics and artificial intelligence. Before looking into some of these technologies, it is worth understanding something about the defence technologies and industries as they pertain to India.

1985: Defence technology and industry

In India, both the Defence Research & Development Organization and defence industries started experiencing certain restrictions on acquisition of technology and products from the developed countries, particularly from 1985 onwards. At the same time, developed countries wanted to make India one of their main customers for arms and defence equipment. Obsolescent systems were offered for sale coupled with licensed production for a political price. Liberal credit and deferred payments were provided to propagate the business and make us perennially indebted.

What was the situation in India then? The industrial ambience had led to excellence in fabrication in limited areas. This means that after a design had been converted into fabrication drawings, our industry was in a position to convert it into a finished product. For low- and medium-level technology, there were large industrial complexes where most of the facilities were established under licensed production. In defence production, the private sector played only a limited role. As far as the academic and R&D institutions were concerned, they were interested in working towards self-reliance and to break away from the licensed production syndrome. The DRDO itself was preoccupied with a large number of single discipline projects concentrating on self-reliance through import substitution and/or indigenization. The end users often would like to see full systems.

1985-95: The period of stand-alone sub-system development

During the next ten years, that is, by 1995, certain industries graduated to design and development of sub-systems. This was due to the active partnership of the national science and technology agencies such as ISRO, DAE, DRDO and the industries. Many in the private sector who were hesitant to enter this field ten years earlier, started vying with defence

PSUs and other public sector companies to take up defence R&D tasks at the sub-system level. For example, private sector industries were in a position to develop phase shifters, displays, tankage, communication systems, certain types of electronic warfare systems, on-board computers, on-board transmitters, thermal batteries and even air frames. This marked a very important step for both the DRDO and Indian industry. Because of such interaction between R&D and industry, the enthusiasm and confidence of industrial establishments grew and enabled them to design sub-systems and to absorb the specified stringent processes of technology. Above all it enhanced their willingness to take risks and go through the rigorous quality assurance and certification processes required for military systems.

2005: Graduation to systems engineering

During the progress of large R&D projects, there were undoubtedly delays and cost overruns. There was some criticism in the press about this. But here it needs to be underlined that these projects needed support through the difficult phases of their development. In fact, R&D in India survived only because of the efforts of a few visionary scientists and leaders. But for them the nation would have been satisfied with making small items, surrendering to business interests that would use all means to convert India into a perpetual 'buying nation'. Defence R&D is now taking the lead to reverse this trend through its self-reliance mission in defence systems. In DAE and ISRO too such an impulse for self-reliance is in the forefront.

We forecast that by 2005, more industries will be in a position to take up stand-alone mode systems engineering and systems integration to the specified requirements of R&D organizations. Sub-systems like multi-mode radar, 'kaveri' class aircraft engines, all composite carbon fibre composite wings, display systems, fly-by-wire systems for Light Combat Aircraft (LCA) and for futuristic aircraft, mission computers and air frames will be developed, engineered, produced and delivered for integration and checkout. Of course, this is the DRDO's vision. We believe that the Indian industry will respond given the national will on other fronts. We believe that when Indian industry becomes strong in systems engineering and systems integration as well as sub-system development and fabrication, the nation will have multiple options on choice of systems and industries to make them competitive and cost effective. In certain sub-systems or technologies we can even compete globally. There would also be a number of civilian commercial spin-off products and services which can be marketed domestically and in foreign markets.

Growth of technology capability in DRDO

The DRDO was established in the 1960s. Its major task was to build science-based capability towards making improvements in the available imported systems and weaponry. In the '70s we saw development in ammunition and gun design, leading to production and in the '80s a tremendous thrust was given to major system programmes in design and development which lead to productionization of electronic warfare system, communication systems, missile systems, aircraft, main battle tanks and radars. These programmes gave a new impetus to multiple design and technology development centres resulting in the production of design capability for an integrated weapons system in the nineties. Now the vision for the DRDO is to promote the corporate strength of the organization, and to make the nation independent of foreign technology in critical spheres. Technology innovation is expected to lead the DRDO and its industrial partners to global competitiveness in systems design and realization. Let us look at the technological growth of a completed missile project, Prithvi and an advanced developmental project, LCA, under progress. The following observations are drawn from some of my talks on these projects.

Prithvi missile system

In 1982, a detailed study was carried out for evolving advanced missile systems in order to counter the emerging threats to the security of India. Experts and members of the armed forces took part in this study and it resulted in the Integrated Guided Missile Development Programme comprising five projects. In July 1983, the government approved the programme, whereby a unique management structure was to be established, integrating the development, production, and the user services, with government machinery for expeditious implementation.

The Guided Missile Development Programme

The Guided Missile Development Programme envisaged the design and development of our missile systems, Prithvi, Trishul, Akash and Nag, leading to their production. It also established the re-entry technology capability through Agni. The re-entry technology demonstration was completed by 1992, through flight tests of Agni. Prithvi was the first of the four operational missile systems to be inducted into the armed forces.

The technological goal of the programme is to ensure that the systems will be contemporary at the time of their induction into the armed forces. The systems have been designed to be multi-purpose, multi-user and multi-role in nature. The programme has adopted the philosophy of concurrent development and production to reduce the time-cycle from development to induction.

Brief description of the Prithvi system

Prithvi is an all-weather, mobile and surface-to-surface guided missile which can engage targets quickly and accurately over a range of 40–250 km. The weapon system is designed to engage targets beyond the range of field guns and unguided rockets. The system is highly mobile with a minimum reaction time and has a capability of being deployed at short notice at desired locations. Its mobility also provides fire and scoot capability.

The Prithvi missile is a single stage system and uses two liquid propulsion engines of three ton thrust capability each. The guidance system of Prithvi is based on a strapdown inertial navigation system along with an on-board computer, which offers integrated solutions to navigation, control and guidance requirements.

It's flight control system allows the missile to follow the desired trajectory, by controlling the vehicle in three mutually perpendicular planes viz. pitch, yaw and control. The electro-hydraulic actuation system is used to control the positioning error. The errors induced due to weather conditions such as wind, shear and gust can be corrected by the guidance and control systems of the missile. It is also possible to manoeuvre the missile in the final phase. The ground support system is equipped with special vehicles to carry out the mission, command and control, maintenance, logistic support and survey. The modular design and built in check-out and calibration facilities help in equipping the missile in the deployment area with the desired warhead and for carrying out a quick check of the missile's operational readiness.

The effectiveness of Prithvi

A manoeuvrable trajectory, its high mobility, low reaction time, its self-contained and self-supporting features and low footprint area make the Prithvi missile system difficult to counter. Besides, the high accuracy of its system, its high warhead capabilities and absence of vulnerability to counter-measures, including Electronic Counter Measures (ECM), make the Prithvi missile system potentially dangerous for the enemy. Possession and deployment of a large number of Prithvi missiles can act as a deterrent and prevent a missile attack from our adversaries.

In case of war, the powerful explosive and high accuracy of the Prithvi missile has enormous potential to bring life to a standstill in cities and urban areas, to affect the morale of the enemy. Also, a sizeable portion of the enemy air force would be engaged in neutralizing the mobile missile launchers (as borne out by the experience of Allied air forces in the recent Gulf war against mobile Scud sites).

Prithvi is a cost-effective weapon

Usually, Vital Areas (VAs) and Vital Points (VPs) which are of high tactical and strategic importance have a high level of air defence protection. Much of this air cover is multi-layered, with some overlapping redundancy and is networked through computer communication links for ensuring effective command and control.

The deep penetration capability of the Prithvi missile, up to 250 km range, will enhance the firepower of the air force against heavily defended targets in adverse weather conditions. In addition, the night attack capability of this missile will be useful for attacking targets like factories, petroleum dumps, marshalling yards and other static installations.

The accuracy of the system at 250 km will be further improved upon in Phase II, when terminal homing guidance or anti-radiation systems will be integrated into the Prithvi system. A scheme for retrofit is being contemplated and designed. This capability will be an asset in attacking hard targets like armoured concentrations in their parking sites.

The development and production experience of Prithvi

India had certain strengths in design, materials and engineering when the project was initiated in 1983. However, the development of Prithvi required aerospace quality materials like magnesium alloys for wings and certain special aluminium alloys for airframe and tankages, and navigational sensors of a certain accuracy, all of which were not available within the country. The Missile Technology Control Regime, though not formally declared, was in effect in some form or the other. All these drove us to deliberately adopt an indigenous route right from the beginning. A number of critical technologies, materials and processes were developed by harnessing the available talents within the country and using innovative management methods. The development of the Prithvi Inertial Navigation System is an example of this. Though we were able to get only the coarse class of sensors for the inertial navigation, our scientists came up with innovations to enhance their accuracy using software. The use of simulation in the design phase, and the hardware in loop simulation to fly the missile on ground, as well as the association of users at every stage, greatly helped in improving the effectiveness of the missile and reduced the number of user trials.

Throughout, the project was driven by goals of excellence in performance and of meeting schedules. Concurrency was built into every activity of the programme to reduce the time from development to induction.

Aside from strengthening the country to face the threats from across our borders, Prithvi has demonstrated that India can develop world-class high technology systems and devices by using its own indigenous strength, and thereby defeating the control regimes. An important benefit of the Prithvi programme is the new breed of technologists and leaders, who can make our country stronger and self-reliant.

Light Combat Aircraft (LCA)

One of the largest programmes of the DRDO is the Light Combat Aircraft (LCA). It has got all the potential elements of high technology; thirty-three R&D establishments, sixty major industries and eleven academic institutions are integrated and working together on this project.

There are two types of fighter aircraft, Light Combat Aircraft and the Medium Combat Aircraft. The Medium Combat Aircraft weighs about 15 tonnes at take-off, whereas the Light Combat Aircraft has below 10 tonnes take-off weight. This new generation aircraft has primary structures made of composite materials and advanced avionics. The LCA has technologies of composite wing, fly-by-wire flight control system, multi-processor based mission computer, low RCS, high weapon carrying capability, high manoeuvrability powered by a uniquely designed 'kaveri' engine. The LCA design caters for top-class manoeuverability and high performance. In addition, its mission capability and survivability characteristics will be superior to those of the heavier aircraft that would come into the market within the next few years. The LCA will be the most cost-effective aircraft in relation to performance considering the fact that our R&D cost is one-third of that of the developed countries for similar programmes. The LCA tops the lightweight fighters in its capabilities with the unique feature of full-user commitment. The LCA can be marketed at much lower cost than the combat aircraft of similar class.

DRDO-Navy participation

Let us look at a few other cases of building up a strategic technological strength. During 1995, in the Bay of Bengal, despite rough weather conditions, our defence scientists and engineers from Bharat Electronics Limited (BEL) worked with a naval team on a ship to commission the modified electronic warfare system for user trials. In Chandipore-at-Sea, in stormy conditions, DRDO aeronautical and electronics engineers engaged in the final phase of user trials of Pilotless Target Aircraft (PTA) 'Lakshya' for the three services. Also during 1995 we had a successful flight of the PTA whose jet engine was designed and developed within the country. The naval ships gave full support in this mission for deploying the simulated missile to encounter IR targets fitted with the PTA. An experimental laboratory on the sea, Sagardhwani, sailed from the west to the east coast with a mission of characterizing the ocean depth with particular reference to temperature gradient.

Another exciting achievement of the Navy is imminent. Work has been completed for the state-of-the-art submarine sonar, Panchendriya, by the Naval Physical and Oceanography Laboratory (NPOL) situated on the western coast. The new ships being built will be armed with our Trishul missile system and the hull-mounted sonar Hamsa. It will have its first Modulated Data Bus which is mostly linked by fibre optics. The Government has also approved the Naval Integrated Electronic Warfare Programme (NIEWP). In four years, ships, submarines and naval aircraft would be provided with the latest electronic surveillance system coupled with electronic counter-measures.

Action plan for the Army

Strategic technological action by the Army has been equally

exemplary. Phased induction of various systems and equipments needs to be linked and dovetailed with the defence self-reliance plan. This is a sure way for Indian industries to achieve the goals and the direction for preparing the business plan and for ensuring participation. Likewise, the dependence of our armed forces on imported systems needs to progressively decrease. Also, as is done elsewhere, India has to follow the induction of products in phases like Mark I, Mark II, etc. so that technology capability and production infrastructure are built in a phased way. This situation will cut down the delay of systems readiness. Technological uncertainty will be removed and willing investment by industries may be possible. The industries should be given a clear mandate—will they be developers? Will they be fabricators of an integrated system house and for what possible areas? Once this policy is enunciated, industry can fully participate as the financial aspects would be clear. Recently the DRDO opened seven of its laboratories for industries to pick up technologies already developed. These industries have to shape the technologies for commercial application.

User trials of the systems developed is an important part of their induction by the armed forces. Normally, user trials pose a big challenge for the R&D and also the industrial establishments. We are no exception. But the outcome of this exercise could help the country to become independent and self-reliant. If the Army has to gain in self-reliance, rethinking is required in its plans of user trials and also of the mission requirements. In view of the onset of the performance evaluation through extensive combined environmental simulation, would it be possible to plan for reduced scale user trial tests for high altitude, and desert conditions? This will result in industries moving over to series production within a short time followed by full-scale production for domestic and international markets. Of course, a series of technological and military considerations would be vital for taking such decisions.

The future

The above has given a glimpse of defence research and its

interface with operational systems. Future defence operations are going to be based on multiple networks of Army, Navy, Air Force and space systems. Information technology is going to be used in unprecedented ways, in the planning stages, in various simulation exercises, as well as during actual operations when the need arises. Continual surveillance is going to be another feature in the years to come. This is done through remote sensing, communications and several other means. Continual improvement of systems with higher precision, speed and maneouvrability would also be a part of this complex picture. All the critical elements are driven by advances in materials, electronics, advanced sensors, information processing, robotics, and artificial intelligence.

Advanced sensors

Advanced sensor technology has been identified the world over as one of the critical technologies for the future. Advanced sensors require ultra-pure materials and ultra-clean manufacturing conditions. Integrated electronic devices are using microsensors on surface mounted devices. Advanced sensors will be used in every segment of human endeavour covering, agriculture, health services, advanced manufacturing systems, advanced avionics, optical communications, space satellites, super smart highways, biotechnology, genetic engineering, pollution control, diagnostics and so on. Molecular and supramolecular systems for sensing and actuation are creating new sensors capable of measuring physical, chemical and biological parameters. In view of the strategic importance of sensors for industrial, aerospace and health applications, it is necessary to have a national mission on advanced sensors. We will lose out in all areas including agriculture or trade if we do not have sufficient national capability in sensors, since quality improvement, productivity enhancement and enforcement of standards will require use of advanced sensors. Environmental monitoring is another area based primarily on sensors continually looking at the quality of air, land and water.

A detailed assessment of the state of the art of advanced

sensors indicates that the following are major technological trends.

* development of intelligent or smart sensing devices
* emergence of integrated multifunctional sensors
* smart sensors systems capable of performing integration self-compensation and self-correction
* sensors integrated with actuators, and
* development of artificial noses which can create olfactory images, i.e. sensors can smell and quantify the smell!

It is estimated that the worldwide demand for sensors was of the order of $ 5 billion in 1994; USA has about 55 per cent share of the world market. An analysis of the world market for sensors indicate that industrial control, medical and scientific instruments account for 50 per cent of the global market of sensors. Temperature sensors account for 36 per cent; pressure sensors 34 per cent and flow sensors 28 per cent of the world demand. The world market for chemical and biochemical sensors is rapidly growing and this is one of the emerging end-use applications. The demand for sensors in India will be about Rs. 500 million in 2000 and the dominant use will be in industrial control and automation applications. In spite of the fact that it is strategically important for industrial and defence applications, India has a negligible presence in the advanced sensors market, even in the use of sensors, not to mention in their manufacture and development.

Though there are a large number of institutions active in sensors development programmes in India, most of them have not as yet aimed their efforts at a specific product or service. There is no programme which is oriented towards industry or the health sector. A number of organizations have strong capabilities in one or other element of sensors: for example, for material development or sensor element development or sensor-device integration. There needs to be a sharper focus for the sensors programme besides closer networking and a joint development programme. Perhaps national teams, as is being done for LCA, could be a model to follow.

National programme in advanced sensors

India has to mount a sharply defined national programme on advanced sensors. If India has to become a major player in advanced sensors there has to be comprehensive national mission implemented in the consortia mode. Several disciplines have to be integrated into developing a focussed product. Among the new capabilities required are micro-fabrication and manufacture. All application segments of advanced sensors need special attention with specific focus on market development.

The mission may be implemented through the existing institutions or through a new mechanism. However, the mission has to be very clearly defined and it has to be end-use oriented. It is preferable, if industries take a lead in this mission. Unless India has strong national capabilities in advanced sensors we may lose out in all areas to newly industrializing countries, since both industrial competitiveness and trade competitiveness are going to depend upon the capabilities in advanced sensors. In future, the competitive edge in the manufacturing sector as well as in services is going to be greatly determined by the large-scale use and innovative applications of sensors. Tables 9.2 and 9.3 provide a glimpse of some of strategically and industrially important sensors. It is crucial India develops major industries in these areas, with commercial level operations in the domestic and foreign markets.

Let us now look at a few examples of space systems, which would form a core of strategic sector industries.

Cryogenic engine for GSLV

For the satellite launch vehicles, all-solid multi-stage rocket systems or solid plus liquid multi-stage rocket systems or all-liquid multi-stage rocket systems can be used. The cost per launch is in a way controlled by the take-off weight of the launch vehicle system for a given payload and type of orbit required. The cost-effectiveness in commercial launch vehicles, that is, the cost of injecting a satellite into a geo-stationary orbit will decide the choice of the propellant system for individual

TABLE 9.2

Strategically Important Sensors

Area	Sensor to be developed	Trends	Action needed
Strategically important sensors	Inertial sensors for navigation and avionics	a) laser gyros	Development of ultra noise-free and stable lasers
		b) fibre optic gyro	Development of integrated optic chips surface micro machining
		c) micro accelerometer	
	Sensors for submarine detection	SQUID based systems	Development of SQUID sensor and associated noise-free electronics
	Sensors for detecting explosives such as RDX & narcotics	Combining nuclear magnetic resonance	SQUID sensors for sensing ultra and weak electro-magnetic fields nuclear quadrupole arising from nuclear magnetic resonance (NMR)/nuclear quadrupole resonance (NQR) resonance principles
	Piezoresistive microsensors	Surface micro machining of poly-silicon micro structures	Development of monolithic silicon transducer including signal conditioning and calibration

TABLE 9.3

Sensors Needed for Industrial Applications

Area	Sensor to be developed	Trends	Action needed
	Humidity sensors	Polymer electrolytic, heat treated polymer dielectric, inorganic substance distributed polymer distributed polymer (change in resistance due to humidity absorption)	Humidity sensors using changes in permitivity and resistance need to be developed. This will require first development of sensors material and related electronic circuitry
		Cellulose system polymer (change in permitivity)	Metal oxide silicon field effect transistor (MOSFET) using humidity absorption polymer to be developed
Industrial process control and safety		Carbon particle distributed humidity absorption resin (sharp change in resistance with absorption of humidity)	

Area	Sensor to be developed	Trends	Action needed
Gas sensors for process control		MOSFET + humidity absorption polymer (change in characteristics of transistor)	Surface acoustic wave sensors to be developed
		Quartz oscillator + polyamid (change in load of oscillator)	
		Organic semiconductor (increase in conductivity due to adsorption of gas)	
		Colouring matter membrane LB membrane (fluorescence quench)	
		Quartz oscillator + organic thin film (change in load on vibrator)	
		Gas transmission polymer membrane + electroide (selective permiation of gas, electrochemical reaction)	

Area	Sensor to be developed	Trends	Action needed
Sensors for monitoring toxic gases		Artificial noses	Development of multicomponent molecular recognition systems
Industrial process control and safety	Inductive proximity sensors	Non-contact metal detection sensors with wide operating range and fast response	Development of proximity sensors and sensor alignment techniques
	Semiconductor displacement laser sensors	Light-emitting diode or semiconductor laser based sensors	Light source and position sensitive detector development

stages. Normally, a liquid rocket system will be of a lower weight and with a cryogenic upper stage further weight reduction is achieved.

For example, to place a 2.5 ton payload in a geo-transfer Orbit, an all-solid multi-stage launch vehicle will have a take-off weight of 525 tons. This will reduce to 470 tons if the liquid stage replaces the solid upper stages. It will further reduce to 450 tons with all-liquid stages and eventually to less than 300 tons when the upper stage is replaced by a cryogenic engine. The major differences in take-off weight are evident. It is said in the space community that for every additional kilogram of payload, the cost will be reduced by a few lakhs of rupees when utilizing the cryogenic engine. The propellant used in the cryogenic engine is a combination of liquid oxygen and liquid hydrogen in specific ratios. The proposed cryogenic engine for India's Geosynchronous Satellite Launch Vehicle, GSLV is of 12-ton thrust class. The engine weighs only 250 kg and has a length of 3.1 metres. The engine has to be very compact with proper insulation, regenerative cooling and sealing for handling liquid oxygen and hydrogen.

The engine has to be closely coupled to the tankages and flow control devices to form the upper stage. The propellant loading, transfer, insulating and pressurizing systems are integrated into one integral system for modular handling and operation. The technological challenges in realizing this stage are many. The materials selected have to work at minus 253° Celsius as well as at high temperatures of 1750° Celsius continuously. The nozzle and thrust chamber have to be regeneratively cooled using the liquid hydrogen itself. For the liquid hydrogen turbo pump, speed has to be maintained above 50000 revolutions per minute (rpm). Compare it with the revolutions of your motor car engine which is 5000 rpm and of a commercial jet aircraft engine which is almost 15000 rpm. Considering the fabrication, material technology, which is sealing, bearing, insulating technologies and the process of making the various cryogenic sub-systems, the country has yet to develop all these and our industries and R&D laboratories have to work together for this important task. A design and manufacturing database has to be established so that no country can come in the way of our space programmes. In this context, it is essential to note that cryogenic engines cannot be used for any missile application as their storage life is limited, the filling operations can be sensed in advance and no mobility is possible. The argument that cryogenic engines can be used for missiles, quoting Missile Technology Control Regime, is non-technical and commercially motivated.

Where are we in aero propulsion?

Where are we in aeroengines and propulsion? India with its LCA programme, is now developing a uniquely configured GT engine as described earlier. Similarly, for GSLV, India has to develop within schedule, a cryogenic engine and stand on its own its feet in the area of satellite launching. It can be seen that in both these areas we are lagging behind the developed countries because we did not feel their importance, given the level of aerospace technology missions taken up in the country in the past. Today, the priority given to commercial and military aircraft as well as GSLV, cryogenic engines and jet engines has become vital. Bridging the gap in technologies, to become a part of the leaders in the game is not an impossible task. The partnership between our institutions and industries can accelerate development and our technology acquisition. It will also help tailor the technology acquired to our infrastructure and needs. It can be seen that with the launch of Polar Satellite Launch Vehicle (PSLV), we are almost at par with the developed countries in the area of solid propellant power plants. The PSLV has also established the technologies of storable liquid propellants and related propulsion.

Hyperplanes of the future

DRDO has entered into ramrocket systems where much higher energy levels (of above 500 sec with solid propellants and upto 1000 sec with liquid propellants) will be realized. The scramjet engine will give energy level of 3000 sec. Compare this with 450 sec of cryoengines! This is not only for military application. These supersonic combustion engines have application for cruise missiles, launch vehicles and hyperplanes of the future. India's proposed scramjet is designed for operating up to Mach 12. In the long term it could become part and parcel of our jet aircraft too. Currently, only a few countries are working in this area. Based on our experience with LCA and GSLV, India should at least take initiative in the elements of the hyperplane programme so that India's hyperplane and future aerospace vehicles can be built around this power plant. The hyperplane can deliver a payload of above 30 tons for a take-off weight of 250 tons, giving a quantum jump for the existing payload/take off ratios of max 3 per cent to 15 per cent through mass addition.

A future hyperplane mission can have an integrated power plant complex working in three modes.

— Fan ramjet engine mode in low altitude, low speed flight regimes
— Scramjet engine mode in Mach number range 3 to 12 along with in-flight airliquification and mass addition
— Rocket engine mode till payload launching.

In the critical technology areas of scramjet engines, our aerospace scientists start with the design, development and integration of fixed geometry air intakes for a wide Mach number range supported extensively by analytical tools like Computational Fluid Dynamics (CFD) and experimental set up like hypersonic wind tunnels. The combustor development including the material, fabrication technology and combustion kinetics has just begun. Test and evaluation facilities are to be planned for prototype and full scale engine testing.

By 2010, commercial jet aircraft, military fighters reusable satellite launch vehicle and the reusable terrestrial payload delivery vehicle will have one common feature, that is, the usage of supersonic combustion engines for flying in hypersonic flight regimes.

The real proliferators

Recently I addressed diplomats in Delhi on the subject of nuclear proliferation. I offer an extract: 'During my tenure in Delhi, I made a study of the proliferation doctrine initiated by the five nations. The USA for the last four decades, upto 1990, accumulated about 10,000 nuclear warheads and almost an equal number was accumulated by the erstwhile Soviet Union. And this cruel fanaticism was justified in the name of ideology of Capitalism versus Communism! The seeds of nuclear proliferation were thus sown. These two nations used nuclear weapons as a tool to subordinate or influence many national politics by giving so-called nuclear technology for peaceful application or nuclear power stations. For China, nuclear weapon technology was given by the Soviet Union and we have witnessed recently that the same developed countries have ensured that Pakistan will have a certain number of nuclear weapons.This has been reported by a former prime minister of Pakistan.

The five nuclear weapon countries proclaimed that they were the nations solely approved to possess nuclear weapons. They evolved certain international policies. The total number of warheads they possessed were so many that they created safety and security problems of tremendous magnitude for the world. These two nations driven by the people, negotiated START-II (Strategic Arms Reduction Treaty). They signed a treaty for reducing the warheads, including the delivery carriers to 3000. When I asked Dr William Perry, US secretary for defence, during his visit to India, why 3000 and not zero as Pandit Jawaharlal Nehru had put forth the concept of complete nuclear disarmament in the 1960s, Dr Perry answered zero nuclear weapons is a dream. He meant that the nuclear weapons should always be with the club of five and be a dream for others. We can assume that at no time will the five nations come to zero level of nuclear weapons. Nuclear weapons are a strong component of the global strategy they visualize. For them they are weapons of political strength and by propagating a non-proliferation doctrine they claim to generate peace. It was a delightful privilege for DAE and DRDO teams, backed up by the political leadership, to break this dangerous and self-centred monopoly of nuclear weapon states.

Similarly, in the area of chemical or biological weapons or missile systems, the origin of their proliferation is the same. If one opens the Pandora's box of proliferation, one would see USA and the former Soviet Union, with the recent addition of China. If there could be an impartial world body, not driven by the superpowers, the developing countries affected by this dangerous proliferation can seek justice and compensation. Can we dream for such a new and just world?

Strategic industries—the future of India

We are able to provide only a glimpse of a few important elements of strategic industries to be developed in India. The ones described are well within our reach—technologically, investmentwise and schedulewise. If industries and institutions work together with clear vision and goals in mind and with assiduous build-up of markets right from the word go, Indian industries can reap rich commercial benefits. Also, let us not forget the fact that a strategic technology or industry today, will have day-to-day applications in many walks of life two decades hence. Therefore, it is our duty to build the necessary technologies today so that the future generation of Indians will have new worlds to conquer and not have to struggle with the problems of 'bridging the past gaps' as we are doing today! We owe it to the future generations that we hand them over by 2020 only the excitement and challenges of the future and not the weight of problems of the past or the crises of the present. Only then will India have truly arrived as a developed country populated with proud people confident of their future.

Chapter 10

Health Care for All

> *Don't give a place to disease.*
> — Auvaiyyar, Tamil saint-poetess

Former Prime Minister I.K. Gujral, in his address to the 1998 Science Congress at Hyderabad, made a revealing remark on the state of our basic amenities. 'I see before me the bottled water kept for the dignitaries on the dais. It reminds me of three classes of Indians: one who can afford bottled water; others who manage to get some water in their taps or in a nearby tap or a pump irrespective of its quality or regularity of supply; the third set of Indians are those for whom drinking water is a daily problem and who will be ready to drink any polluted water.' For such a situation to persist after fifty years of independence was a national shame, he added. Unfortunately, if we do not do enough on this front, and the related one of health care, ten years down the road we might still be saying the same thing.

In the ultimate analysis, any society will be judged by its ability to provide universal health care for its people. This does not merely entail the ability to treat diseases and ailments but also to prevent their onset by means of suitable systems and measures. We are aware that not all diseases are entirely preventible. For example, we do not fully know what causes cancer, or diabetes. We do not have cures for many genetic disorders. Permanent cures may not be possible even for many allergies and respiratory problems such as asthma. However, through regular medication and precautionary measures, most patients can lead normal lives.

Disease prevention

Most communicable diseases, however, can be prevented by suitable sanitation systems, control of disease-spreading materials (such as foul water) or vectors (like mosquitoes), and by immunization programmes carried out on a large scale. A number of diseases can be controlled by paying adequate attention to nutrition and dietary supplements. For example, the use of iodized salt can prevent goitre, which is rampant in many parts of the country. The intake of vitamin A can prevent blindness. Globally, 25 per cent of blind and visually handicapped persons are in India! And, of course, among people who can afford it, a balanced food intake and physical exercise can help prevent several forms of heart disease.

The rich at least have access to information about health-related issues in many ways: through journals and magazines, discussions with others and visits to doctors and medical specialists. That is not the case with many lower-income groups and poorer people. There is a total absence of health education among these sections. And even if they want to, many of them cannot afford a visit to a doctor, or afford regular medication when it is urgently required. More often than not, they end up relying on quacks. Barring a small percentage, most primary health care (PHC) centres do not provide any tangible health care to people. There are many reasons for this: irregular and limited supply of medicines, not enough doctors or paramedical staff, callous and apathetic medical staff, the leverage of influential local individuals, the excessively bureaucratic operation of the system. Despite all this it is creditable that the death rate in India has come down to 9 (per thousand) in 1995 as compared to 14.9 in 1971.

Sanitation

Proper drainage of dirty water, disposal of garbage, sewage and human and industrial wastes are crucial for a clean micro-environment, which is a prerequisite for preventive health care. We have simply to visit the slums of Mumbai or Delhi to witness the urgency of such measures. Even in rural India, most women have to wait until it is dark so that they can relieve themselves in the open. The filth in these places renders them rife with diseases.

My co-author Y.S. Rajan narrates his experience with a Department of Science and Technology project at Mumbai for setting up a big plant for garbage processing and installation of simple latrines in slums. The latrines had about ten modules built around a central pillar. To decide on their location, Rajan visited many slums in Mumbai. An incredible amount of putrid water collected and stood for days around the huts even when it was not raining. Added to this dirty water and excreta were various other forms of garbage thrown out by the slum dwellers. How could they and their children be healthy and free from diseases? Above all, what could be expected of their attitude towards keeping general public conveniences like latrines clean? Many poverty removal schemes are not applicable to the Mumbai slums because the earnings of the people who live there are above the poverty line! They may earn more than they would back in the village. They have better clothes and more food. But the appalling sanitary conditions negate all other aspects of progress. A similar situation exists in most big cities. The response of elite Indians is to remove the slums from view and send the occupants many kilometres away. Or simply to ignore them by building high walls to block these dirty areas from sight!

Drinking water

A recent event demonstrated how technology can assist in meeting drinking water needs. One of the DRDO laboratories at Jodhpur has developed an electrohydrolysis or desalination process that is used to convert salty brackish water into potable water. Many districts of Rajasthan have brackish water. A similar situation prevails in several districts of Tamil Nadu and Gujarat. The technology developed by DRDO labs was promoted by the Department of Rural Development (DRD) and the Government of Rajasthan. Two desalination plants of 20000 and 40000 litres respectively have been installed and production has commenced. More than 100 villages now have potable water. I found the villagers jubilant when I went to inaugurate one of the desalination plants. This example is replicable in many parts of the country.

Health for all

Better sanitary conditions and an improved micro-environment in the habitat or workplace are the most important requirements for health. In the coming years we also need to pay attention to the working conditions within factories as well as open workplaces, be they coalmines, quarries or roads. Removing health hazards to which our people are exposed is a crucial national mission. It is not enough to consider 'global quality levels' of living or working places only for the well-to-do. Ordinary Indians too deserve and have a right to live and to work in a good environment.

After a good and clean environment comes the need for better nutrition, with necessary food supplements. Preventive healthcare systems—inoculation, vaccination, immunization, periodic health checks and medical treatment are the next steps. These should be made available and affordable to all Indians. Employers, Central, state and local governments should bear the responsibility to assure people of this health security cover. But how is this to be implemented?

It is true that public health services are under severe strain. There is also a tendency towards the commercialization of medical services, which by itself is not bad if there are countervailing insurance or social security covers that make them affordable for most. Nevertheless, there are also a number of bright spots. Many medical professionals who run expensive medical care systems to cater to the needs and fancies of the affluent, also subsidize the weaker sections by providing them with good services. The authors have seen such philanthropy being practised at the L.V. Prasad Eye Institute at Hyderabad. Those who are well off pay for their treatment while those who register themselves under the category 'not affordable' receive free treatment. Some of these private initiatives are very efficient and humane. There are also many NGOs and a number of local initiatives that work well. Even the doctors and the staff in many government-run medical centres have a number of good ideas to make the existing systems functional and service-oriented. There are also a number of systems using alternative and holistic medicine which are promoted by well-trained specialists; some of these can bring down the costs of running the general health care system. Given all this, we do not believe that India cannot take up the challenge of 'health for all'. We can make the systems work; we can change them to help people, despite the growth of the population and multiple challenges in the task of removing poverty and accelerating economic growth.

It is with this firm and considered belief that we describe some facts about the projected scenario of diseases and disabilities and describe how to combat the problems.

Towards the vision: the two Indias

Soon we will have one billion Indians. A few tens of millions of them have lifestyles equivalent to or even more luxurious than the upper strata of the developed world. They enjoy the material wealth and the facilities offered by modern technologies, and simultaneously enjoy the benefits of cheap labour. Another 200 to 300 million Indians, the so-called middle class, have a varied lifestyle, often aspiring to copy the developed world but having only limited resources. They face the stress of modern life but often do not have the facilities for good living. The rest of the population is engaged in jobs which leave it confronted with constant insecurity about making ends meet. This majority does not have economic surplus and has just enough for covering its bare necessities. Investment in health care is an impossible luxury.

A TIFAC survey of the future scenario of Indian epidemiology as perceived by medical practitioners reflects this reality. India would have the diseases of the developing world—many communicable and infectious diseases—as well as the diseases of the developed world!

Among the infectious, maternal, perinatal and nutritional diseases, tuberculosis (TB) is perceived as the one requiring top priority in the short term till the turn of the century; followed by AIDS, vector-borne diseases, and diarrhoea. Then come nutritional diseases, hepatitis, diseases related to pregnancy and childbirth, diseases preventable by vaccination, acute respiratory infections, prenatal disorders, leprosy and sexually transmitted diseases.

Experts also indicate that the application of new developments in technologies could substantially reduce the incidence of these diseases by the year 2020. Even by 2010, we can substantially reduce the 'diseases of the developing country', except for AIDS, provided we act immediately.

Non-communicable diseases such as ischaemic heart diseases, strokes and female cancers are perceived to be of major concern in the short run, while these are likely to decline considerably by 2020. The decline is expected to be much faster for female cancers, which is particularly good news for a country which still has an adverse sex ratio for females. However, experts also envisage an increase in suicides and homicides, as also psychiatric disorders and accidents, making these areas of high priority.

Even as India would struggle to eradicate the diseases born of poor living conditions and poverty, some of the stress typical of modern developed countries is expected to increase. Is this something which can be prevented by reorienting ourselves as we make progress? Can some elements of our cultural heritage and simple living be retained to prevent or avoid some of this stress? Or, as some cynics would say, is it that our simple living and emphasis on values is only a manifestation of our poverty rather than an affirmation of a fundamental conviction in austerity?

Immediate steps for the new vision

One thing is definitely clear—halting the spread of TB, AIDS, diarrhoea, etc. must become a priority. Our vision should be to eradicate, before or by 2020, the infectious, maternal, perinatal and nutritional diseases. The action plan can be simple and effective. Let us look at some examples.

Experts opine that the information on TB mortality is quite sketchy, despite the considerable number of epidemiological studies on the disease. There is an immense need to develop a reliable TB database.

At present, polyvalent BCG vaccine, which is vulnerable to interference caused by non-tuberculosis mycobacteria, is used. An effective vaccine for the prevention of tuberculosis must become a priority. Monoclonal BCG vaccination and the identification of specific clones for development of more efficient vaccines are some of the preventive technologies that have been identified. Guidelines for identifying high-risk individuals and protocols for chemoprophylaxis also need to be developed. Health education programmes need to be undertaken for specific target groups. Many NGOs and youth organizations can be fruitfully utilized to fulfil major life-saving missions. The television and film media could also be tapped to spread the message, and there could be corporate sponsorship for such programmes. In the awareness campaign, let us also invoke some of the fears raised by the recent 'Surat plague'. Let us make all Indians aware that TB is not a disease confined to the lower classes.

TB is diagnosed by screening for specific symptoms of the disease and by sputum microscopy for acid-fast bacillus. Culture facilities facilitating detection of the disease are available only at specialized institutions. The diagnostic tools of endoscopy and bronchography are available only in tertiary hospitals. Rifamycin, the mainstay in short-course chemotherapy, is produced indigenously but is quite expensive. Some of the future technological requirements for TB diagnosis and treatment are R&D investment for developing Elisa kits and cost-effective process technology for producing Rifamycin, immunoassay of mycobacterial antigens, water-soluble dyes for bronchoscopy and bronchography.

Similarly AIDS, another major killer, would need to be tackled frontally. Fortunately, there is a much greater awareness campaign for AIDS than for TB. To date, a vaccine to prevent HIV infection has not been found, though clinical trials have started. AZT is the only drug currently in use to inhibit the replication of HIV. It inhibits the enzyme reverse transcriptase and thereby the viral genome. However, viral mutations lead to drug resistance within twelve to eighteen months. This occurs when AZT is used in combination with other drugs.

The option available for India to contain the AIDS epidemic lies in preventive measures such as the identification of high-risk individuals through screening, screening of blood used in blood transfusion, community awareness about the disease, and so on. We also need to focus on research to produce indigenous drugs based on traditional medicine.

Gastro-intestinal disorders are responsible for more than one-tenth of the disease burden in India. Much of it can be tackled by providing sanitary living conditions and good, clean drinking water to all Indians. In addition, we need to concentrate on finding simple, safe and inexpensive methods of diagnosis.

The search for such inexpensive diagnostic tools and vaccines is combined with other challenges. One is straightforward: the protection of intellectual property rights (IPR). If somebody or some company has already invented a new drug and patented it in India, permission has to be obtained from the party concerned before it can be used. The party may charge heavily for IPR, upsetting our cost calculations. Or a new drug not covered by such patents would have to be discovered; this may not always be easy, as research and its qualification through various regulatory tests takes considerable time.

There could also be unforeseen challenges. When a smaller company manages to invent and to produce an important vaccine, a bigger company selling vaccines may try to use underhand means to prevent its rival company from establishing itself on the market. So genuine companies trying to provide inexpensive vaccines and medicines may have problems in overcoming such illegal and immoral 'competitive' practices.

This brings us to another important area. Most vaccines would require good delivery and storage mechanisms. They lose their effectiveness or potency when not stored at particular, often low, temperatures. So as with milk or fruit, we need good refrigeration or chilling systems to enable the vaccines to reach villages.

Also, how do we ensure that the vaccines have indeed been stored at proper temperatures through various phases of handling, from the factory in which they are manufactured upto the point of the consumer? Here too there are technologies to help us keep control. There are thermal sensitive paints which can change colour; a strip of such paint can be put on the medicine or vaccine cover. If the instructions regarding the exact temperature and permissible time without refrigeration are violated, the colour will change irreversibly.

Fortunately, in India there are groups working on vaccines and irreversible thermal sensitive paints. But when it comes to stable and reliable electric power supply to the rural areas and towns, enabling the operation of good chilling systems in the rural areas, one is assailed by doubts.

A reliable refrigeration system presumes a stable supply of electric power. Electric power is a vital component for operating most machines. The entire electronics industry depends on it, though modern-day systems consume less and less electric power for greater performance. It is time we as a nation learn to appreciate the importance of electric power for industry. The current crisis in the power sector cannot be allowed to continue. In our march towards becoming a developed country, we need to drastically transform our electric power operations. It is not merely for agriculture or industry, but for the very health of our people. What this suggests is the importance of interlinkages. In the past few decades, many government departments, agencies and individuals have begun to function autonomously. The concept of self-reliance should be for the country as a whole, not for departments, agencies or individuals alone! But in India, many of the agencies do not see beyond their allocated areas. Someone concentrates on the purchase of a vaccine; another on development; another 'deals with' distribution without trying to understand the special character of the item to be distributed. There is enough 'paper work' to protect everybody. 'I have done my task!' the representative of any department might say. Of course there are also problems in such a system for those with initiative. On the pretext of coordination, many irrelevant questions are raised and often months pass before a decision is taken. We have heard many sincere people telling us that they have sent detailed proposals with specific linkages spelt out to the department concerned in Delhi or the state capital. Often Delhi has something to say even when proposals are sent to the state capital. It may take three to six years for the proposals to be cleared; often the clearance comes after the subject matter has become partially or fully obsolete.

If we want to achieve a developed India, we have to learn to get out of this pitiable state of inaction. If laws, rules and procedures have to be changed, this should be done. The rate at which technologies offer new solutions and new windows of opportunity is fortunately very high in the current phase of human development. We can make up the lost time and missed opportunities, provided we learn to move fast. Such opportunities are not waiting around for us. Others grab them. We need to think holistically and innovatively, and not in our closed compartments. And above all, we need to learn to act fast and protect those who make genuine mistakes. Failure is a part of any venture! The authors can cite from their experience of three mission-oriented organizations: the Department of Atomic Energy, the Indian Space Research Organisation and the Defence Research & Development Organisation, which have project-oriented management for time-bound achievements in high technology, and also their societal application. Defence lasers can be used surgically to treat glaucoma or cataract. Atomic energy is used for irradiating, for example, groundnut seeds for higher productivity; and space research has led to an accurate prediction of the onset of the monsoon. The unique characteristic of all these three departments is that their scientists are not afraid of taking decisions and above all are not afraid of failures. But they have indeed succeeded, thanks to visionaries like Dr Homi Bhabha, Prof Vikram Sarabhai, Prof Satish Dhawan and Dr Nag Chaudhri.

For example, satellite remote sensing offers a medium to map out areas where mosquitoes breed or such areas from which other diseases can spread. There have been a few successful experiments over limited areas. We have our remote sensing satellite whose data is being sold commercially worldwide. We have many experts in remote sensing applications! Many entrepreneurial scientists and technologists have started small companies and provide services even to foreign clients. Why don't we deploy these talents to benefit the country as a whole, in the big battle ahead to combat diseases? We are aware that satellite mapping alone cannot solve all problems. It can monitor, and present a quick picture and help us to develop microplans. Similarly, there are other tools. Also there may be several sources of local knowledge available with our tribal communities or village elders about the control of vectors. Why not deploy this after a quick study? DRDO had an interesting experience in the north-eastern state of Assam, where the organizatioh has a Defence Research Laboratory especially devoted to preventing malaria and its treatment. It is a small laboratory with less than fifty members. It has been established to keep our armed forces healthy. This laboratory has done something unique in health care. It has characterized the vector of the mosquito prevalent in that region based on their own medical knowledge and the experience of the local people. The laboratory, in turn, has treated the people in the villages and helped them to be free of malaria.

TABLE 10.1

Estimated and Projected Mortality Rates (per 100000) by Sex, for Major Causes of Death in India

Causes	1985 M	1985 F	2000 M	2000 F	2015 M	2015 F
All causes	1158	1165	879	790	846	745
Infectious	478	476	215	239	152	175
Neoplasms	43	51	88	74	108	91
Circulatory	145	126	253	204	295	239
Pregnancy	–	22	–	12	–	10
Prenatal	168	132	60	48	40	30
Injury	85	65	82	28	84	29
Others	239	293	280	285	167	171

Source: World Bank Health Sectoral Priorities Review

Non-infectious diseases

Let us now address non-infectious diseases, some of which are considered 'developed country' (post-transitional) diseases! Since these diseases are significant in developed countries, there is also a vast knowledge base utilized to tackle them. Heart diseases are perceived to be the ones which will receive major attention for many years to come.

Urbanization and altered lifestyles are indicators of socio-economic development and lead to risk factors for cardiovascular diseases (CVD). At present, pre-transitional diseases like rheumatic heart disease, mostly the problem of the poor, co-exist as a major cardiovascular disease along with post-transitional diseases such as coronary heart disease and hypertension. In India nearly 2.4 million deaths are caused by cardiovascular disorders. Small-scale community-based studies indicate the prevalence of CVD in adults, ranging from 2–6 per cent in rural and 6–10 per cent in urban areas. The health sector review of the World Bank projects that CVD mortality rates would double between 1985–2015 (table 10.1).

Studies of overseas Indians in many countries reveal excess coronary mortality in persons of Indian origin. These studies conducted in several countries and involving different generations of migrants from India/South Asia suggest a special susceptibility to CVD as persons of Indian origin face the challenges of epidemiologic transition. When a community's status changes from being poor to affluent, both genetic, environmental and perhaps nutritional factors appear to play a role in the special vulnerability of people of a particular community, in this case of Indian origin. Other factors include the stresses due to living in a different cultural setting. Experts believe that an epidemiologic transition is therefore likely to result in a major CVD epidemic in India.

It is critically important to develop relatively inexpensive diagnostic aids for detecting coronary heart disease (CHD). These include ECG (electrocardiogram), stress ECG, nuclear cardiology, echocardiography, holter monitoring and cardiac catheterization with coronary angiography. Technologies like magnetic resonance angiography of the coronary arteries are still under investigation. ECG recorders and simple stress equipment are manufactured in India and are easily available. However, if the diagnostic facilities have to be extended to the primary care (ECG) and secondary care (stress ECG) levels, in response to the coronary epidemic, their manufacture in larger numbers and reduced cost per unit would be necessary. Medical therapy of CHD may involve anti-anginal drugs (nitrates, calcium channel and beta blockers), anti-thrombotic agents (aspirin, heparin, etc), ACE-inhibitors, thrombolytic agents (streptokinase, urokinase, etc) and antioxidants. Primary health care centres are not presently geared to provide emergency care. Development of treatment protocols for CHD and training of appropriate manpower at primary levels needs to be taken up on a priority basis. Let us remember that CHD or CVD is not merely the problem of the very top strata, of a few tens of millions. (No doubt this strata can not only afford private treatment in India but also afford periodic check-ups and treatment in the UK and USA. It is sad to note that this strata have confidence only in foreign facilities, despite the presence of expert doctors in India and all such imported equipment with which foreign-returned Indian specialists are operating world-class facilities!)

CVD or CHD is going to become a common illness, from the lower to the upper middle class and even among many rural people. Therefore, it is not a disease of the affluent; it is a disease which may also attack many Indians, who have just marginally escaped death from severe infectious diseases or nutritional disorders. The Kalam–Raju stent, used to prevent arteries from closing up, was one such attempt to target the treatment of this group. We need many more measures for diagnosis. Since most primary health centres (PHCs) may not have access to excellent specialists, advances in modern communication and information technologies also would need to be deployed innovatively to provide such tele-access (that is, access at a distance). Most readings of the diagnostic equipment, ECG or others are electrical signals. These can be transmitted to the specialists in a very economical form with modern digital technologies. The opinion and advice of the specialists can be retransmitted to the PHC. We understand that many of those who operate costly nursing homes in cities would be willing to provide such advisory services at a nominal cost as a part of their contribution to society. Let us try many such methods to reach out to people. In addition, the advice of specialists regarding dietary habits, exercises and practices for mental stress relief (including yoga) may have to be popularized in the media.

Another CVD which is prevalent now in India and arises mostly due to poverty or neglect of illnesses at a young age is rheumatic heart disease (RHD). It is a major cause of cardiovascular morbidity and mortality. The prevention of RHD requires early diagnosis and prompt treatment of streptococcal pharyngitis, especially in children aged 5-16 years. Though a streptococcal vaccine is under investigation, clinical trials are yet to take shape. A multivalent, non-cross reactive, long lasting and inexpensive vaccine would be ideal for prophylaxis, but does not appear to be feasible. Secondary prophylaxis with penicillin is an available technology whose compliance needs to be improved. Clinical trials on the efficacy of immuno-modulatory therapy for rheumatic fever is required. While balloon valvoplasty and surgery are presently available at most tertiary centres, the equipment and disposables are mostly imported. Indigenously developed prosthetic valves must be promoted and technologies for production of indigenous equipment and disposables must be developed. On all these fronts, given targets and good organization, India can easily measure up to the problem.

Other non-communicable diseases such as diabetes may be a cause for concern. About 5 to 10 per cent of the population in India suffers from diabetes. Preventive measures include genetic counselling and dietary and lifestyle counselling. Blood glucose detecting devices have been simplified and miniaturized. However, a high running cost and the need for changing the equipment are limiting factors. Standardized glucose measuring

TABLE 10.2

Projected Number of Cancer Incidences in India

Cancer Site	Year 2001 M	2001 F	2011 M	2011 F	2021 M	2021 F
Oral Cavity	44875	23670	59560	24515	75299	24261
Pharynx	41541	11073	56898	15175	73638	19669
Oesophagus	39981	33496	56539	48099	74838	64418
Larynx	18836	1590	23785	1074	28898	346
Lung	47634	6963	67969	9138	90517	11459
Urinary bladder	11861	2998	16603	4167	21822	5456
TRC*	204728	79798	281354	102168	365012	125609
Breast	–	99941	–	140603	–	185677
Cervix	–	83283	–	82495	–	76963
Lymphona	25892	16053	35366	24428	45679	33958
Leukemia	19013	14701	25902	21152	33392	28366
All sites	476308	448482	655787	574181	851904	705896

*Tobacco Related Cancer

M—Males; F—Females

(*Source: Srinivasan K.; Demographic and epidemiological transition in India, Institute of Population Sciences, Deonar, Mumbai*

devices and diagnostic kits would greatly help in the management of the disease. The projected requirements of insulin for 2010, estimated at about 168 billion units annually, indicates the importance of developing indigenous technology for low-cost human recombinant and other newer forms of insulin. It may incidentally be pointed out that much of this equipment, medicines and diagnostic kits, be it for diabetes, CVDs or other diseases, can be exported. Domestic consumption alone can form a reasonably profitable business venture.

Cancer is another area that would require special attention. Amongst many high-level non-medical decision makers there is a general opinion that cancer is a disease of the rich and they can take care of it. But the facts are otherwise. Cancer is a degenerative disease influenced by age, environment, and lifestyles. Also, increased life expectancy means an increased incidence of cancer! Table 10.2 indicates the incidences of cancer in India and the future projections.

Indian incidences as per the current records appear to indicate that if we look at the common sites of cancer in the population, their proportions and trends, over 40 per cent of cancers in males and 20 per cent of females can be directly attributed to the use of tobacco. Most of these cancer cases are presented only at the late stage of the disease and very few at the early localized stage, increasing the incidence of death by the disease. A relatively high incidence of stomach cancer in the south and gall bladder cancer in the north is observed, thus making studies on cancer etiology and epidemiology imperative. It is essential to generate information on baseline parameters for different regions of the country in order to assess the risk factors and develop measures to create awareness. Effective diagnostic and therapeutic facilities are essential all over the country. For example, endoscopes are an essential part of diagnostic services for cancer. They are available only at specialized institutions. A set of endoscopes costs about Rs. 2.5 million now. We believe that the cost can be brought down partly by economies of scale and partly through innovative design to cater to essential needs. Often the vision of those who plan the programme is limited to procurement of the equipment in a few urban centres and in a few other areas to prove that we have it elsewhere too! This narrow vision should change.

Yet again, availability of external radiotherapy Cobalt-60 units is limited to specialized units. There are only 120 units in the country and these are also not uniformly distributed. With the increasing incidence of cancer, it is estimated that for every one million people, at least one unit will be required. That is about 1000 units, with increasing demands in the future. With our tremendous capabilities in nuclear technologies and many other supporting Indian industries, can this problem not be solved by innovative and inexpensive designs? Experts believe that it can. If there is a mission, a demand will be generated.

If a nuclear technologist is shown foreign equipment and asked if he or she can manufacture it in India, the answer will be 'yes'; he will come up with an innovative design and an estimate of the cost which may often be very high. It is a pity, but it is only very rarely that the same technologist would be faced with a project stating that our vision is to reach the whole of India. 'Can you sit with doctors, production specialists, businessmen and others to come up with minimum essential features to create technology available at a lesser cost, on a large scale and more speedily?' That is a question which is never asked. Over a period, our system has lost the capability to enthuse people; to pose challenging problems for our youth; to harness a large vision.

Let the coming fifty years be a period of expanded vision for India, faith in ourselves, a bold desire to carve new paths and create an environment for the youth to excel. Such a new developed India will inspire confidence in people of other countries as well. Let us look for a strong, healthy and wealthy India radiating its well-being to all people.

Sight for all

Even as we speak of vision, it is depressing to acknowledge that India has one-fourth of the world's blind or visually handicapped. About 12 million people are fully blind and 20 million suffer from various forms of serious visual handicaps, rendering them virtually ineffective.

At K.G. Hospital at Coimbatore, a well-to-do person along with a few doctors is providing eye care to many poor people, including those in nearby towns and villages. The vans go for tests and pick up cases requiring treatment. While going on a round of some of the patients, I came to an elderly man and asked him in Tamil what his name was and where he was from. The man replied, 'I have heard about you, Kalam Sir; I am happy to be near you though I cannot see you!' I asked him how old he was. That made the elderly man tearful. He said, 'I don't know my age and I don't care about it now. I have been in darkness for so many years that it appears to me that many *yugas* are over. Losing your own vision is such a bad thing because you own children taunt you as a *kurudan* (a blind man).' Indicating his bandaged eyes he said, 'These *punyavans* (holy souls) appear to care for me. They brought me in a van, examined my eyes and did some operations. Once they opened the bandages to do a check-up; it looked to me that I was able to see though hazily. They told me that in a couple of days my bandages would be opened and they would give me glasses. May God bless those who will save me from the miserable state of being a *kurudan* . . . Kalam Sir, I am confident that I will see you with my eyes and glasses during my lifetime . . . my faith in God has gone up; he comes through kind human beings . . .'

The man was obviously suffering from a cataract. Probably his children either did not care or he could not afford to go in for an operation.

Almost 80 per cent of blindness in India is due to cataract. The other significant causes are corneal diseases, glaucoma, diabetes and other vitreoretinal disorders. Intraocular lens (IOL) implantation is an ideal method for rehabilitation of cataract patients after surgery. Extracapsular cataract surgery with IOL is one of the most cost-effective therapies, in terms of quality of life, since vision with as good as 6/9 is possible. In India mostly intracapsular extraction is practised. However,

IOL implantation is also becoming increasingly popular. According to a survey, of the cataract operations reported in the country in 1992, 42 per cent were extracapsular and about half of these received IOLs. The projected requirements for IOLs in the country would be close to 2 million every year. This necessitates production of better quality IOLs indigenously. Another modern technique of cataract surgery employed in over 75 per cent of the cases in the USA is phacoemulsification, where surgery is performed through a 3 mm incision and the lens inserted through a slightly enlarged incision (5.5 mm). Alternatively, a foldable silicon IOL is implanted through a 3.5 mm incision. Phacoemulsification technology needs to be made available in India. There is also scope for development of small incision technologies such as lasers and mechanical endolenticular fragmentation.

The DRDO has made a small contribution to eye care through the development of 'Drishti' eye laser equipment. The DRDO has formed the Society for Biomedical Technology (SBMT) with the objective of creating conditions under which cost-effective, life-saving medical products can be indigenously produced and made available to the common man at affordable prices. The spin-offs of defence technology are the basic strength of SBMT. The society binds together scientists, engineers, doctors, social workers and administrators in a shared mission. In less than three years time, DRDO/SBMT, along with others, have successfully developed an external cardiac pacemaker which is one-third of the cost of its imported counterpart, an automated cancer detection device for mass cancer screening, and a low-cost cardiac stress test system to take this important screening tool of diagnosing coronary artery disease to small towns and community health centres. The technologies for these systems have been transferred to industry for production. The laboratory systems of Drishti and coronary catheters are under clinical validation. The Jaipur foot for polio-affected children developed by Dr P.K. Sethi has been made ultra-light by using an advanced composite material that goes into making missile heat shields. The coronary stent is under production.

Plans are afoot to enlarge these efforts, using a spin-off of defence technology for launching indigenous development of a hollow-fibre dialyser, coronary stents, drug delivery implants and microprocessor-based in-canal hearing aids. The mission is enormous. The partners are medical institutions and industries. We desire that all the available technology forces and philanthropists must come together to make it happen.

There are other solid institutions and industries in India capable of doing more. BARC is not merely devoted to nuclear devices or systems. It has the knowledge and capabilities for many medical technologies. The Centre for Advanced Technology (CAT) at Indore has world-class capabilities in laser devices and applications. Dr M.S. Valiathan, who led the Health Care Technology Vision 2020 studies, is an eminent scientist and technologist of India. More than three decades ago he came back from USA after his advanced studies to build an institution called Sri Chitra Tirunal Medical Centre located at Thiruvananthapuram. Operating from there against heavy odds, he and his team have developed many biomedical devices ranging from blood bags to heart valves, bringing down the costs several fold. These devices are under commercial production in India and some of the devices are also produced abroad under successful technology export contracts. The institute has developed several unique capabilities in biomedical devices.

Similarly, the co-chairperson of the Vision 2020 exercise, the eminent nutritionist Dr Mahtab Bamji, has extensive experience in rural areas. After retirement she spends much of her time in rural areas, contributing towards the vision. There are extremely capable medical personnel, scientists and engineers all over the country. There are many NGOs and youth in search of challenging human missions. There are many persons like Dr V. Sudarsan of Mysore who combine modern knowledge and scientific methodologies with the inherited wisdom of our people. Also, most experts believe that many older forms of medicines and medicinal plants will have an important role to play in future medicare systems not only in India but in the world. That is the reason many foreign multinational companies invest in research and development of herbal drugs. A few of our experts opine that much of its knowledge has not been fully exploited because of the limited prevalence of Sanskrit and Indian languages. With its ancient knowledge base and excellent biodiversity, India can really become a world leader in herbal and other natural medicare systems.

Maternal and child health

Let us end this chapter by addressing a crucial element of the health care system, that is maternal and child health. Women of child-bearing age and children under five represent the maternal and child category in any population profile. As per the 1991 census, 56 per cent of the population in India fall under this category. The projected Maternal and Child Health (MCH) population is given in table 10.3. Anaemia, chronic under-nutrition and complications during pregnancy and childbirth are the orders of priority for maternal health. In the case of children, the priorities are diarrhoeal diseases, anaemia, perinatal disorders and vitamin A deficiency. Effective antenatal care, prophylactic iron and folic acid supplements, food security, improved sanitation and drinking water facilities, universal immunization coverage are some of the measures which would reduce the problems in MCH. (see table 10.3.)

In fact, none of the medicare required for maternal and child health demands breakthrough technologies. What is required is a large-scale production and distribution system. Even anaemia diagnostics have become simpler, thanks to development in the technologies of advanced sensors. We require a new vision regarding our children and mothers. The very foundation of our future depends on their health.

The vision

The vision for health for all Indians is realizable well before 2020. We have discussed some details with a few examples.

TABLE 10.3

Projected Maternal and Child Population at Different Points of Time

Year	Children (0–4 years)		Adult Female (15–44 years)	
	Number (millions)	per cent of total population	Number (millions)	per cent of total female population
1991	111.4	13.2	186.3	45.8
2001	114.5	11.3	231.8	47.2
2011	106.4	9.1	275.7	48.6
2021	108.5	8.3	302.3	47.5

Source: K Srinivasan; Demographic & epidemiological transition in India;
(Assumption: NRR of one by 2011)

While one needs numbers and statistics, technical evaluation and investments, we believe that a change in thinking would lead to a miraculous transformation. The richer and more powerful sections of our society should realize that the health of their less-privileged countrymen is their problem as well. They can go to the USA or UK for a cardiac examination or surgery but they cannot escape an infectious epidemic in India very long. Enlightened self-interest should make businessmen realize that a sick worker cannot give his or her best even with the most modern equipment. High productivity requires a healthy workforce. Health administrators should learn to treat health as people's pain and agony, not as files. Similarly, politicians at all levels should learn to look at pain removal as a part of their duty.

I would like to conclude this chapter with a quote from a convocation address I delivered at the Tamil Nadu Dr M.G.R. Medical University, Madras, on 21 March 1996.

> I conclude by recalling the great saying of the Jesuit St Ignatius Loyola to St Paul. St Paul asked for a message from his guru before taking up the assignment of preaching. St Ignatius Loyola said, 'Go to all parts of the earth and ignite their minds and give light.' Dr M.G.R. Medical University gives the message: My young children, go to all parts of the country, particularly beyond cities, remove the pain of mind and body. Indeed, a health mission is ahead of you. My best wishes.

Chapter 11

The Enabling Infrastructure

Indeed one's faith in one's plans and methods are truly tested when the horizon before one is the blackest.

—Mahatma Gandhi

The various chapters so far flesh out the vision of a developed India: poverty being eradicated by about 2010 and the building up of a robust and fast-growing economy through our core competencies. We have illustrated possible trajectories through a few interlinkages between various sectors. Agriculture and agrofood processing will require some of the finest inputs from engineering industries, materials sectors and even sensors and electronics, in addition, of course, to the life sciences and biotechnology. In the modern world every usable product or service is based on a blending of multiple technologies, which are shaped to one or several end uses. Design capability is integral to this and without it we would remain merely at the level of licensed producers. In the long run, that would be a form of enslavement to the developed world.

There are other types of linkages too, that of trade, for example. It is not much use having higher productivity, say of crops, fruit, vegetables, fish and eggs, if these cannot be supplied in time to the consumers. They cannot all be consumed at the place where they are produced. Traders have to sell the products outside and buy other products with the money made. The world today, thanks to the technologies of transportation and telecommunication, has become connected in a much more complex way. The time taken to fly around the globe can be less than a day. Messages, including images of people, can be transmitted almost instantaneously. Competitiveness in such a complex world can be sustained only at a high level of the knowledge and skill bases at all levels. Many resources have to be usefully deployed to generate and utilize such knowledge and skill levels. Also, those who have such knowledge and skill levels aspire for better living conditions. We have observed that persons enjoying a better standard of living are able to work more. A simple truth is that a modern developed economy cannot be built on a large number of people living just above the poverty line, producing agricultural products alone and cut off from the rest of the manufacturing and business centres. This means that every production centre in the country should have speedy economic connectivity with other parts of the country. At every centre there has to be more and more value addition.

Value addition is simply enhancement of the value of a material with processes attached. It means doing something more to satisfy the ultimate user or consumer. Innovation can add more features to kindle the imagination of a user or consumer. For example, a farmer can grow a particular variety of mango that is in great demand. There can be value addition if he can provide consistency in taste, shape, size; people would be ready to pay more for such an assurance. Value addition can be done through selection, sorting and packaging of mangoes at the production centre. If such a value addition has to be achieved on a large scale, then some forms of semi-mechanization, testing, etc. are involved. These are technological inputs.

Nowadays, there are packages designed through computer simulation which consider the types of shock, vibration and thermal conditions the contents and the packages are likely to undergo in transit. We carry out such simulations and design for military equipment, satellites, launch vehicles and missiles. With the increasing presence of computers these techniques are being applied to ordinary civilian life. That is the beauty of technology. As it grows and matures, it spreads to more and more people and provides benefits to all, thus bringing down the costs of application of technologies.

Coming back to our example of value addition, in addition to good sorting and packaging, transportation in containers with controlled atmospheric conditions, or where necessary under chilled conditions, keeps the mangoes fresh. This too is value addition.

Such a continual value addition at each centre of economic activity can be achieved only when they are interconnected, by road, rail, waterways or air. For instance, exotic flowers may have to be flown in by air to fetch the best price. There was a time when jasmine flowers from Madurai used to be flown into Delhi from Madras (now Chennai) by the morning Indian Airlines flight to be sold in Delhi's Connaught Place!

Such physical transportation systems are a part of the enabling infrastructure. Naturally, bus or truck stations, railway stations, airports and ports (coastal and inland) are also a part of the infrastructure. As better and better technologies are deployed in these infrastructure sectors, they can provide improved services. 'Better' means not merely having a good road without potholes! When goods move by truck, precious hours are lost at checkpoints and weighing-posts. The hours spent in these posts are really negative value additions. In addition, some of the delays lead to loss of quality of agriproducts or even decay. Activities at such checkpoints can be speeded up tremendously through use of electronic aids such as electronic weighing machines, computers and electronically controlled signals and displays. Indians have a right to have good roads, quick clearing facilities and freedom from daily pinpricks. Modern technologies can make this happen. At all levels we have to dream and will that India shall have such systems; we have to change our mindset; and, as important, change the obsolete administrative and legal systems.

We have looked at the important infrastructural elements of internal connectivity: road, rail and aviation. But in addition to moving goods within India we need to move them to other lands as exports and to receive goods as imports from other countries. Ports are crucial for this activity. In ancient times, Indian ports attracted many traders: Arabs, Persians, Greek, Chinese, Portuguese and many other Europeans. Indian traders also travelled overseas. Most of our ports today have not kept up with the technological changes taking place in the rest of the world. Much smaller countries like Singapore handle much more value added trade in their ports which are computerized and where many operations are automated. Our ports are considered very slow in comparison. If they are not upgraded India will become irrelevant as a trading country. Hence, ports form a very important element of infrastructure.

Both domestic and global economic and physical connectivities (through road, rail, aircraft, ports and airports) depend vitally on telecommunication networking. Instant transfer of information is essential for any business today. Telegraph and radio once gave a great fillip to speedier communication. Then came the telephone. Nowadays satellites, fibre optic cables and other improved forms of wireless communication and, more importantly, improvements in micro-electronics and computers have revolutionized the way we seek and exchange information. Thousands of tonnes of different kinds of cargo and their movement can be monitored almost instantaneously, thanks to the advances in communications and information technology (IT). Thus telecommunications and IT are two of the most critical elements of the modern economy. That is the reason why many countries are concentrating on a National Information Infrastructure (NII) and linkages to the Global Information Infrastructure (GII).

These infrastructures and related technologies and services are evolving so rapidly as to form a completely different world in themselves. Some call it a virtual world. Of course, we cannot eat or have many other physical comforts in the virtual world. But this virtual world created by IT has become as real as the real world in all activities: agriculture to health to education to manufacturing to security. India cannot afford to ignore this newly emerging area. One is happy to note the significant national resolve to make India a major IT power.

All the above depend crucially on energy and especially the assurance of quality electric power to all Indians and for all sectors of economic activity. Sometimes one wonders whether we can have such a vision at all! How many power cuts plagued us while we wrote this book! How many times the computers were down! Many in Delhi told me after the successful nuclear tests, 'Sir, when will Delhi be without power cuts?' The problem, of course, is nationwide. The situation needs to be changed radically if we are to realize the vision of a developed India.

Investments in infrastructure

The aggregate level of investment infrastructure increased from about Rs. 6000 crores in 1980–81 to about Rs. 29000 crores in 1990-91 and to about Rs. 50000 crores in 1994–95. As a proportion of GDP, the investments in infrastructure ranged from about 4.5 per cent to 6 per cent. Of the total annual investments in the country about 25 per cent are in infrastructure projects. It is estimated that the investments in infrastructure during 1997–2002 may be about Rs. 500000 crores and about Rs. 750000 crores during the next five years.

Figures of this magnitude may seem intimidating but the truth is that for all the inefficiencies of administration, and even one might say, a certain lack of commitment to make this a great nation, our economy has grown to huge proportions.

The share of the railways has been only about 0.6 per cent of the GDP and has remained stagnant over decades. There is a great need to increase it because railways are an extremely energy efficient mode of communication. Of late the number of railway accidents is increasing and it also appears that most line expansion projects are moving very slowly. There are a number of technologies for high-speed trains which are possible and have been talked of at various fora. It is essential to modernize many parts of our railway tracks, signalling system and even facilities for passenger comforts. For the movement of goods, it is possible to have multimodal containers, that is, containers which are standard for railways, roads, ships or aircraft. Investments in road transport and waterways have ranged between 1.3 to 1.6 per cent of GDP. Investment in electricity has been on the average about 2.5 per cent of GDP. For telecommunications, it has grown from 0.3 per cent to 0.8 per cent of GDP. How do we increase these rapidly is the question.

One way is to increase GDP. But without improving infrastructure GDP cannot grow! Without investments, roads or electric power or telecommunications or ports cannot come up. Does that puts us in a catch-22 situation? Not really. There are many private investors in India and abroad who would be ready to investigate projects which would yield returns over a long period. It is necessary to attract them to invest in these projects. Since 1991, the government has been granting several concessions to attract them. But much of this investment has come in bits and pieces. Some of these investors had unrealistic assumptions. Nevertheless, private investors do seek profit. It is necessary to assure them of reasonable profits and to give them cover for certain risks. The government has to ensure that the long term interests of the country or the public are not unduly compromised. Considering the fact that the development of infrastructure is integral to speedy economic growth—the only way our people can break out of centuries of poverty—the country has to learn to be innovative in offering packages which will attract investments.

Investors complain that the path to investment is riddled with time-consuming procedures. The only way to put in place attractive policies and make them work is to simplify procedures. The authors are not unaware of the various vested interests that have been built up over time. Many in India believe that from the lowermost counter, which gives out important application forms which the government requires to be filled, to the highest levels there are a large number of avenues to convert 'authority' into money. We believe a call for a new vision for India with a higher aim and sincerity, resulting in jobs for almost everyone, and with the makings of a movement, would remove many of the present cobwebs. In pre-independence India, Indians were after all only viewed as fighting with each other over caste, religion, language and more. Did the people not join a great movement without any guns or arms to dislodge a mighty empire?

Coming back again to the investment question, even while private sector investment will be essential to build up infrastructure, the government has to invest too. Estimates indicate that the funds required to improve the existing national highways as well as to expand them would be about Rs. 150000 crores. The private sector could contribute a proportion, but the remainder will have to come from the government (both central and the states). But here we need to question whether most of the funds indicated are really required. Some assumptions need to be re-examined: should widening of an existing road from single lane to double lane cost about Rs. 50 lakh per kilometre? And is the same amount again needed for improving the double lane pavements of existing roads? Should the cost of widening double lanes to four be about Rs. 250 lakh per kilometre? Should a new expressway cost Rs. 800 lakh per kilometre? We are not questioning the capability of our engineers and accountants. Such estimates are worked out since nobody wants to be accused of not using materials of a particular standard, even when this is not exactly relevant. Therefore a lot of 'padding' has been built into the system over the years.

It is time that these basics are questioned and some innovative methods are used at least in the short run, say five to seven years. In many areas where there are no roads or terrible roads, some improvement is much better than no improvement awaiting sanction of huge budgets. Some 'standards' can be relaxed: some innovative mechanisms for reducing costs can be experimented with countrywide. Let us not wait for some special wisdom to emanate from the capitals.

Even with all these standards in place, has the country achieved what it wants? We ought not to be afraid of some initial low performance resulting from empowering various functionaries in different parts of the country. They could consult public-spirited citizens around their areas and help in decision making. The media has a special role too. Instead of only emphasizing failures and horrors, let them also play up a few successes; some of them will serve as role models for others to follow. Let us spread hope; let us work with determination.

The reason I am emphasizing these aspects is simple. India can launch itself into a developed status only when the economic machinery starts 'real movement' through the infrastructure. Once the machinery moves, the process of economic growth will create more money in about five to seven years. That money can be reinvested in further improvements. Those of traditional thinking may find this difficult to accept. But let us learn the lessons of the past fifty years. The poor people cannot wait for a whole millennium to pass to have a better and more secure living. If a reasonable infrastructure is in place, our innovative people would find avenues to a better life. Money in the hands of our hundreds of million Indians constitutes a huge market. While the 250 million Indian middle class may aspire for foreign goods, the Indians below the poverty line would be very happy with Indian goods. In fact it is the Indian industrialists who do not necessarily have major export ambitions who should spearhead the movement converting these 750 million into a new huge market. Once they become a force, India will be a billion-plus market that will attract the whole world!

It will be difficult to look at details of all the sectors of infrastructure. Let us examine a few. First, the electricity sector which is so crucial.

Quality electric power for all

No nation can aspire to be modern and developed without the availability of quality power for all. No modern machinery can run without uninterrupted and quality power systems. The whole magic wand of Information Technology (IT) will be at naught if there is no electric power. Imagine New York or London or Tokyo having just one day without power or a week of interrupted power supply. It just cannot happen. If it did, it could bring down the government. When we look at the power situation in India, 'depressing' or 'gloomy' appear to be mild words to describe it. Hundreds of thousands of precious human hours are lost because of lack of quality electric power (not to talk of many others who have not been covered by electricity at all!). At a time when equipment models change so rapidly, an investor would want to obtain the maximum advantage from a particular kind of equipment, even with three shifts. But the quality of our power supply often makes sophisticated equipment lie idle for hours. Those who manage to continue production do so by investing in electric supply regulators and a standby power system. What a waste of productive capital resources!

India's first hydroelectric power plant of 130 MW was commissioned near Darjeeling, West Bengal, in 1897. At the time of independence the sum of installed capacities at various pockets was above 1300 MW. A tenfold increase in five decades! The present installed power generation capacity is about 85000 MW, or a sixty-five fold increase in five decades. The power transmission system which started with 78 KV has now matured to 400 KV grids and 500 KV HVDC (high voltage direct current) systems for bulk power transfer. Recently one of our major national laboratories in electric power technology, the Central Power Research Institute (CPRI) with its main laboratory at Bangalore has test-charged a 1500 KV HVDC line. The higher the voltage of transmission in direct current the less the transmission losses. In the future we need to have many HVDC lines. Electric power distribution which had only a few circuit kilometres at the time of independence has now reached a length of nearby 2800 million circuit kilometres.

These figures are impressive in themselves. We remember how we studied and did our homework by the light of kerosene lanterns during our schooldays. From there it is a sea change! But is it enough or adequate? Let us look at China: in the

1950s India and China had roughly the same installed power capacity. Now China has about three times more installed capacity than India! Further, China has been consistently adding a capacity of about 15000 MW a year for several years now whereas our capacity is growing at a rate of 2500 MW per year. Why is this so? Is it because of lack of funds? We believe that the major problem before the nation is that we have stopped thinking big! We are either getting bogged down in petty details, or getting ourselves trapped in big and longwinded talk of policy, promises, and in political games. The latter is not merely limited to politicians but has also spread to several others in the bureaucracy, technocracy and industry. The moment we sincerely think big and start working hard, we can find solutions. Most Indian people respond when there is a lead, and when there is a call before them.

We do not want to go into the details of efficiency of utilization of even the existing capacities, expressed as Plant Load Factor (PLF). We are at about 60 per cent as against 80 per cent for South Korea. The reasons are many. But the stark fact is that of the installed capacity of about 85000 MW, only about 32000 MW reaches the consumer, that too not without interruptions and other variations in quality. Our first and foremost task is to rectify this situation; it may mean that our state electricity boards and other generators should take various steps and also take a look at the transmission and distribution (T&D) systems. Our T&D losses are about 22 per cent whereas developed world standards are about 7 to 8 per cent. Technically and managerially, we have to find solutions.

Let us not overlook successes even in this gloomy situation. Unchahar thermal power station was acquired by the National Thermal Power Corporation (NTPC) from the government of Uttar Pradesh. Performance was improved dramatically by using debottlenecking techniques. Prior to the takeover the Unchahar Station had a PLF of 18 per cent; in six months thereafter it went up to 35.5 per cent and in twelve months to 73.7 per cent! The availability factor which was 27 per cent at the time of the takeover, went up to 49.5 per cent six months later and about 79.5 per cent after twelve months. Specific oil consumption, which is an indication of wastage and inefficiency of operation, which was at 21.8 million litres (Ml) per kilowatt hour (Kwh) at the time of takeover went down to 6.3 Ml/Kwh in six months and 3.3 Ml/Kwh in 12 months.* These dramatic results have been obtained under ordinary or even oppressive circumstances, and despite the absence of recognition by the system. While a day's power breakdown or an audit report on delay or excessive project costs hits headlines, nobody even bothers to mention these achievements in a small column of a newspaper. Nor even is such achievement talked about by politicians or bureaucrats! We don't know who are the heroes and heroines who made these achievements possible through teamwork!

Now imagine a situation where we create a national climate to think *big* and praise every *small* success which contributes towards the *big* goal and where every team which attempts improvement and succeeds is recognized nationally. When we give the teams at least the attention equal to that given to Prithvi, Agni, Insat, PSLV, Pokhran or that of a major national or international award for an eminent scientist, we will have multiplier effects! In about three years we will have maximum utilization of existing capacities as per developed country norms. Let the electric power stations do it themselves or let them be taken over by public or private entities to make this happen. We would even say that let some enterprising companies from anywhere take them over to set an example of standards, if they can trigger our inherent pride and mobilize it for action! Of course, early enaction of relevant legal measures are required to allow private and local initiatives.

Similarly, improvements in the transmission and distribution (T&D) systems requires priority attention. With the present level of installed capacity, and assuming they work very efficiently on the lines discussed earlier, every 1 per cent improvement in T&D losses would mean availability of an additional 600 MW to

---

*This example draws on an article by Rajendra Singh, Chairman, NTPC, in *Technorama* (January 1997).

the consumer. As we have discussed earlier, there is scope to bring down the transmission losses by about 14 per cent if we consider world standards. Part of this has to be achieved through reconductoring with better materials, installation of shunt capacitors on the distribution system to correct power factors, use of better transformers, use of high voltage distribution systems (single phase), systematic planning during the addition of sub-stations and lines, and partly through better management to avoid pilferage. All these are well within the capabilities of Indian industries and laboratories. But there is no sense of urgency in the execution of the projects. If the T&D losses are cut down to the world level, almost about 70 per cent of the peak power deficit will be wiped out and there will be no average power shortage which is estimated to be about 10 per cent. The economic advantage is obvious: the cost of establishment of a 10000 MW power generation unit could easily be Rs. 60000 crores.

There has been an overemphasis on generation relative to transmission and distribution. As a result of this, T&D losses continue to be high. Even if new capacities are added, they will reach the consumer with a 10 to 15 per cent cut over what is acceptable internationally. What a way to waste a capital intensive and precious resource! There is also a real danger that plants put up with great difficulty and expected to go on stream in the next few years, will not be able to operate optimally due to absence or inadequacy of these T&D evacuation systems. Here again the resource scarcity of the State Electricity Boards figures in deterring immediate investments for the renovation of T&D systems. There is an urgent need to enact laws to enable private sector entrepreneurs to enter the T&D business.

On the power generation side we need to step up the contribution of nuclear power generation as well. The pollution generated is minimum compared to that from thermal power generation. According to the DAE's projection, 20000 MW will be added by 2020. Our view is that this projection should be doubled in view of the urgency and magnitude of our power needs.

In the vision for the electric power sector, we are thus

dominated by much needed short-term measures which relate to immediate capacity additions and increased power availability. The crucial ones are:

- Setting up many small projects in the range of 25 to 100 MW.
- Refurbishment of the existing power plants. These will be on the lines done by the NTPC for the Unchahar station.
- Attention to all the T&D systems on the lines discussed above.

In the medium and long term:

- Our hydro-power capacities are not fully utilized. The country should augment its hydro-generation capability as it is crucial in the long run.
- Several cleaner energy generation technologies like the Integrated Gas Combined Cycle (IGCC) are necessary. These need to be specially designed to match Indian coal with high ash. We should learn to use our abundant supplies of coal by suitably treating them rather than resorting to import of coal or fuel from outside. Even the USA has set itself a target of energy security with least dependence on foreign sources of supply.
- Nuclear power, including that with fast breeder technology, is crucial in India's search for energy sources.
- To further enhance the carrying capacity of the transmission lines, microprocessor-based compensation systems are envisaged.
- New sub-stations where land is scarce, a situation which is likely to increase with growing urbanization. Design and manufacturing capabilities for constructing gas insulated sub-stations are required to be developed in the country.

New sources of electricity

Our vision for the electric power sector will not be complete without a major emphasis on the new sources of energies which are clean and renewable. The principal forms of these are: biomass, wind, solar, and small hydros. India's wind potential is estimated at 20000 MW. See table 11.1 for other potentials.

TABLE 11.1

Estimated Potential for Various Renewable Energy Technologies

Sources/system	Approximate potential
Biogas plants (in millions)	12
Improved woodstoves (in millions)	120
Biogas (MW)	17000
Solar energy (MW/km^2)	20
Wind energy (MW)	20000
Small hydro power (MW)	10000
Ocean energy (MW)	50000

Source: TERI Energy Data Directory and Year Book 1997–98

Renewable energy sources should be seen not merely in terms of units of power but as saviours for areas which might not have had access to power. If this location specific approach is used and such systems are chosen to provide people with power, a tremendous economic and social role change will be brought about by these energy sources. The technology vision for such a service is therefore a right mix of these technologies along with other conventional sources like batteries, diesel or kerosene engines.

In the much longer term, fuel cells, organic energy sources, hydrogen energy fission power and fusion power would play an important role and Indian researchers have immense opportunities to create new systems.

Energy efficiency

In the short, medium and long term, efficiency in the use of energy will be a crucial part of the technological milieu of all sectors. For example, the waste heat from steel plants today is rejected at relatively high absolute temperature levels (sometimes ranging from 800° C to 1500° C). If, say, 20 per cent of this energy is recovered in the form of waste heat, this could be used to fuel a medium-sized power plant. In every walk of life, including our homes, there can be many examples of energy conservation. For example, if a milk vessel is taken from the refrigerator and kept outside at room temperature for some time before being put on the stove, the additional energy required for heating a cold vessel will be reduced. More important, many of the electric gadgets we see in our homes and factories are not designed for efficient use of power. Most of our fans, for example, consume about twice the electric power they need to run at a particular speed. Many incremental technological inductions in such systems will mean more power being available for others to consume. The agricultural sector is also an area where such energy conservation would need to be addressed immediately. Even if power is given free or at subsidized rates for agricultural operations, it is desirable to utilize minimum energy for the same task through the use of energy-efficient electric pumps. In the long run the aim should be to avoid excessive subsidies because the nation and the people have to realize that electric power is the lifeline of the country's economy.

Other issues

There are a number of complex political and legal issues which are required to be solved to ensure the vision of quality power for all. Private sector participation could also lead to competition in servicing the users. There are also possibilities of transborder flows of electricity as a regular business. Technologies are well within reach to make India a power-rich country which is able to provide quality power for all at affordable prices. But the nation and several stake-holders have to evolve the priorities in infrastructure technology and break the nexus of vested interests and inertia, often built up by the stakeholders themselves. We believe that the country can accomplish this vision for electric power, when it wills itself into becoming a developed nation.

The waters

Rivers have great mythic significance for us. However we have not treated our water resources with the care they deserve. The need for water for agriculture, industry and personal consumption is understood by all, especially when big cities and rural areas reel under water shortages in the summer. The pollution of our rivers and water bodies is also reflected in the health problems that occur in many parts of the country. Urgent attention is needed to overcome these problems in the coming years. Recycling of water and water conservation will be a critical component of our daily lives in the coming millennium.

We would like to share with the readers another aspect of water: water as a transport medium. Waterways are one of the most energy-efficient forms of transport. Road transport services and railways occupy a prominent place in our transport system accounting for 53.3 per cent and 31.7 per cent respectively of the total GDP of the entire transport sector in 1992–93. On the other hand, water transport has a share of only 6.5 per cent. The GDP in the road transport sector has been growing at an annual rate of 8.8 per cent between 1980–81 and 1992–93 as compared to the growth rate of just 3 per cent in water transport.

There are several factors which explain the diminishing importance of waterways. The main disadvantage of waterways is that they can transport goods only on fixed and limited routes unlike the road and railway systems which have the capacity to provide services between a large number of points to suit the requirements of the users. Secondly, there has been a rapid expansion of the railway and road networks during the past four decades, while waterways have remained almost neglected. Public sector investment in inland waterways transport (IWT) has been very small in comparison to the investment on other modes of transport. It was only in the Seventh Plan that some attention was paid to the development of waterways and water transport. The use of IWT is confined only to certain areas like the Mandovi river in Goa, Ganga in the eastern regions, the canals and backwaters of Kerala, Karnataka, Maharashtra and Andhra Pradesh.

The spatial limitation of waterways cannot, however, be considered a major constraint in the development of water transport as 61 per cent of the extent of navigable waterways remains unutilized. Attention, therefore, needs to be focussed on how best the current navigable water system of 14544 km can be utilized to develop an efficient transport system. It is imperative to identify and remove the physical and infrastructural constraints. Some of the major constraints are given below:

- Navigational hazards due to bank erosion, siltation and deterioration of channels
- Shallow water and narrow width of rivers
- Lack of adequate navigational aids
- Inadequacy of horizontal and vertical clearance, inadequacy of hydraulic structure (locks), and old vessels; and
- Loss in the cost of advantage of IWT when the place of origin and destination is not located on the river bank.

An analysis of the current status of the two major waterways in the country, viz. the Ganga–Bhagirathi–Hooghly (GBH) river system and the Brahmaputra river reveals that presently mostly bulky and non-perishable commodities are being transported on these two river systems. There is, however, a great potential for increasing the volume of traffic on them. But this potential can be exploited only through development of an integrated network of rail, road and IWT. This would also require the establishment of efficient mechanical cargo-handling facilities at various points of the multimodal transport network. Although some waterways in the country have been classified as national waterways, there is a need to modernize these by making appropriate use of available technology, such as position location and communication systems, so that they become 'smart waterways'.

Smart waterways should have sufficient navigable depth and width so that larger vessels with higher draft may be able to navigate them. The condition of the waterways should permit navigation throughout the year. They should have smooth bends and minimum siltation, with sufficient vertical clearance so that the vessel's movement is not hindered. Vessels should be able to navigate at least eighteen hours per day on the waterways. Efficient loading and unloading facilities should be available at several points. The waterways should be adequately lighted and equipped with modern navigational and communication aids.

If we have smart waterways, movement of cargo, be it food materials or cement, even from Punjab to neighbouring Bangladesh, can be done very effectively.

Among other things, the technology imperatives for waterways are:

- Designing terminals to take care of both bulk handling and general handling and storage, introduction of mobile grab cranes and conveyor belt loaders; introduction of lighterage system for transferring cargo as well as containers; construction of floating jetties to provide flexibility in movement and designing appropriate jetties with necessary equipment depending on the nature, weight and volume of the cargo.

- Introduction of modern electronics, satellite communication and information technology applications such as radio communication (short range) from shore to ship and ship to ship; long-range communication using satellite links; navigation using the satellite-based global positioning system (GPS); fleet management using a combination of satellite communication and navigation systems; electronic charts for convenient positioning of vessels during their transit; use of satellite systems for emergency situations and on-board equipment like low-cost navigation radars, echo sounders and VHF communication receivers.

Thus modern electronic technologies can impart new vigour to an ancient transport system and also save considerable energy in the process.

The oceans

We can extend the idea of river navigation to coastal waterways. Very few countries are blessed with oceans on three sides and a set of islands on two of them. For tourism or for trade, these provide excellent infrastructure in themselves. India has eleven major ports and 139 operable minor ports. The major ports are the responsibility of the Central government and the minor ports that of the state governments. The eleven major ports are: Kandla, Mumbai, Jawaharlal Nehru Port, Mumbai, Marmagao, New Mangalore, Kochi, Tuticorin, Chennai, Visakhapatnam, Paradip and Calcutta. Marked on a map, they form a beautiful garland. These ports account for 95 per cent of the total traffic handled. The annual traffic during 1996–97 was around 225 million tonnes; it is projected that it will be about 390 million tonnes by 2000–01 and 650 million tonnes by 2005–06. The growth of traffic at Indian ports has been on the upswing over the last few years. However, productivity in terms of the Average Ship Turn Around (ASTA) and the Average Ship Berth Output (ASBO) need to be improved to reach international standards. Considerable privatization is taking place at a number of minor ports. We believe that Indian ports should aim at much more. India can easily be an excellent destination for handling major international traffic. Our oceans and islands can also, if tapped effectively, be a rich source of a number of products of high economic value.

Networking the rivers

In addition there is a much greater need for networking rivers. They would not only provide new water routes but also help distribute water from areas of excess to those that are deficient. We know that there are emotional and political issues involved. But we believe that as a nation marching towards developed country status, we should also learn how to share largesse and resources amongst ourselves and evolve an efficient water management policy. What we now have to aim at is creating more wealth and prosperity to share, and not reduce ourselves to petty squabbling over distributing poverty and cornering a few privileges.

The IT mission

So far we have discussed the conventional forms of infrastructure. In terms of modern infrastructure, telecommunications is crucial to any competitive economy. With the emergence of digital technology (which includes computers) data transmission has pervaded all aspects of life, under the name information technology (IT). We have seen how a whole range of service sectors have been opened up through IT. There are good possibilities for India to emerge as an IT superpower, with a large share of world business and also by being the originator of many new IT and software systems in the world.

For the past few years several committees and fora have addressed the issues relating to India becoming a major IT and software player in the world. India has become a destination for many of the world's software companies. Indian experts are being 'job-shopped' for by many companies. Indian software exports are growing by percentages of almost tens per year. The potential is far more. The Prime Minister's Office has recently set up a National Task Force to address the issues involved and speed up the process of expansion of the IT sector in India.

This means action on several fronts. The setting up of the backbone fibre optic networks has to be speeded up. The exclusive communication infrastructure available with many government agencies such as railways, oil, and the Oil and Natural Gas Commission (ONGC) has to be deployed as a data transport medium. The private sector has to be encouraged and enabled to enter such activities. Also, innovative systems have to be allowed to bridge the 'last-mile problems' of reaching the network to the actual user. All these would mean removal of various existing monopolies and allowing the Indian entrepreneurial spirit to flourish.

In addition, steps have to be taken by the government to remove several irritating procedural bottlenecks to make even single person units of the IT industry come up all over the country. With a right mix of fiscal incentives, computers can be made available to a large number of Indians. In fact as the revolution in telephone facilities has already linked towns and a large number of villages, it is possible to have the STD/ISD booths thereby set up equipped with computers to send e-mail and receive data. Such activities can be run on a commercial basis, if government agencies reduce excessive entry fees and tariff rates at least for the next five years. We may soon have a situation where software export companies are located in India's villages!

India's strengths in software and IT are due to its talented youth. Despite many problems, our schools and colleges have prepared them for the new challenges. Many private initiatives have trained them for taking up specific jobs. Many poor families spend several thousands of rupees on their children to equip them for a computer job. Most of them are rewarded.

Development of software and IT technologies is progressing worldwide in a direction suitable to advanced countries: increased automation; much less dependence on manual entries; increasing use of higher end software for design, simulation, analyses and synthesis. Already the share of the developing world in the overall IT and software output or activities is at a low percentage. Our value added share in the IT sector may go down further if we do not address the matter of acquiring core strengths in the design and production of higher end systems. As one learned academic put it, 'We may import a large number of computers or computer components in SKD (Semi-Knocked Down) form along with other IT systems and software. We may spread them across the country. If we calculate the value added benefit to the economy and minus the import value, are we plus or minus? That is the crucial question to answer.'

We believe we simultaneously need rapid expansion and attention to large-scale commercial activities in the higher end value adding IT and software systems. Then alone can India keep the balance between imports and exports in the IT and software sector. In fact, we can create a major and sustained surplus in India's favour in a few years' time. Speed is of the essence since a few late starters over the globe are trying to become IT giants and are working hard.

One of the elements necessary to make India a major IT power is to strengthen IT education in the country. Many engineering and science colleges have to be facilitated to introduce modern IT courses with the private sector and even with foreign funded initiatives. Constraining monopolies have to be removed and we should try new approaches.

The key should be to create a large human resources cadre in all aspects of IT. That is the crucial infrastructure for India to become a major IT power.

In order to realize this vision, telecommunications forms the bedrock. Again, in the not-so-distant past, telephones were considered a luxury. Thanks to Sam Pitroda who brought telecommunications to the national centre stage and launched the C-DoT project, telecommunication access and penetration has grown by leaps and bounds. The policy of opening up telecommunications to the private sector can speed up the process. Unfortunately however, monopolies do not break down easily. We hope the special focus on IT will lead to acceleration of telecommunication networks and extension of better services. A positive feature of the Indian telecommunications network is that the proportion of digital lines in the overall network is close to the world's best.

The telecommunications network is therefore in need of substantial expansion as well as quality improvement. This is crucial if it is to support the wide range of services that are now becoming available. The new services such as those involving multimedia applications will require a much higher capacity than what is provided by conventional copper lines and most switching systems. Ideally then, the country requires a predominantly digital network of sufficient bandwidth to facilitate voice applications, data applications and multimedia applications in rural or urban settings, at the workplace or at home, and even in remote, hilly or isolated areas or in the islands, ensuring affordability, ease of use, mobility and confidentiality.

For these services to be available to the maximum number of subscribers it is necessary to increase the number of lines, increase the proportion of digital lines, use digital switching technologies, increase the capacity of the access and transmission network, and improve the quality of Customer Premises Equipment (CPE).

India could, by 2015, have a network which could be totally digital; provide full coverage within the country; provide mobile services based on the Personal Communication System; provide personal communications services including global mobile communication services by satellite; and provide end-to-end high bandwidth capability at commercial centres.

We could witness the following in the Indian access network by the year 2000: the beginnings of fibre to the kerb and fibre to the building; the beginning of large-scale deployment of HDSL13 technologies on existing copper lines; the beginnings of voice and data communications on the cable network.

It is expected that by the year 2015 the access network would be able to support full mobility access throughout the network, the provision of personal phone numbers and that optical fibres would reach the subscriber's home.

A very wide range of CPE should be available and in use in the country. Specifically, we are likely to witness the widespread use of broadband CPE for applications running on the Integrated Services Digital Network (ISDN) and the beginnings of computer-telephony integration. We can expect routine use of multimedia terminals by 2015 providing video telephony and video-conferencing applications on demand.

Services and applications are expected to expand from voice, video-conferencing and high bandwidth data applications in 2000 to extensive high bandwidth services available in the bigger cities at least, and several serious applications in education, health and entertainment will be available. The overall vision includes continual efforts to spread services to a large number of rural areas. That would call for innovative systems and flexibility in policies.

Rural connectivity

Over a period, a number of modern scientific and technological achievements have helped the rural areas as well. They have also affected rural life-styles, sometimes irreversibly. Modern fertilizer and agro-chemicals based high yield agriculture, health services, electricity, radio, television, bus services, agro machinery and plastic footwear are a few examples. However, there has been an asymmetry between the rural and urban areas. Since urban areas are centres of industrial and business activities and also seats of political power, many facilities for better life are first established there. The economies of scale would also be cited as being influential in people taking such a decisions. Wealth begets wealth. Higher economic activity begets more economic activities and therefore more employment.

Therefore, migration from rural areas begins. Many underemployed persons move to the other cities in search of a better life. Per se this is not bad. But on the other hand attention given to modern facilities in the rural areas is poor. A good doctor would not like to stay in a village, nor would a good teacher. The asymmetry that is thus created takes a toll on the cities as well. Most cities are becoming unlivable as about 50 per cent of their inhabitants live in slums or near-slum conditions, or live so far away that they tire themselves in commuting. A number of studies have shown that beyond a size, it becomes much costlier to provide services to the increasing population in a city than to establish a new city!

The new cities need not be brand new. Let us look at the nature of modern industries and the emerging scenario. The mass production of yesteryears is only confined to a few areas. It is possible to have a number of decentralized industries which maintain world-class levels and become part of a globally competitive industry. Electricity can be supplied anywhere. The vital modern telecommunication and IT infrastructure have made global connectivity instantaneous.

Therefore it is possible to connect clusters of villages through a nearly annular ring of roads, with traffic designed in such a way that movement from one village to another can be quick and convenient. This helps in many ways. Many agro industries, services industries and even high tech concerns, can be relocated in such villages by moving a few government offices and providing special concessions for industries. Once the process starts, economic activities will take care of the rest. These clusters have to be managed in an imaginative fashion, involving local people, panchayats, business persons and the intelligentsia which will move in. The vision includes the building of many such clusters all over India. Some states have already shown interest in developing a few clusters.

Indian technology and foreign claimants

One aspect which is interesting is how, whenever India achieves something that is commendable, the developed nations tend to trace it to some knowhow, equipment or manpower that was provided by the west. For instance, in July 1980, when we launched our first satellite launch vehicle and put the Rohini satellite into orbit, India became one of four nations to have a satellite launch facility. But within a week, a news item originated from the USA saying that I had had a few months' training at NASA and that is where I picked up the technology that was used for the launch. This was supported by the rest of the western press. In Germany they claimed that the wind tunnel test was carried out in their facility, and so they had indirectly enabled the launch.

When we heard the news about the reactions of the western scientists, technologists and the press, the general response of my team of scientists and technologists at Vikram Sarabhai Space Centre (VSSC), Trivandrum was one of great amusement. We knew that thousands of scientists, engineers and staff had worked on the project from the drawing board to the development stage and right through till the launch. The technology was completely indigenous. The SLV used proportional control for its first stage control systems with a sharing logic software. This was a first in the world. Similarly, we had made other innovations in comparison to any launch vehicle at that point of time. As for the Scout, the American satellite launch vehicle from which our technology was alleged to be lifted, only the fifth launch of the Scout had proved successful. In comparison, our second, third and fourth launches were all successful. This is a pointer to the technological strength of our nation.

Again, when I was involved in the Guided Missile Programme and we successfully launched the Prithvi missile several times, the western press including some of our own analysts insisted that we were using a Russian technology. In fact, Prithvi had a distinctive design, using a particular gyro system with a uniquely configured software, which nobody in the world had tried; when the flight is in progress, the drift can be monitored through the on-board computer. It had other innovations too: the type of thrust termination is so innovatively configured that for a multiple payload, multiple ranges can be achieved. Today, Prithvi is comparable to any world class missile system, and probably is the best of its class in payload capability.

Let us come now to a third, very important milestone, namely Agni. We launched Agni in 1989 and it was successful. We have so far done three launches. Surprisingly, again, there were two claimants who wanted to take credit for the success. Germany said that their guided system which was used for scientific experiments in India had gone into the making of

Agni. And the USA claimed again that my NASA training was responsible for Agni. Actually, in Agni, there were innovations made in the guidance technology. We can manoeuvre the payload and the complete re-entry hypersonic flow was simulated in the Computational Fluid Dynamics in one of the best computers that we ourselves had designed. The re-entry structure, in fact, has used a specially designed material to withstand the 3500° C heat generated upon re-entering the atmosphere. It is really amusing that the Americans think that it is only with their technology that India can succeed.

Recently two departments, the Department of Atomic Energy and the DRDO, working in an excellent partnership, tested several nuclear devices in Pokhran. Three tests were carried out simultaneously; there were two more tests subsequently. We had excellent results, well reported universally by nearly 125 seismic stations. This indicates that India has reached the stage of nuclear weaponization. We were extremely happy with our achievement. But the next day we found the western press alleging that Israeli technology had gone into the triggering system of the nuclear device. There was also the familiar accusation that the scientists and technicians who had visited the USA had helped India achieve this breakthrough. This was puzzling because nobody in the world has used the type of triggering mechanism we have developed. Multiple innovations have gone into the nuclear technology and nuclear device testing area.

In all four of these cases, I was fortunate to be continuously involved directly or indirectly in various teams of ISRO, DAE and DRDO. I find myself asking why in spite of innovative and excellent design capabilities in India, an impression is created by the west that no one other than the developed nations can achieve such technological excellence. Just as there has been a racial element in human history, it would appear that this element is entering into the technological arena too. Developed nations feel that only they are capable of developing certain types of aerospace, missile and nuclear technology. But we should ignore this and go ahead with our technology development.

Chapter 12

Realizing the Vision

I have learnt to use the word 'impossible' with the greatest caution.

—Wernher Von Braum

A very high-level committee, working on a matter of vital importance for India, once called a press conference to share their forthcoming recommendations with media persons. A young reporter got up and asked, 'We have seen or heard of many such reports. When will action be taken on them?' The chairman of the committee gave an evasive reply. Then a member of the committee intervened, 'We generate many reports. There are many reporters like you to report the news. Reports and reporters—do we need action!'

Somehow over the years, we have developed a habit of giving low priority to actual action on the ground. Often people are keen on getting huge publicity in the newspapers or the electronic media, while announcing their programmes or policies. Public memory is short. Nobody bothers to ask whether something is being done to implement them even after a year! Still, there are a number of persons who do keep pushing against heavy odds to do something concrete. Because of them, despite our missing out on a large number of big opportunities, there is some progress in our country. We would like to see that in the coming years actual achievements should far exceed what we have been able to convey in this book or what are contained in the TIFAC Technology Vision 2020 reports.

Can the country be geared up for action to realize the new

vision for India 2020? We believe that it can. People may ask why we think there will be action now, when earlier there was a relative slack. The answer, we believe, lies in appreciating that a large part of our population is young and raring for change. The missed opportunities are history for them. Besides, even those who had earlier worked for 'blocking' some initiatives would like to see an 'opening up'. The earlier systems whereby all initiatives were left to a few departments in New Delhi has fast undergone a change. The licence-permit-quota raj has been substantially dismantled. This has unleashed a large amount of entrepreneurial talent and adventurous spirit in India. Many youngsters are prepared to explore new avenues of work and employment and not wait for a secure job in government. The explosive growth in television, thanks primarily to satellite communications, exposes people to the realities existing elsewhere, the world over. 'Why not in India?' is a natural question that arises in the minds of the viewers. While some, of course, become pessimistic and aver that India can't improve because of the pervasive corruption, mindless bureaucracy and greedy politicians, there are also others who want to try and make things better because the post-liberalization economy gives them an opportunity. Many of them have tasted the benefits of economic growth and the resultant affluence and this has served to trigger their imagination. There is also substantial political devolution of power to the states. The seventy-fourth constitutional amendment which empowers the panchayats adds another dimension to political and economic liberalization. We look at these as opportunities for enabling a large number of initiatives all around the country.

We believe that a spate of actions would follow along the lines which will be described here.

A restatement of the vision

Let us have a brief overview of the vision which we envisage for our people.

- India should become a developed nation by 2020.
- A developed India means, that India will be one of the five biggest economic powers, having self-reliance in

national security. Above all, the nation will have a standing in world economic and political fora.

- To achieve this status, several steps are to be taken in agriculture such as making eastern India a wheat granary and increasing the use of hybrid rice, as also for improving the quality and yield of various crops, vegetables and other products. Environmental considerations in agriculture gain attention.

- Capitalize on the agricultural core strengths to establish a major value-adding agro-food industry based on cereals, milk, fruits, and vegetables, to generate domestic wealth. Also, make India a major exporter of value-added agro-food products. Agro-food industry and distribution systems should absorb a number of persons rendered surplus from increasingly productive and efficient agriculture.

- A number of engineering industries and service businesses to grow around the agro-food sector.

- India to capitalize on its vast mineral wealth to emerge as a major techno-industrial global power in various advanced and commercial materials: steel, titanium, aluminium, rare earths, etc.

- Indian chemical industry to be transformed into a global technological innovator in clean processes and speciality chemicals, and new drugs and pharmaceuticals; a major business should be created in natural products. Vast biodiversity should be transformed into wealth of people and the nation through selective technological interventions; Indian marine resources are to be transformed into economic strength.

- There is to be a resurgence of Indian engineering industry: machine tools, textiles, foundry, electrical machinery, and transport-equipment. India is to become a net exporter of technology by 2010 in these areas and an important world leader in embodied software for manufacturing and design; also a key contributor to the field of flexible manufacturing and intelligent manufacturing.

- India should emerge as a global leader in the services sector with its vast and skilled human resources base being its core strength. The services will range from the simple to the most sophisticated ones using the emerging digital and communication revolution. The services sector is not only to be a money-spinner but will also employ a good proportion of our people, often in self-employment, with abilities ranging from simple skills to super skills.

- While India needs to pay most attention to economic areas and employment generation, both crucial to making her a developed country, attention should also be to the strategic sectors. The confluence of civilian and defence technologies is leading to a situation where most new technologies are basically 'dual use' in nature. A carbon-composite material can go into making a tennis racquet or a FRO-caliper device for polio-affected patients and also for a missile system. A computer can do simulations for a civilian product, for rapid prototyping or the suitability of market conditions for a future product; it can also simulate performance of a fighter aircraft or weapon performance. These 'dual technologies' are closely guarded by the developed countries under the premise of non-proliferation of nuclear weapons or missiles. But they are the basis for their market dominance as well! Therefore countries like India should master technologies relating to space, atomic energy or defence and even many complex machine tools or electronics. These will lead to domestic and foreign business orders for Indian companies even when they are not necessarily for the use of ISRO, DRDO or the Atomic Energy Department. The value additions would be very high. To continue as an economic power, therefore, India has to master the strategic technologies as well, though in the short run they may appear to be high-cost technologies. Fortunately, Indian laboratories and industries have an excellent base in these technologies and have assumed a leading position globally in a number of areas of materials, electronics, propulsion, simulation, among others. India needs to further strengthen these areas with concrete missions focussed on dual use capabilities. That is, to develop a generic technology common to defence while simultaneously developing multiple civilian applications on a commercial scale. Therefore, it is necessary to draw Indian industry, especially the private sector, into these high-tech areas not merely for fabrication but for design, development, production, marketing and post-sale services. India should also emerge as a major exporter of products and services resulting from its capabilities in high-tech areas.

- The health of all our people is vital even while we are pursuing the all-round rapid growth of the economy and technological prowess. People's health leads to better economic and social progress. Many recent technological inventions are making it possible to reach health services to all. Sensors and information technologies in particular, are making it possible for access of specialist attention to even remote areas— popularly called 'telemedicine'. India should attend to short-term rapid action and emerge as a nation with excellent health service cover which would be an example to the world.

- In order to achieve the vision, several crucial actions need to be taken to ensure speedier growth of infrastructure: energy, quality electric power in particular, roads, waterways, airways, telecommunication, ports, etc. Several short-term measures and some unconventional steps need to be taken. The long-term action should be aimed at providing world-class facilities for all parts of India. Rural connectivity is crucial even in the short run if the boom in agriculture and agro-food sector is to be utilized fully. In addition, the progress in information technologies is leading to the possibility of very advanced world-class industries and businesses being established in a village. Highly creative projects in software, information technology, design and other creative work can in fact be better done in a rural environment which has good facilities and good connectivity. The persons who live there should have access to the latest information available globally if they have to be creative and current. Such connectivity can be provided by electronic means even today. Thus, there is a true possibility of many of our well-connected rural areas becoming world-class centres of excellence and also making for a lot of value-added exports or vigorous domestic business, besides giving us food and other products which normally come from rural areas. There are also excellent possibilities that such well-connected rural areas may be host to a number of biotechnology factories which will produce value-added natural products for sale globally. But all these are possible only with an excellent rural connectivity which means good roads, telecommunications and, of course, quality electric power.

- Given the devolution of power to the panchayats, they can also play a major role, with competition as well as cooperation between the village panchayat enhancing performance.

Now, let us look at how this vision can be realized and who all will have to propel it towards fulfilment.

Our actions

Before writing this chapter we had a lot of discussion amongst ourselves about the action to be undertaken. We also had the benefit of discussions with many people, from well-educated housewives to professionals and to social scientists in the fields of history, psychology and economics. We also spoke to a number of 'ordinary' people who are concerned about India, as also with some youngsters and a few politicians. Dr Kalam had the benefit of discussions with number of those who were and are in power. Everywhere there was a genuine interest to act, to break the vicious cycle of pessimism and inaction.

However, a major but unstated problem is how to initiate such action. There were a number of suggestions for others to act upon: somebody should write a report or should convene a meeting or hold a workshop or bring it up before the cabinet or should write to the Prime Minister, a chief minister, or the Planning Commission. On one hand, we were very happy with people's positive attitude and willingness to work for a new vision for India. It appeared that many people would be ready to make some sacrifices. On the other hand, after a lot of thinking, we decided that we should not put forth a general set of programmes for action. Given the present situation in India, we cannot expect an ideal, well-synchronized set of activities. Looking back at India's struggle for the first vision for independence, we do not believe that all actions took place simultaneously. People acted spontaneously, sometimes even clumsily and the freedom movement was launched. We believe that all of us Indians should actually do something. We need to initiate action with an overall vision of developed India particularly on the lines given above. For this, some part of our time and energy too should be devoted to doing a specific task which would be in keeping with this vision.

There is a tendency in our country to advise others. In a way, this is good. However, we believe that those who advise, should also act. Then the advice becomes much more effective. We decided that we should also take action and in the past two years we have been doing this within our limited capabilities. One of our endeavours has been the creation of awareness that India has to become big and strong. And to reach that status, we do not always have to take big steps. There are several small steps which can take the present India to a status of a big India. This is an important message that we have been successful in conveying to people. In addition, the Technology Information, Forecasting and Assessment Council (TIFAC) has formed action teams to formulate concrete projects in most sectors. These will become the exemplars in the short, medium and the long-term. Eminent Indians are participating in these action teams. We have the benefit of being partners in the evolution of many such projects. We are also aware of the number of people who volunteered to lead and be members of such action teams. It is a thrilling experience. In many places we have visited, many fine scientists and specialists are putting science into use, to transform the lot of the poor. Such persons have sacrificed their own comforts to engage in such activity for many years. We call them 'punyatmas' (good souls). We also found that there are many able persons at various levels in the administration who help in this process. We may call them 'punyadhikaris'. We have met and talked to them. We have understood the trials and tribulations they often go through. We also received many good suggestions from them. We are now in search of 'punyanetas'.

Our job is to make this golden triangle of *punyatmas*, *punyadhikaris* and *punyanetas* work countrywide, so that a lot of actions can be initiated and promoted at the grassroots level. These actions in conjunction with the work done by the action teams of TIFAC can encourage a number of demonstrative efforts. In addition, we are also trying to convince many of the agency heads to mount major mission-oriented projects during the Ninth Plan period and we are assisting them in whatever way we are asked to and we can. We are putting in extra effort on weekends, holidays and even beyond office hours to help such a process. We cannot claim that these efforts are meeting with complete success. The slowness of our system makes us feel exasperated sometimes. But there is also a positive feeling because there are some who are ready to move. We are hopeful. In our own way, we will continue to put in our efforts. We would also welcome suggestions from readers on what else we can do in our individual capacity or otherwise.

What industries can do

While individual efforts is crucial, another golden triangle, of industry, government and R&D institutions, really forms the base of a country's development. They set into motion technology-based business activity, employment, demand creation through policies which will help businesses, and as a consequence wealth creation. This golden triangle is crucial in our competing in global markets, as well as in bringing wealth and prosperity to our people.

Having said this, let us see what we include under industries. In India we have several categories of industries. Those which are set up by the Central government are generally called central public sector units (PSUs). The PSUs are technologically and managerially strong. Then there are a large number of small sized state-level Public Sector Units (PSU-S). They fulfil very useful functions but their technological capabilities are not as much as PSUs. There are a number of big private industry groups. Many of them are family-owned and a few of them are also professionally managed public limited companies. Then there are a very large number of small-scale industries, some exceptionally good, some just about surviving, and some which are also sick and which have gone under. There are also a number of multinational companies (MNCs) which operate in India. They are regulated by the Indian laws. All these industries have a definite role to play. In addition to the existing ones, many more will spring up in the coming years. Some of the existing ones may also cease operations or may graduate from one class to another. We consider all of them as partners in the national Indian vision and progress. However, all of them cannot be doing the same kinds of activities. These will vary since their capabilities, their roles and their aspirations will be different. It is with this in view that we suggest a few steps which can be taken by industries in different categories. Also to be taken into account are a large number of tiny units in the informal sector, some of them being almost cottage-industries or even one-person industries.

The PSUs have done this country proud on a number of occasions. We should remember that our country was not manufacturing even simple pins prior to independence. Thus to have major industries to manufacture sophisticated equipment, machine tools, electronic products and defence machinery was a big dream. Central PSUs have purchased technologies from abroad, to a large extent from the erstwhile Soviet Union, and also from a number of other developed countries to put India firmly on the industrial map. Today many sophisticated aircraft are manufactured in our country though they are under licensed production. This capability gives us the confidence that when an Indian-designed Light

Combat Aircraft (LCA) is successfully tested, Indian industry can take up the production. The same is true of radars, submarines, electric power plants, or complicated machine tools. However, in the past two decades there has definitely been a slackening in most of the PSUs, in their technological efficiency, human productivity, raw material consumption, management leadership or export capability. It is difficult to pin-point where the problem lies. Over a period we have got into a vicious circle, not having trusted those who work and contribute. With the emphasis on checks and balances and public accountability, and with the belief that micro-procedures are more important than results, a system has developed where the empowering process is not fully operational. The chairman and managing director of a PSU feels that he gets too many instructions from the ministry; the ministry officials feel that they have got bogged down in various procedures which have been set up to meet various norms of accountability. The politicians in power feel frustrated that the entire procedure has become so unwieldy that they are not able to effect changes even in a full term of five years! There is a definite need to break this vicious circle. Recently, there have been steps to improve public sector efficiency. While welcoming these steps, we believe that these actions are too small for India. We have to make all our industries into ratnas and not just a few. It will require considerable amount of empowerment. We are also aware that the closure of some PSUs will be involved. This can be done by transforming the existing operations or mode of operations, and changing or discarding some of the legal, administrative and financial procedural systems!

The managements of the PSUs and those responsible for labour affairs and many of the labour leaders have to think how they can transform themselves or get rid of their dead wood, or how they can get rid of their weaknesses and utilize their strengths to excel in order to realize a vision. They should be able to make an important contribution even if by means of a partnership with another PSU, another industry, or an industry in the small-scale sector or an R&D lab or MNC.

PSUs: What can they do?

Even while people are working for these overall changes in the PSU system, we suggest that steps to realize the vision should not cease to be taken. A few bold persons should start working towards such changes, and should be strong enough to speak about them. In addition, more important even within the existing constraints, a few like-minded persons should affirm their readiness to take action and formulate a few projects which can contribute in developing the technological core strengths of India. Then, they could work to transform the core strengths of the enterprise into wealth which would indirectly flow to the people. Such a targeted approach would need to he pursued by each of the PSUs. If we map the strengths of the PSUs with respect to a number of items given for the Technology Vision which we have described in the earlier chapters, we would find that there would at least be five projects for each of the PSUs in multiple areas! That means a lot of projects. We would suggest that each PSU takes up at least one major project in one major sector. This is an appeal to the top and middle management as well as to the workers and the ministry officials. If they take a sincere decision amongst themselves, they can find the resources, partly internally and partly from the financial markets.

State-level PSUs

Much of what we have said for the Central PSUs would also be applicable to the state-level PSUs. However, we have to recognize the fact that state-level PSUs are not as strong as the Central-level PSUs in technology, management and financial resources. But they have the advantage of working in close proximity to the people of the state. This is a strength. However, often in the past, many government-supported systems have not learnt to find out and to listen to the problems of the users and beneficiaries. Elaborate rules and procedures and guidelines are drawn up in closed office rooms. Often good ideas are generated but they do not relate to the realities on the ground. Thus, most contact programmes have become routine exercises. In some sense, the newer ideas of 'responding to market' basically means the need to learn how people are reacting, what people want and what people expect. The state-level PSUs have a very good possibility of fulfilling this role in terms of providing extension services and in introducing newer products of technology generated by themselves or others and also for providing many post-sale services. This means, many of them have to transform their character and pattern of working and network with other national and international actors in order to provide useful economic services in the state, outside the state and even globally. If that is done, the beneficiaries will be many. In addition, it will also provide a number of employment opportunities within the state.

But the state-level PSUs need not confine themselves to merely activities within their region. Some of the state-level PSUs can also aspire to be as competitive globally as the Central PSUs or any other private sector industries. PSUs which can rise to the occasion should aim for this and should not be afraid of the many problems which will come in their way.

We have suggested and requested that the Central PSUs take up at least one project each in crucial sectors. Similarly, in the case of state-level PSUs, it may be good if a cluster of few PSUs takes up one project each in a crucial sector. This will entail working together. The proposals put forth by such PSUs will definitely generate enthusiasm though there could be some cases where they could face discouragement. But they should try. Since state-level PSUs are very large in number, there will be several thousand such projects or tasks.

Big and medium-size industries

Certain private industries have played an important role in India's industrialization even before independence. Despite constraints posed by the planned and regulated nature of the economy, our private sector has expanded in almost all sectors. Like the public sector, it also depended on import of technologies, though many companies have subsequently been successful in increasing the local content as well as in marginal innovations. Some private sector industries have taken strides in technological development and have capabilities which are comparable to those of international levels. By and large, by the very nature of the private sector, there is a good deal of flexibility in their operations and they also have good management systems. Some of the private sector industries have also instituted good training programmes to upgrade their personnel.

In recent times, after the liberalization in 1991, the private sector started playing an increasingly major role in the Indian economy. The contribution of this sector has been recognized not only in the consumer sector, but also in infrastructure and strategic industries. In the coming years it has a most crucial role if India is to realize the vision. Since it does not have the number of procedural and institutional constraints of the PSUs, which we hope will be removed in a few years' time, we feel that the medium and big-size private sector industries should each own one major project in a sector to realize a vision for India. It could be in agricultural, it could be in agro-food processing, health, materials or chemicals or natural products or any other area which they think will make for a strong Indian presence globally. Since licensing has been dispensed with in most of these areas, they have the freedom to choose. We are aware of several other constraints in the system in terms of land acquisition or environment clearance or other clearances which do take time. Let this not deter them, especially for vision projects. Let them have within their own management system a fast clearance track for those projects connected with what they think will make India a developed country. They need not even be constrained by what we say in this book or any other books or reports.

While we would like to see lot of technological development taking place in India, we would even be happy if they can get a jump-start on vision-related projects with technologies either from Indian labs or in certain cases with foreign collaboration. But they should bear one thing in mind: making a beginning with imported technology, they should not be satisfied and stop there. Nor should they be satisfied with marginal technological changes which can limit profits. Their goal should be to have a global presence and also to operate on such a scale that a large number of Indians would be benefitted and gain employment. If each of the top and medium-sized industrialists makes this decision, that they will implement this irrespective of what others do, we are sure they will be doing India and Indian people a great service. It is not a service without profits. They will have a lot of future business and good profits even in the short term.

Therefore, we would appeal to the big and medium-sizes industries to mount at least one project each on their own, specially to realize the vision, in addition to their business operations and expansion plans. Some may say that it may just be a different title for an old project. Granted there may be a few such cases. But the fact that a private industry address a Vision 2020 project and gives it a special status, will give a signal for many others. For any project or programme to succeed, the minimum requirements are infrastructure development such as electric power, communication and transportation. Industries, particularly in the private sector, individual or consortium mode should enter into a mission mode, combining it with a business code. Similarly, the service sector offers great business opportunity.

Small industries

Small industries (SI) contribute more than 40 per cent of Indian industrial output. As much as 30 per cent of engineering products exports come from SI. This sector is a large source of employment for our people. Nearly eighteen million people get direct employment. SI's have helped a great deal in import substitution, often themselves working at a very low margins of profit. However, a large number of them are not technologically strong. This situation by and large has been due to the policies of the past which did not create a climate in which technological innovations were rewarded. Having said this, we cannot leave most of these small industries to market forces alone with a philosophy of let them perish or survive. One does not plead for protecting the inefficient, but it is our duty to enable them to be efficient because in the past we have not provided a policy framework to support efficiency. So generally most people adopted soft options. Now we don't have the time to follow such options. We would therefore suggest that most of these industries themselves start trying out what else can be done. Fortunately, there are several schemes by governmental agencies as well as industry associations to help the small-scale sector for enhancing its technology and management capabilities.

One of them is the formation of and progress made in the Technology Development Board. In addition, let these SI's learn to contact nearby academic institutions or a laboratory. Let them knock at their doors and ask them for help or cooperation. A few of the labs or institutions will refuse, a few will charge exorbitantly, a few will say no, and a few will talk positively but may give a delayed response. But let this not discourage them. If they keep trying, there will be definitely some response: some state governments have already started Technology Promotion Centres.

Of course, a number of small industries have to learn how to change their method of functioning. They may have to change their product lines. Those who are very sick may have to think of closing down and take up a new line of activity. Let each person from the small-scale sector industry, let the owner or entrepreneur decide that he or she has to have a vision for his or her company to excel, to contribute to change and if necessary to innovate and to grow stronger. Even if 10 per cent of them succeed in the beginning that itself will be a large change. In the meanwhile, we believe that the movement starting with various individual actions will pick up momentum, giving a special boost for the other 90 per cent to follow. In addition, we would like to appeal to the youth to try to get into newer enterprises. Information technology and software have been given a thrust in this country. There is likelihood of easier procedures and better enabling environment, and easier availability of venture capital or bank loans. Many young entrepreneurs can enter these areas. Once they make a profit, they can also enter other areas of business. A new class of small enterprises would need to emerge in India.

We would like to emphasize that high-tech activity does not mean that it has to be 'jazzy'. There are many things done within India which are very good and useful. Often one is not aware of them. In addition to developing strengths and starting new things we should also explore what we have and make that knowledge accessible to as many persons as possible. The initiative to tell others about what we have accomplished should come from the industries themselves. Let us look at examples cited by Dr G. Venkataraman, vice-chancellor, Sri Sathya Sai Institute of Higher Learning. He was the key person and the architect of the DRDO effort to beat the technology control regime which disallowed sale of supercomputers to DRDO. We have now Anurag which provides a hardware platform for solving defence problems. In a letter to Y.S. Rajan he says, 'One problem I have faced as a scientist is the lack of information about what is available where. For example, aluminized nylon (made mainly for the zari industry and supplied to saree manufacturers), happens to be very useful as a radiation shield in cryogenic systems. We used to use the stuff in Trombay. By sheer chance we discovered a small outfit in Ahmedabad which made the product and were able to procure our needs from that company. Similarly, one often needs electrically-conducting paste. I once stumbled on a company in Bangalore making this product. This again was by sheer chance. Suppose a scientist in Dehra Dun wants this paste. He is not aware that it is made in India. But he knows about a company in Boston which makes the same. So he imports it, when it is really not necessary. I think the time has come for our industry to prepare exhaustive product directories covering all sectors, especially related to the components level. If this information is put on a website and the web availability is widely publicized, it would be of *great* help to many.'

G. Venkataraman implies that there would be thousands of such small industries in India. Let us explore them! Also let them awake to see their own strengths!

Tiny sectors

To a certain extent the pressures of the small-scale sector

would have an effect on the tiny sectors. Also a growing nation would have many changes in consumption patterns and demands. These changes could help some tiny sectors and some may be adversely affected. One cannot leave these tiny sectors to themselves. This is where governmental and social interventions are definitely called for. In this vital area we think the role of non-governmental organizations (NGO), and the governmental support, including through its administration, is very important. Their scope should not be merely to make them survive, but also to enable them to change to newer patterns. This would require marketing of skills. This is a complex task. Government policy has to evolve in this respect. The private sector can also take initiative in adopting tiny sectors nearby and help them to upgrade skills by assuring them of a market for their products. In the coming months and years, we also, in our small way, would like to concentrate on and remove the bottlenecks in some of these areas because the people of this sector need help. We are attempting to do this in a number of places in the country. If they are not taken care of, as India grows, they may relapse into poverty. It is more painful to slip back into poverty after enjoying some benefits of life. It is much more painful than being born poor and living in poverty. The tiny industries sector can be used to take development technology into the rural areas.

MNCs and foreign entities

Our vision of India, in keeping with our great traditions of the past, is not xenophobic. While we emphasize the Indian core strengths and 'made in India' concepts, these are to ensure employment for our people, to create prosperity for them and to ensure the long-term viability of such prosperity. A number of MNCs came to India in the past and contributed significantly to it. Many more are coming in, with a number of them thinking in terms of a long-term relationship. In a way the 'sanctions' being 'imposed' would also help to identify which foreign companies desire a long-term relationship with India! India needs foreign direct investments and foreign technologies without a time lag. In about a decade Indian technological and business strengths will grow tremendously. Indian companies may also emerge as MNCs operating in different parts of the world. They would sell technology-intensive products and services as well as export technologies. Even beyond 2020, India would continue to attract foreign direct investment. A developed and technologically strong country with a one-billion-plus prosperous population would definitely be the *ideal market* for any business person or entrepreneurs. We also feel that many foreign researchers would come in search of projects or partners in India.

The immediate actions for MNCs and foreign entities would be for them to have their mission compatible with India's interests and its core strengths. To create a win-win situation, they should, of their own, initiate projects which will enhance technological capabilities and spread the effects of prosperity. Their large publicity mechanism can also attend to specific Indian concerns. In order to initiate action in this direction, they need to interact with many Indian groups to understand their concerns. We do realize that foreign companies are here to do business, make profit and to create conditions for continued and growing profit. But they can also set apart 10 per cent of their operations for creating conditions in India for it to become a *developed nation* and for its people to be prosperous without continued dependence on others for technology. In turn, market potential will increase. Is it Utopian to think thus? Will somebody strong make somebody not-so-strong, strong enough to be equal? In the long run India is going to become strong! Those who are partners in that venture *now* will definitely stand to gain. We have the above thoughts for MNCs and foreign entities presently in India and who may come in the near future. They have their'think-tanks'. We hope they will capture the message for actions. Sanctions from certain foreign countries are against the concept of global village. Global markets are opening up and those affected should wage a war against this tendency.

Academic and R&D labs

The nation is proud of its scientists and scholars, though, of course, many of them would reply they doubt whether the nation cares for them at all. When asked why many of our best and brightest have gone abroad to make a living, they opine that this is because as a nation we have not cared for the talented and meritorious. There is some truth in what they say. However, by and large, compared to the situation before independence, government assistance has provided a tremendous opportunity for higher education. If today Indian scientists, technologists and scholars in different fields are respected worldwide, it is because of the education system we have built up. Our excellence is evident even within the confines of the limited opportunities which are available for research and development in the universities and the national R&D laboratories. We believe and appeal that scientists, researchers and scholars should shed their pessimism. There are many reasons for being pessimistic and cynical. We are both a part of their community. We know the problems they face, especially the younger ones, and also those who are not in positions of power in these institutions, the so-called middle levels and the lower levels. We appeal to these people to think big, because they are the only ones who understand the forces of technological modernization and the new energies that can be unleashed through technologies. They also have the capability to absorb the knowledge base which is growing at an explosive rate.

There are some studies which indicate that from around the beginning of the new millennium, the knowledge base will be doubling in less than a quarter of a year! We would request the scientists, technologists, scholars, teachers and others to ponder that in a country which is so poor, they have been enabled to have world-class knowledge. Therefore, even within the several constraints they face daily, they should take it up as a challenge to make India a developed country. They will have to spearhead the movement by talking about what can be done, encouraging people that we can overcome the difficulties and offer help to industries, government administrators and others that Indian science can help to smoothen the difficulties arising out of a faster pace of economic development.

Those who are specialists in the humanities should be the

vehicle for communication to the people about the need to have a new vision and the ways of realizing it. We have got tremendous opportunities to do several actions. We do not say that large-scale liberalization and empowerment have to be done in our academic system and national laboratories and wait for it to take place. Even when all of us have to keep pushing for such liberalization and empowerment, we should also push a few projects. There are number of avenues available in the government system including the recently constituted Technology Development Board to promote commercializable technology development. We would sincerely hope that each scientific group picks one project on its own to realize the vision. To show immediate results to our industries and to local administrators, let them not wait for somebody to recognize a project from Delhi or elsewhere. Let these actions be taken. If the scientists feel confident that it will lead to very good results, there will often be success. Once there is a success with good economic and social impact, everyone will claim ownership of the project. Success has many parents!

The government's role

There is a Central government with many ministries and departments, there are many state governments and there are many government agencies. In any modern country, the government has to be present to create enabling environment, to ensure law and order, and to conduct activities of public good. There is rightly a general feeling in the country that there is an overpresence of the government. Also, most government institutions do not grow in actions; they grow in size! They think that they rule and not serve. There are some exceptions too! But the government surely also has many officers, who themselves feel bad about the situation. They feel that there are many constraints which are troubling them. We are addressing some of the individual perceptions in a later section on what we can do. But there is a need to treat the government as a whole. There is a need now to look at the country as a whole. Though, in principle, the government is considered as *one*, in practice, there are many departments and divisions in the departments and there are a number of officers or staff. It is well known that there are turfs. There are also a number of coordination mechanisms, but these are often used as instruments for delaying actions. The government also includes the political system. During the past fifty years India's development has greatly depended on the government. It was the strength of the country and also its weakness. Many initiatives were taken by the government. But the planned and regulated nature of the economy over a period have inhibited others from taking initiative. Therefore, one important role for the government is to shed its presence and to empower various agencies within itself and also to empower private initiatives. The government should also take care of activities of public good like education and health. It should also no doubt create viable mechanisms for bringing up the weaker sections. For all these, it has to enable conditions for faster growth which would mean a lot of private initiatives and even foreign investment. There are also possibilities of raising a large amount of private domestic investment in the country, provided one is bold and, if necessary, unconventional. It is essential for the government to do this. Let us not take a strong moralistic posture. Let the past mistakes be redeemed as we act towards making the country a *developed one, and the only one totally free of poverty.*

In addition, we believe that many departments within the government have talent and capabilities. This is not only true of technocrats, but also of administrators and other staff. We believe that each of the departments should mount a major mission which will consist of number of projects in a particular sector with which they are broadly concerned. If necessary they should work with multiple departments. Often this is more effective. Having worked within the government system for very long, we can also say that if top administrators have the will, and if four or five of them get together, the systems are flexible enough that speedy decisions can be taken. We believe that one of the crucial motive factors in realizing the vision would depend upon how a few government departments take the lead immediately to mount such a vision. We don't have to teach them what such missions are. The blueprints are available in terms of Technology Vision 2020 document. They have the talents to mount such missions. They can generate more documents, as necessary, but the actions are neded. These need to be done efficiently and the results should be visible immediately. These should be the criteria. The reason for immediately visible results is to generate the confidence in people that we can do it. Then the movement will start after which people would be ready to wait for long-term results. Otherwise, a pervasive cynicism, now evident in the system, will continue.

Non-Governmental Organizations (NGOs)

Under the category of NGOs come many important academic, educational and R&D organizations created under private auspicies. There are social service organizations. There are activist groups that fight for certain type of rights in many areas. There are religious bodies which serve their communities; there are some which serve all communities. Some NGOs target particular activities: bringing vision to the blind, for example. Many have contributed excellently primarily to higher education; the mission schools and colleges, particularly in the rural and coastal areas for example. Some work with tribes. Some have a particular environmental concern. Some NGOs are large; some are tiny, one-person operations; others are registered and have 'government recognition' for tax benefits, etc. Still others shun any organized institutional framework.

If we look at all of them, we can capture the spirit, the energy and the very texture of a resurgent India. We see some individuals working in them radiating a calmness and a grace which borders on a spiritual message. There are also many dedicated individuals, some of them great intellectuals, reflecting upon out the problems of the system. We have seen a number of persons who have sacrificed brilliant careers to carry on the struggle. When you still see the pain in their faces after two decades of their struggles, tears come to your eyes. We have had a number of such experiences. We are putting forth the concept of *punyathmas* for rural transformation.

Despite the multifarious approaches, the NGOs collectively represent a large part of India. We believe NGOs have an immense role to play, not merely as conscience-keepers but also in creating a mood to think ahead and create a climate for a developed India. They can become powerful messengers of hope and a positive synergistic mechanism between the organized sectors and individual initiatives — in metropolises, cities, towns and villages; in schools, colleges and universities; in fields, factories and markets.

NGOs have many creative people full of energy. This team can participate in the movement for a developed India, concentrating on action projects to spread health and educational services as well as to create a climate to make all Indians think as one.

What *we* can do

We have illustrated earlier a few large segments of institutions whose actions are vital. We have suggested how each of them can decide and act, irrespective of what others do. There are also many other important institutions in the financial sector and the services sector. We request all of them to think about our proposition. However, we notice that there is one very important element which is common to all these sectors. That is the people who work in these institutions. They may be top managers or good working staff, highly skilled professionals or those with limited capabilities. There are those who do private contract jobs for others. There are people who function as intermediaries. In addition there are a large number of people who do not contribute directly to production or GDP figures. These are people who work at home without any salary. There are many who do voluntary services. All these persons, the human beings behind all activities, can be clubbed as 'WE'. We try to illustrate in some ways what We can do. This We is so wide that it encompasses most Indians. In a way it can cover foreigners who work in India or are working on an Indian contract!

We know that there are several pressures on a top manager's

time but he can set apart a few hours in a week to think and decide how India can become a developed country. Often as a top manager, he is in a powerful position to do something different within his agency. As a banker, he could take interest in some innovative projects which can have a beneficial impact when they fructify, or one can help out a local administration where there is a good administrator trying to solve people's problems. Take another case: you would have come across youth who are very capable and are enthusiastic about taking up something new. Why not encourage them? You could create some small groups which can discuss possibilities of contributing to a new, emerging India. And act on the conclusions of such discussions. It may well be that some of you join together, upgrade your skills for creating a new India or give your knowledge to youngsters in your organization. Or you could train people who are less equipped than yourself, maybe in your company or even in your neighbourhood. Devote maybe two days in a month for such efforts as a joint project. When you plant many such saplings, some may die, but many would grow.

If you are a clerk in, say, a government department, you can decide to work slightly more efficiently in clearing a public demand or a new project. If you can be an instrument in creating a feeling that the government (Central, state or municipal) works speedily and justly, you have created necessary conditions for a developed India. Don't think what can one person do. Many drops make a flood. A worker in a factory can decide to increase his or her productivity a little more and give attention to quality. The Japanese have an organized system to obtain and act upon the suggestions at the grass roots level. We don't have such a system. You can be the initiator of such an effort. At every level a feeling of contributing concretely towards a developed India is a must. The larger the number of persons who act, the better it is.

My co-author Y.S. Rajan was recently in a meeting to discuss the effects of sanctions. This was before the USA had announced the details. All were Indian and working for foreign banks. One elderly gentleman emphatically said how we all have to learn to be proud of ourselves and take actions to nullify the sanctions. He narrated an episode about his visit to Japan. A leaking tap in his hotel room disturbed his sleep. He complained. Two people came, worked for half an hour and made it right. They showed the performance to him and he was satisfied. Then they apologized deeply for the inconvenience caused to him and informed him of the hotel management's decision not to charge room rent for that night. So far one can perhaps explain this as normal professionalism. But then, with a bow, the two workers showed the tap piece to him and said 'Sir! Please see, the trouble caused to you is not by a Japanese product but an imported. We will continue to do better, Sir!' The message is that most Japanese are proud of their country's capability. They want to excel in their work. If each of us attempts to do so in our spheres of work the status of developed India will arrive sooner than we expect, because our country has many natural core strengths and competitive advantages.

A positive media

The media plays an important role in any modern society in moulding public opinion. It has its own constraints. Like any enterprise, it has to make a profit. The media presents news, views and analyses tailored to suit what the readers would like. It also has to create headlines, look for something shocking, exciting or thrilling. But Pokhran, or an Indian victory in a cricket match, or some other positive event does not occur every day. Generally, the focus is on the negative: a gory event, on worrying developments. Such coverage has gone to a point that a situation much more worse than is actually the case is being presented.

We do not at all believe that the press role is not to criticize and not to highlight problems. There is also at times a need to exaggerate events to make a point. But we feel too that it is time now that the media attempts a more positive outlook, reporting at least one positive event a day! Devote a part of the paper to say something good about India which is real and not false. If the major papers do this, there will be a great attitudinal change in the country. Similarly the electronic media can also help to create a new climate: report one good event a day not just from a metropolis or city but from different parts of the country. Let us discover our heroes and heroines who silently work all over the country.

Rediscovering our gurus

If you are teacher in whatever capacity, you have a very special role to play, because more than anybody else you are shaping generations. There was a time in this country when teachers were respected as gurus. Now, however, the teacher's is often a neglected lot. Many of them work under miserable conditions. We are aware of the need to solve their problems, but even given these, we request that teachers do two things. First, let them think about a developed India in their own ways and enthuse the students. Secondly, they should update their own knowledge because the student is only as good as the teacher. Let them constantly try to upgrade their skills so that they can enthuse the children to think big. Let us not transmit our frustration to them. I attended one parent-teacher association in a school and was asked to talk to younger children about some aspects of technology and how India can be transformed. I said, 'Well I would not like to give any special message to young children because they themselves are born with the message. They are fresh. I would therefore appeal to the parents and teachers not to pollute their fresh minds with our own frustrations. If we can instead convey to them a message about a bright future and encourage them, that will be a great service we will be doing to them and also to the country.' It is the message we would like to give our readers as well.

Political system and the Parliament

Lastly our appeal for actions will not end without an appeal to the political system and especially to legislative assemblies and the Parliament. In fact all the panchayats also come under this

73rd amendment, the ruling party, the opposition party and also all the political activists have got a great role to play. Technologies are changing at a rapid pace across the world. They are changing the lives of people. We have tried to give a glimpse of this in earlier chapters. India is fortunate to be blessed with many resources of biodiversity, material resources and above all human resources. We have also got a technology and industry base. However, it is not enough to say that we have these and then also say that we have everything, we will take care of ourselves without making too much of an effort. We have to work hard. We have to work together as a country. While the various industries, government agencies, private individuals, R&D labs, the NGOs and media all can contribute, the major source of inspiration and enabling comes from our legislative bodies. Therefore we look forward to a day where our Parliament and the legislative assemblies will proclaim to the nation 'India's second vision is Developed India before 2020'. This vision statement to the nation is essential. It will trigger the birth of a movement for a prosperous India.

One India: Different actions

We have described many actions that are possible. We have not listed out some obvious examples: if you are a doctor you can extend the benefits of free and inexpensive medical aid to the poor at least to a limited extent; if you are a rich building contractor, make it a point to spend on your own or in a cooperative way to improve some parts of a town or contribute to rural connectivity around a few villages; similarly, ex-servicemen can attempt to organize a few productive activities in villages or small towns. Writers of textbooks can make a point of adding a few pages on a developed India and emphasizing that all of us have a role in making it. A great nation is made of contributions from a large number of ordinary persons.

Recently a powerful administrator was talking to us about the applications of technologies and information technology, in particular for the agricultural sector. We were explaining about the need to reach 350 million tonnes of foodgrain production by 2020 and the fact that it cannot be achieved without selective injection of technologies of water management such as drip irrigation, controlled used of fertilizers, micro-nutrients and pesticides and many post-harvest technologies. All these technologies are multi-disciplinary: for example, a drip irrigation system would involve plastics, advanced metals, hydraulic system designs, water treatment technologies, soil analysis systems, computers, sensors and even automatic control systems.

The reaction of the administrator was to narrate a whole series of subsidies to the farmers, the political patronage at village, state and national levels and other issues of law and order. How can you introduce these technologies? The generation and use of technologies for national development has to be initiated politically. But, we believe, it is equally important that technologies have to be marketed to the political system.

This is not typical of the agricultural scene alone. Look at manufacturing. We have discussed at some length the concepts of Computer Aided Manufacturing (CAM) and Flexible Manufacturing Systems (FMS). We have discussed about laser cutting and waterjet cutting as new tools. We have discussed about the ever-increasing role of software and IT in the manufacturing sector. Now look at the village or town artisans; they do not have a lathe or drilling machine. Most small-scale units have obsolete equipment. Even in the corporate sector there are factories using machinery which is two or three generations old. We all know about the Maruti story: while it has done a tremendous job in developing manufacturers of small components within the country, for the key subsystems of the car the company has to rely upon its Japanese parent company. Telco has been relatively successful in building up an in-house design capability, though it may not as yet be at the cutting edge of automobile technology. For many Indian companies, the dependence on external knowhow for design and technology remains very high.

Yes, we have in the agricultural sector visible signs of the oppressive problems of the past — poverty and feudalism. However, even severe critics will agree that there are many bright spots. Similarly, the manufacturing sector exhibits the effects of colonial domination and the uneven policies of the past fifty years. The general Indian method of taking the soft option through imports on the conditions laid out by the principals is evident too. Still, it is showing increasing dynamism.

It is not possible nor relevant to talk of one single set of actions for the whole of India. There are many actions which need to be taken. It is not necessary all of them should be started at the same time with a single trigger shot 'GO!' Or that they conflict with one another.

For example, we need to tackle the problems of small and marginal farmers: even for this, solutions are many. It may not be possible to solve them all at the technological level as the holdings are so small. Therefore experimenting with some organizational mechanisms of working out cooperatives or corporate partnerships will be useful. There are also intermediate solutions of having marginal improvements at the level of small holdings. Even while doing these, India has to prepare for higher technological level actions for realizing the full potential of the land-water-weather system in a sustainable manner. This may be called high-science or high-tech agriculture.

In a similar manner, we need to help a large number of tiny manufacturers and thousands of small-scale units through ancillarization, marketing channels as well as technological inputs. Even while doing so, we need to take action to capture the world markets with high-tech manufacturing. We cannot afford to take our pre-eminence in the manufacturing world of the future for granted.

We were touched by the recent observations by C. Subramanian to a group of industrialists. While discussing newer initiatives in agriculture, he said the Technology Vision 2020 documents contain a rich source of information and action points. We should not wait for general policies to emerge but launch demonstration projects; there is plenty of scope for such local or regional initiatives. CS is the architect of India's food security. He started the actions through specific demonstration projects and thousands of farmers saw the successes. The Green Revolution followed. With his recent observations we are doubly convinced of the approach we are suggesting: that is all of us have a role to play; actions are many; but the goal is one.

Therefore, we find a role for every action aimed at making ONE DEVELOPED INDIA.

Our appeal and request described here is briefly as under:

You (A teacher, banker, doctor, administrator or other professional)	Devote a few days in a month to doing something better; something speedier; something of high quality; something which will make you proud; something which will make a poorer or suffering person's life a little better.
Government ministries/ departments	One mission each to realize the vision of developed India with internal core strength. Preferably in partnership with other departments, agencies, NGOs and private sector. Don't wait to start.
Central PSUs	One project each to make a developed India. Unleash your technological strengths. This is in addition to the mission your ministry may launch and for which you will contribute.
State PSUs	At least in one area transform yourself to service the people in your area. If possible launch one

India 2020

	project with partners on similar lines that goes beyond your region.
R&D labs/Academic institutions	You have the unique opportunity to be the front runner. Each lab or institution to launch such a project of your own, in addition to contributing to missions, PSU projects, etc. You will find financial contributions even around your area.
Private sector (large industry)	Each launch a project to similar what is suggested for PSUs, in addition to its own corporate plans and other demands placed on it by government sponsored missions and projects. Also create projects to uplift our small-scale industries technologically and even agriculture.
Small-scale sector	Even though your problems are many look ahead. Learn to capture a few technological strengths. Catch hold of a nearby academic institution or laboratory. You will find some persons with innovative 'fire' in them. Once you find a knowledge source relevant to your business, you will find that life is being transformed for you.
MNCs	You have a role to play. In addition to your own concerns of profit and your global strategies, look at the one-billion-plus

country with inherent strengths as a partner and not as a short-term market. Demonstrate clearly through one or two projects each that you want to and can create core competitive technological strengths within India, to help its march towards a developed status. A small help at the right time is better than a larger help to a person who does not need it at that time! You have an opportunity to contribute to a momentous task.

NGOs

Your role is as multifarious and as complex as India. Try to help in creating a climate for positive actions and a rapid change for the better

Media

Spread the message of success, however small the successes are. There are many grim events and developments that you have to cover, but the positive can also be news. Build up an image of an India with hundreds and thousands of heroes and heroines who are changing the country's destiny.

Integrated action: Possibilities

In these twelve chapters, we have discussed our vision for a developed India and the possible ways of transforming it into reality in two decades. A number of areas have been covered.

Here, we wish to suggest how each and every Indian, in different walks of life, can contribute towards realizing the vision for the nation.

The authors held discussions with economists, agricultural experts, technologists from different fields, from industry, government administrators at various levels, non-governmental professionals and activists, media persons, and political leaders at different fora. We concluded that concerted efforts in five areas can lead to a major movement towards transformation of the nation. These five areas are marked by strong interlinkages and progress in any one of them will lead to simultaneous action, in other areas as well. The five areas are highlighted below.

Agriculture and food processing: India should have a mission to achieve a production of a minimum of 360 million tons of foodgrains in two decades. This will allow for good domestic consumption and still leave a sufficient margin for food exports and aid to other countries. This mission will demand a great revolution in research, technology development, agricultural extension services, and above all a major network of marketing, storage and distribution.

Electric power: This is the most important part of the infrastructure. Besides assuring people of domestic comfort, it is imperative for increasing food production, and to support a whole host of manufacturing operations, in the engineering and chemical and material processing industries, as well as in the smooth operation of the entire transport, communications and information sector, all of which are vital to economic growth and employment. The growth of a nation's GDP is vitally linked to the availability of electric power. India's installed power capacity today is about 85000 MW. Only about 32000 MW reaches the consumer. There is shortage of about 15 per cent in the peak power requirement. The requirement of electric power will only multiply because of the growth in the demand from various sectors. Immediate action is needed to greatly step-up the generation of electricity from coal, gas, hydro and nuclear sources. Research on other sources of energy also has to be enhanced.

Apart from generation of power, another major mission is to ensure its efficient transmission. The consumer is interested in the actual quality of power that is available, and not in the statistics of the installed capacity of generation. Here the technologies and systems management for countrywide distribution is of crucial importance.

Consumers too have to be careful. Precious power should not be wasted by inefficient equipment, fans, lights or other industrial and domestic appliances or agricultural equipment. Therefore, technologies for energy-efficient end use appliances are of crucial importance to India.

Education and health: In the first chapter we spoke of Kuppu and Karuppan. They are representative of about 60 per cent of India's people. These two have the urge and the willingness to work hard. But because of the lack of education they are unable to utilize the available opportunities for better employment or to improve their standard of living. People like Kuppu and Karuppan have to improve their educational levels. In turn, their children also have to break out of their educational handicap. The lack of educational opportunities and their poor quality of life perpetuates their poverty. Non-availability of preventive health care further weakens their bodies and therefore their capabilities. Can we break this vicious circle?

Prof Indiresan, who led the TIFAC panel to identify the driving forces and impedances, has tried to point the way out. Indians should be provided access to first-rate education and skill development opportunities. This cannot be done by the prevalent methods of village schools or other schools and institutes in towns and cities. We need to create clusters of villages with excellent internal connectivity through roads and communications which are also linked to nearby urban centres. These rural clusters would have quality centres of education, and health support facilities. People can easily commute between the villages and acquire the best skills and education. Their access to well-equipped health care centres will be the necessity.

These centres would have the knowledge base to advise them on preventive health care methods. The teachers or medical personnel in these quality centres would also have access to other experts in India and even abroad through communication connectivity. Let us not forget India's excellent achievements in satellite communications. Besides technological expertise, what is required is good political and managerial leadership all over the country to implement this mission. Let not the children and grandchildren of Kuppus and Karuppans be handicapped. We can achieve an India without such handicaps by 2020.

Information technology: In the Technology Vision document, software engineering and associated IT products and services are important core competencies. Fortunately, already a decision has been taken at the national level to make India an information technology superpower in about a decade. When this task force of IT is deliberating its final report, two important items may be considered by them for special action. All of us feel that India has the intellectual power for higher levels of software. High level software provides a challenge for our best minds and at the same time it is a wealth generator. This should be focussed upon as a mission area in IT. If the necessary enabling conditions are provided, this single area can transform our IT, electronics and manufacturing sector into a major economic entity. Another item relates to actions for the spread of IT applications countrywide for purposes ranging from boosting business to spreading knowledge about fundamental rights and responsibilities, to impart skills, to provide preventive health care information and for several such items pertaining to acquiring a better standard of living. It can be a very useful tool for transmission of education to even the remotest parts of our country. India's system of education and skill-generation can be transformed in a decade if we can creatively and purposefully deploy IT technologies.

Strategic sectors: To reach the status of a developed India, in addition to the four mega-missions mentioned before, there is an equally important mission for national security. In today's environment, national security is derived from the technological strength of the nation; that alone will give us the real strength. It is India's experience, be it in agriculture or in the areas of the nuclear, space and defence research, that when visionaries set a mission, results are achieved. This strength is to be further expanded with the creation of a few major industries in aerospace, advanced electronics, advanced sensors and advanced materials. These industries should operate in a market-driven environment winning global markets. For example, India should be in the business of building small passenger jets even with an international consortium. Likewise we should be in the business of selling satellites and providing commercial launch services. Marketing of aerospace systems, providing aircraft sub-systems, maintenance services to global customers, as well as business in products with advanced sensors and advanced materials, should become a part of our normal business. We should also begin aggressive marketing of various defence systems such as main battle tank, guns, LCA type aircraft and certain types of missiles. The thrust towards self-reliance should be coupled with global marketing. Such an approach should become the focus in the strategic sector. In this direction, the Ministry of Defence has a ten-year profile for indigenization of defence systems to achieve 70 per cent indigenous production from the present 30 per cent. To achieve this goal, the defence R&D and production infrastructure is already being geared up and the partnership of Indian corporate sector has been sought to accomplish this major task. Similarly, other departments having technologies pertaining to strategic industries have to open up their technologies to establish major industries which serve the multiple needs of domestic and global markets.

Implementation: Our suggestions for these major missions, do not envisage the present methods of departmental implementation or expanding the governmental structures. In order that India marches towards the cherished goal of a developed nation, there is an urgent need to change the present methods of working and the mindset that has developed because of centralized power. Many existing governmental structures would need to be drastically reduced. There should be reduction of monopolies and a greater competition in the implementation of many packages of these mega-missions. Therefore, private sector participation would be required along with more liberal and simplified procedures. Healthy competition leads to greater efficiency and innovation. Empowerment of implementing teams would lead to speed in action and enhance capability to take risks. Wherever there is a government presence, its mode of operation should be made a facilitating one and the public accountability systems should be changed accordingly.

In conclusion, we believe that the five mega-missions when integrated and implemented with a national focus, will result in actions which will shape the second vision of the nation. The necessary financial, managerial and human resources would flow from those whose minds are ignited, including those in the government and industrial sectors.

We therefore have a dream. Our dream is that both our houses of Parliament would adopt a resolution for the second vision of a great nation: 'India will transform into a developed nation before the year 2020. A billion people are our resource for this national transformation.' This event will inspire the nation.

Afterword

India is a nation of a billion people. A nation's progress depends upon how its people think. It is thoughts which are transformed into actions. India has to think as a nation of a billion people. Let the young minds blossom—full of thoughts, the thoughts of prosperity.

Appendix

List of Chairpersons and Co-chairpersons Technology Vision 2020

Task Forces	Chairperson	Co-chairperson	Member Secretary
Agro-food Processing	Lila Poonawalla New Delhi	C.K. Basu New Delhi	
Waterways	S.M. Dutta New Delhi	V. Raghuraman New Delhi	
Road Transportation	Deepak Banker New Delhi	Dr Amit Mitra New Delhi	
Civil Aviation	Prof R. Narasimha Bangalore	Y.S. Rajan New Delhi	Dr B.R. Somasekhar Bangalore
Electric Power	Shekhar Dutta New Delhi	Tarun Das New Delhi	
Telecommunications	Dr Bhishnu D. Pradhan New Delhi		
Advanced Sensors	Dr B. Bowonder Hyderabad		

Panels	Chairperson	Co-chairperson	Member Secretary
Food & Agriculture	Prof S.K. Sinha New Delhi	R. Ranganathan Guntur	
Engineering Industries	R. Ramakrishnan Chennai	V. Radhakrishnan Chennai	
Health Care	Dr M.S. Valiathan Manipal	Dr M.S. Bamji Hyderabad	
Life Sciences & Biotechno- logy	I.A. Modi Ahmedabad	Prof Asis Dutta New Delhi	
Materials & Processing	R.K. Mahapatra Hyderabad	Dr B.K. Sarkar Calcutta	
Services	P.S. Rama Mohan Rao Hyderabad	Pramod Kale Ahmedabad	
Strategic Industries	Prof U.R. Rao Bangalore		A. Sivathanu Pillai New Delhi
Electronics & Communi- cation	Satish Kaura New Delhi	Dr A.K. Chakravarti New Delhi	
Chemical Process Industries	Lalitha B. Singh New Delhi	K. Dharam Mumbai	
Driving Forces & Impedances	Prof P.V. Indiresan New Delhi	Rajive Kaul Calcutta	

TIFAC Scientists who were closely associated with the co-ordination tasks of the Technology Vision 2020 Exercise

1. Shri Y.S. Rajan, ED-TIFAC
2. Dr (Smt) A. Amudeswari, Former PSO-TIFAC
3. Dr D.N. Singh, Director-TIFAC
4. Shri Deepak Bhatnagar, Director-TIFAC
5. Shri S. Biswas, Director-TIFAC
6. Shri R. Saha, Director-TIFAC
7. Ms Sunita Wadhwa, Sr. Scientific Officer-TIFAC
8. Shri T. Chandrasekhar, Scientific Officer-TIFAC

The TIFAC Governing Council provided the overall guidance.

References and Further Reading

In conceptualizing and writing this book we have drawn upon a large number of articles and books. Some books and articles are specifically referred to in the text itself. The material from the TIFAC Reports 'Technology Vision 2020' has been used in explaining a number of concepts. In addition the material from a large number of talks delivered by Dr Kalam, especially from 1994, has also been used extensively in the book. Only in a few cases specific talks or addresses have been quoted. For convenience of further reading a full list of Technology Vision 2020 reports are given in this reference. The reports featuring as Economic Intelligence Service, Centre for Monitoring Indian Economy have been of immense value in understanding the multi-dimensional nature of Indian economy and society. For those interested in going into more detail, it will be useful to refer to these reports depending on their interest whether it is in agriculture, energy, infrastructure, industry or social or financial sectors. We are also listing a number of reports, books, journals and articles which have helped us in understanding many issues though specific inputs from many of them have not been carried in this book.

I. REPORTS

A. The TIFAC Reports

Advanced Sensors, Technology Vision 2020, TIFAC

Agro Food Processing—Milk, Cereals, Fruits & Vegetables, Technology Vision 2020, TIFAC

Chemical Process Industries, Technology Vision 2020, TIFAC

Civil Aviation, Technology Vision 2020, TIFAC

Driving Forces—Impedances, Technology Vision 2020, TIFAC

Electric Power, Technology Vision 2020, TIFAC

Electronics & Communication, Technology Vision 2020, TIFAC
Engineering Industries, Technology Vision 2020, TIFAC
Food & Agriculture, Technology Vision 2020, TIFAC
Health Care, Technology Vision 2020, TIFAC
Life Sciences & Biotechnology, Technology Vision 2020, TIFAC
Materials & Processing, Technology Vision 2020, TIFAC
Road Transportation, Technology Vision 2020, TIFAC
Services, Technology Vision 2020, TIFAC
Strategic Industries, Technology Vision 2020, TIFAC
Telecommunications, Technology Vision 2020, TIFAC
Waterways, Technology Vision 2020, TIFAC

B. Other Reports

Status Paper on Indian Railways, Some Issues and Options, Govt. of India,
Ministry of Railways (Railway Board), 27th May, 1998

*Emerging Technologies—A Survey of Technical and Economic Opportunities,
Technology Administration, US Department of Commerce,* Spring 1990

Stewards of the Future: The evolving roles of academia, industry and Government,
Report of the President for the academic year 1996-97, HYPERLINK

Mass Media and Marketing Communication: Perspectives into 2020, Dr N.
Bhaskara Rao, Centre for Media Studies, New Delhi

*Future Technology in Japan toward the year 2020: The fifth technology forecast
survey,* The Institute for Future Technology, 2-6-11 Fukagawa Kohtoh-ku,,
Tokyo 135, Japan, 1993

Profiles of State, Economic Intelligence Service, Centre for Monitoring
Indian Economy Pvt. Ltd, March 1997

Ruy A. Teixeira, Lawrence Mishel, 'Whose Skills Shortage—Workers or
Management?' *Job Skills,* Summer 1993

Infrastructure in India—A Progress Report, IBI Special Report, November,
1997, The Economist Intelligence Unit Limited 1997

National Institute of Science and Technology Policy, Science and
Technology Agency, Japan, *The Sixth Technology Forecast Survey—Future
Technology in Japan Toward the Year 2025,* June 1997

State Science and Technology Commission, the People's Republic of
China, *The National Medium and Long-Term Science and Technology Development
Programme (1990–2000–2020),* State Science and Technology Commission

An Attractive Japan, Keidanren's Vision for 2020, Summary (Revised),
January, 1997

II. BOOKS

Ahluwalia, Esher Judge and I.N.D. Little, *India's Economic Reforms and Development—Essays for Manmohan Singh.* Oxford University Press, Delhi, 1998

Centre for Research in Rural and Industrial Development, Chandigarh, *In search of India's Renaissance, Volume I,* 1988.

Clark, Norman, Francisco Perez-Trejo, Peter Allen and Edward Elgar, *Evolutionary Dynamics and Sustainable Development—A Systems Approach,* Aldershot (UK) and Brookfield (USA).

Gell-Man, Murray, *The Quark and the Jaguar—Adventures in the Simple and the Complex,* Little Brown and Company.

Gowarikar, Vasant, *Science, Population and Development—An Exploration of Interconnectivities and Action Possibilities in India,* Umesh Communications, Pune.

Jain, Ashok, S. Pruthi, K.C. Garg and S.A. Nabi, *Indicators of Indian Science and Technology,* Segment Books, New Delhi.

Kathuria, Sanjay, *Competing through Technology and Management—A study of the Indian commercial vehicles industry,* Oxford University Press, Delhi, 1996.

Krishna Murthy, M.V., N.S. Siddharthan and B.S. Sonde, *Future Directions for Indian Economy—Technology trade and industry,* New Age International Limited, 1996.

Lazonick, William, *Business Organization and the Myth of the Market Economy,* Cambridge University Press, 1991.

Myhavold, Nathan and Peter Rinearson, *Bill Gates—The Road Ahead,* Viking.

Myrdal, Jan, *India Waits,* Sangam Books, Madras.

Nolan, Richard L. and David C. Crosnan, *Creative Destruction—A Six-Stage Process for Transforming the Organization,* Harvard Business School Press, Boston, Massachusetts.

Nath, N.C.B. and L. Mishra, *Transfer of Technology in Indian Agriculture—Experience of Agricultural Universities,* Indus Publishing Company, New Delhi.

Rajaraman, V., *Software Technologies—Challenges and Opportunities,* Tata McGraw Hill, New Delhi.

Srinivas, M.N., *Social Change in Modern India,* University of California Press, Berkeley and Los Angeles, 1967.

Subharayya, B.V., *In the Pursuit of Excellence—A History of the Indian Institute of Science,* Tata McGraw Hill, New Delhi.

Thakurdas, Sir Purshotam, J.R.D. Tata, G.D. Birla, Sir Ardeshir Dalal, Sir